Women in Science

Women in Science
A Report from the Field

Edited by
Jane Butler Kahle
Purdue University

 The Falmer Press

(A member of the Taylor & Francis Group)
Philadelphia and London

UK   The Falmer Press, Falmer House, Barcombe, Lewes, East Sussex, BN8 5DL

USA   The Falmer Press, Taylor & Francis Inc., 242 Cherry Street, Philadelphia, PA 19106-1906

First published 1985

Library of Congress Cataloging in Publication Data

Main entry under title:

Women in science.

  Bibliography: p.
  Includes index.
  1. Women in science. I. Kahle, Jane Butler.
Q130.W658 1984 508'.8042 84-18715
ISBN 1-85000-019-0
ISBN 1-85000-020-4 (pbk.)

Typeset in 11/13 Caledonia by
Imago Publishing Ltd, Thame, Oxon.

Printed in Great Britain by Taylor & Francis (Printers) Ltd, Basingstoke

Contents

Contents

Foreword

In my reply to the students of Stockholm at the Nobel Banquet in 1977, I emphasized that although women in the Western world are represented among students in reasonable proportion to their numbers in the community, they are not equitably represented among scientists, scholars, and leaders of our world. The unfortunate fact that the women of my generation did not achieve to an extent consistent with their abilities was due to both professional and social discrimination. Women were simply not accorded equal access to graduate schools or equal entry to positions in business, science, or government. Although women were needed to replace men who served in the Armed Forces during World War II, there was enormous social pressure for women to leave the job market and return to their homes at the war's end. The current need for two incomes for families as well as the high divorce rate have changed social perceptions of women's roles. The Civil Rights Movement has had a dramatic effect in diminishing, if not ending, legal discrimination. Thus, women now have greater opportunities to choose their fields and to exploit their talents.

I have always opposed reverse discrimination, the setting aside of a certain fraction of spaces in graduate schools or in the professions for women. To request such actions would imply that we are not equally qualified. If we are to succeed, we must believe in ourselves and have the confidence to accept that, given equal opportunities, we will occupy positions in keeping with our competences. Nonetheless, we must make certain that a variety of discriminatory practices, including sex stereotypes and 'old-boy' networks, do not deny opportunities to those who have appropriate aptitudes and who are able and willing to make the effort to achieve.

It is important to recognize that men and women are different and that only women can bear children. Although zero population growth may be desired, negative population growth, particularly among our gifted, does not serve the common good. Society must make greater efforts to assure quality care, especially during the developmental years of children of mothers having aspirations other than to remain in the home. Combining marriage and family with a profession is complicated by the fact that science is a rapidly changing field. One cannot drop out for five to ten years and expect to return as a fully qualified professional scientist. It is, therefore, essential for each woman entering a scientific field to consider the profession and lifestyle that suits her best and to choose a partner in marriage who will accept and support her professional aspirations.

Opportunities in the biological sciences include teaching at all levels, basic or applied research, science writing, medical technologies, medicine and nursing. The different choices require different degrees of education, competence, and commitment. It is important for teachers not only to present the material in a syllabus but also to expose our students to the joy and excitement of science. However, it is even more important to know your students and to help guide them to a career choice that most suits their talents, personalities, and needs.

A fundamental problem of critical importance to science is how to identify the few, those who make the breakthroughs. The most knowledgeable are not necessarily the most imaginative. It is the teachers and preceptors who have the responsibility of finding the few, encouraging them and bringing them to scientific maturity. In return society may offer rewards and prizes. However, to a scientist the greatest reward lies in the intangible — the sheer joy of having the opportunity to dream that each day may bring new knowledge that no one had before, and having realized that dream on occasion.

Rosalyn S. Yalow
Veterans' Administration Medical Center, Bronx, New York

Preface

When one designs a study in education or in the social sciences, concern with historical efforts always lingers in the back of one's mind. What extraneous happenings between the start and the finish of one's carefully designed work will affect its outcome? Although I've never known a researcher to throw up his/her hands in dismay, many a detailed and well executed study has been foiled by everyday occurrences. One solution to this dilemma is simply to conduct esoteric research, studying problems so removed from everyday life that the patterns and processes of the world do not affect the study's outcome. Another possibility is to analyze topics or aspects of life distant from the current social or educational mainstream.

The study reported in this book represents neither of those two sensible approaches. Rather, the authors decided to report on a timely topic currently in flux and certainly in motion. Women have only recently entered the scientific milieu in sufficient numbers to influence it. Furthermore, women scientists have been the topic of three recent books. Our subject, therefore, is both in the mainstream and affected by current cultural and societal changes.

Why select a topic for which one can neither be a definitive source nor report a conclusive result? The answer is concern and commitment. The authors all are concerned about both the number of women in science and about the quality of their lives. They discuss not only entrance patterns but retention and reward systems. They ponder differential pay scales and separate recognition patterns. They analyze both the underemployment and the underutilization of women in science. They review the role and status of women in all sciences, and discuss briefly their employment patterns in academia and industry. However, they focus on what they know best; that is, women in the biological sciences in educational settings. This focus is fortuitous because it is in the biological sciences that the impact of women may be studied. Women now receive 50 per cent of the bachelor degrees awarded in the biological sciences. They are represented in sufficient numbers so that their impact as well as their role and status can be defined, differentiated, and discussed.

However, the recent entry of large numbers of women to any science, even the biological ones, precludes any true synthesis or summary. This book, then, is a beginning. It tells what happens when doors are cracked and it suggests what may occur when they are flung open. It does not pretend, or intend, to be the final analysis, the definitive study, the academic tome. Rather, it is, as the title suggests, a current report. Its data and its findings will change as hopefully the numbers of women in all sciences increase and as their role and status improve.

Jane Butler Kahle
West Lafayette, Indiana
March, 1985

Acknowledgements

With a group project it is difficult to acknowledge all the diverse people and institutions who have contributed to its culmination. Therefore, this listing may be incomplete, although well intended. Initially, both Faith Hickman and Edward Kormondy were instrumental in establishing the Committee on the Role and Status of Women in Biology Education which the Board of Directors of the National Association of Biology Teachers (NABT) approved. In addition, throughout our work the staff of NABT's national headquarters has graciously and ably assisted us. Particular thanks are extended to Lu Bukovskey, who handled our requests and finances.

The last phase of our work, case studies of secondary teachers, was partially supported by the National Science Foundation (NSF Order Number 83–SD–0798). We especially appreciate the efforts of Cecily Cannon Selby, who was instrumental in obtaining the funding as well as in inspiring the project. Her enthusiasm, as well as that of Nobel Laureate, Rosalyn Yalow, encouraged us to devote time and energy to our volunteer committee, although concurrently each of us held a demanding job.

We extend our gratitude to the students, teachers, and parents who helped us by returning our surveys and by inviting us into their classrooms. In addition over 100 science educators evaluated our original survey, which resulted in a much improved instrument. Colleagues at Central Michigan University, Purdue University, and the Biological Sciences Curriculum Study offered many suggestions concerning the experimental phase of our work.

We acknowledge and gratefully appreciate the support, both intrinsic and extrinsic, of our various institutions and employers. In many instances, deadlines were rearranged, priorities were adjusted, and substitutions were accepted which enabled us to continue to work on the project and this book. Many of us received support for travel to committee meetings, for computer analyses, and for secretarial assistance from our respective institutions, and all of us extend our appreciation to them.

Many individuals accepted extra duties or responsibilities in order to complete the manuscript. We particularly acknowledge Joyce Bell's unusual skill with word processing equipment which resulted in a polished manuscript and attractive figures and tables, Maria Doolittle's untiring research efforts and patience in coordinating the efforts of a wide-spread committee, and April Gardner's accurate and careful proof-reading abilities. In addition, Hee-Hyung Cho assisted in the statistical analyses of the data reported in Chapters 2, 3, and 7. His insights and efficiency are gratefully acknowledged.

Finally, each of us was supported by a network of family and friends, who also believe in the equality of humans. Their willingness to assist us and to relieve us of many routine tasks enabled us to focus on the problems of women in science. We hope that we can repay their kindness by contributing to the improvement of both the role and the status of women in science.

Introduction: An Overview of Women in Science

Jane Butler Kahle
Professor of Biological Sciences and Education
Purdue University

In 1981 the National Association of Biology Teachers formed a special committee, the Role and Status of Women in Biology Education Committee, whose title describes its purpose. The first member was Marjorie Behringer, a retired professor dedicated to improving the professional status of women. Her presence encouraged others to accept the challenge of serving on the committee and has continued to inspire our work. Jane Butler Kahle agreed to be chairperson, and Joseph McInerney, Frances Vandervoort, Mildred Collins, and Claudia Douglass were appointed. Later Ann Haley-Oliphant and Marsha Lakes Matyas joined it.

The committee's activities focused on assessing, describing, and improving the role and status of women biology educators. Initially, they conducted the first national comprehensive survey of NABT's members in order to compare and contrast its female and male members. Two articles describe their findings, 'A Profile of NABT: The Results of the 1982 National Survey of the National Association of Biology Teachers' (Douglass and Kahle, 1983) and 'Professional Equity as Reported by Biology Educators' (Douglass, Matyas and Kahle, in press). Next, they undertook an historical, international, and educational review of women in science, especially in biology. This book is the synthesis of their study. More recently, they conducted in-depth case studies of high school teachers who have been successful in encouraging girls to continue in science. This work, partially funded by the National Science Foundation, also is reported in the third chapter of this book.

Collectively their chapters constitute a view of women in science. This view, placed in historical perspective in the opening chapter, focuses on the education and employment of women in science.

ne Butler Kahle

Throughout the book, barriers to women in science are identified and discussed. Some barriers are specific to girls electing to study science in elementary or secondary school, while others affect the pay or promotion policies of women scientists. Some obstacles are societal, while others are unique to specific institutions or industries. In addition, women in various countries face different sets of barriers, while for other groups of women; that is, some minority women, sexual barriers are confounded by racial ones.

By tracing the path and progress of women in science, we hope to identify progress made and changes needed. Bruer (1983) suggests that 'effective change requires a better understanding of why people choose science as a career, how science functions as a social system, and how science rewards participation.' Therefore, not only must barriers to the entrance of women into science studies and scientific careers be delineated, but also obstacles to science's reward and recognition system must be analyzed. Current studies of women in science have described entrance obstacles. A few have discussed retention problems; but none has proposed practical changes, appropriate for girls and women at different educational or professional levels. However, in this book, Matyas presents specific classroom activities which will change the usually negative attitudes toward science of girls. In another chapter, she points out the insidious effect of micro-inequities on the graduate and postgraduate science education of women, and she presents specific strategies for overcoming identified ones. In addition, Douglass documents differences between men and women in a specific workplace, the science classroom. The situation of minority women in the United States is portrayed with the warning that minority women may not be seen as scientists due to the double bind of sexism and racism. An overview of women in science internationally suggests that different educational and employment factors affect women in developed and developing countries. Vandervoort notes that historically many scientific professional societies have discouraged the full participation of women members, and she notes that much will be learned by assessing current changes in and by the American Pharmaceutical Association. Throughout the book, our focus is on educational and employment factors; broader social and cultural ones are left for another work.

Permeating our work is a firm belief in change. We hope that our separate chapters contribute to an understanding of the whole so that change may occur. To that extent, we have included a chapter which describes certain teachers who are contributing to the entrance and retention of women in science. Our observations and data suggest

2

specific teaching behaviors and techniques which may encourage all students, particularly girls, to elect advanced mathematics and science courses in high school. Such enrollments are crucial; for it has been estimated that two-thirds of possible college majors are closed to students who have not completed four years of high school mathematics.

Although we hope that many people will profit from reading our work, we think that the attitudes of educators may determine both the number and the subsequent success of women in science. Therefore, we have targeted our work for teachers — teachers in the broadest sense of that word, that is, those who teach children, adolescents, and adults in schools; those who train neophytes in the workplace; those who interact with friends and peers in professional associations. We have presented the data, we have described the studies, we leave it to the reader to interpret and act upon them. Each reader, then, can be part of the revolution to retain, reward, and recognize women in science.

References

BRUER, J.T. (1983) 'Women in science: Lack of full participation', *Science*, p. 221.

DOUGLASS, C.B. and KAHLE, J.B. (1983) 'A profile of NABT: Results of the 1982 national survey', *American Biology Teacher*, 45, pp. 410–414, 423.

DOUGLASS, C.B., MATYAS, M.L., and KAHLE, J.B. (in press) 'Professional equity as reported by biology educators,' *Journal of Research in Science Teaching*.

1 Women's Role and Status in the Sciences: An Historical Perspective

Marjorie Perrin Behringer
Professor of Biology Emeritus,
University of North Dakota

Historically, many women who either sought to study science or to work in science were aided and abetted in their struggles by concerned men. One of these men, Gunnar Myrdal, a Swedish man of letters, is often quoted for his statement wherein he compares the plight of women in America to that of blacks:

> As in the Negro problem, most men have accepted as self-evident, until recently, the doctrine that women had inferior endowments in most of the respects which carry prestige, power, and advantages in society ... As in the case of the Negro, women themselves have often been brought to believe in their inferiority of endowment. As the Negro was awarded his 'place' in society, so there was a 'woman's place.' In both cases the rationalization was strongly believed that men, in confining them to this place, did not act against the true interest of the subordinate groups. The myth of the 'contented women,' who did not want to have suffrage or other civil rights and equal opportunities, had the same social function as the myth of the 'contented Negro' (Myrdal, 1944, p. 1077).

In 1913 H.K. Mozans, pseudonym for John A. Zahm, wrote a book entitled *Woman in Science: With an Introductory Chapter on Women's Long Struggle for Things of the Mind*. It was an astonishing book in that a man of Zahm's era would write a strong appeal for the case of women, and even more surprising that his appeal was made specifically for women in science, long before their plight became a public issue. It is interesting, however, to theorize that Mozans may have published under the pseudonym because he was hesitant publicly to build a case for women in science.

Few scientists today would deny that the question of women in science is controversial. Because it is difficult to eliminate personal bias, I will for the most part quote from the writings of men; generally the quotations will be from men who are highly regarded for their scholarship in their own fields. As we might expect, though, women writers have published more articles and books than men regarding the topic of this chapter. Therefore, at times I will use statements and data from women authors and researchers. The writing reflects some of my own opinions which are clearly designated as such.

No doubt we recognize that a person cannot establish a career in science, or in any other profession, until he or she has received the appropriate training. Therefore, any history of the status of the American woman in science must first be concerned with the history of women's education in the United States. In the words of Mozans, we must first consider the matter of 'woman's long struggle for things of the mind'.

Review of the History of Education for Women

Zuckerman and Cole (1975) propose that the small number of women in the sciences is the result of accumulative discrepancies in women's education.

> The small numbers of women in the sciences, physical and biological, and in the other learned professions in the United States, result from early and cumulative discrepancies in the extent and character of educational attainment. Women are less likely to attend university or college than men. About a fifth of all women of university age were at university in 1969, compared to more than a third of the males of the same age. Women who attend university or college are slightly less apt than their male classmates to continue to completion of their course of study. Male undergraduates are about three times as likely as women to specialize in science and engineering, thus providing a largely male pool of potential scientists. Finally, men who specialize in science as undergraduates are also more apt than women to go on to graduate studies; about twice the proportion do so (Zuckerman and Cole, 1975, p. 82).

We have records of how such discrepancies in education started long ago. Even during the ancient Greek period, we can find something about their underlying causes. Plato, a philosopher, believed that '...

5

neither a woman as a woman, nor a man as a man has any special function, but the gifts of nature are equally diffused in both sexes; all the pursuits of man are the pursuits of woman also . . . So far as women have the same qualities of character they are to be educated and to be adapted to services in society as men are' (Monroe, 1919, pp. 141–2). But Aristotle, a scientist, disagreed with Plato: 'Basing his argument on a comparative study of the sexes in lower animals he [Aristotle] held that woman was essentially different from man in nature, and hence that the former cannot profit by this higher education to be given citizens' (Monroe, 1919, p. 156). Sadly, in my opinion, this pattern is still evident. Men in the humanities often espouse the cause of equal education for women, while men in the sciences are often hesitant to grant equal opportunities to women.

Throughout the centuries, leaders in learning and politics, most or all of them men, have greatly influenced society's attitudes about the status and education of women. In addition, these men have differed in their views toward women's education. For example, Jean Jacques Rousseau (1712–78), a well-known French writer and social theorist, recorded that 'a woman of culture [education] is the plague of her husband, her children, her family, her servants — everybody' (Monroe, 1919, p. 566). On the other hand, shortly before the time of Rousseau, a practically unknown Frenchman, François Fenelon (1651–1715), a member of a French noble family and a Catholic priest, wrote an unusual treatise, *On the Education of Girls*. The treatise was noteworthy only because '. . . of the very fact it discussed the education of girls at all . . . at a time when "girls were either left uneducated or trained in a narrow illiterate piety in convents"' (Boyd and King, 1975, p. 165). Fenelon, however, had no high ideal of womanhood. Although he did not want girls left in total ignorance, he felt that women had 'no need of much of the knowledge that men possess. . . It is enough if one day they know how to rule their households and obey their husbands without arguing about it' (Boyd and King, 1975, p. 265). Even as late as the early 1900s, after education for women had become fairly well established, the controversy still flourished. Two prominent educational psychologists, G. Stanley Hall and Edward L. Thorndike, expounded opposing views regarding the status of women. Hall (1844–1924) was a romantic and a deeply religious man. He idealized women, considering them 'the keepers of the hearth, the guardians of civilization and, through their roles as mothers, the keys to the future of humanity' (Seller, 1981, p. 366). Yet, his academic interests in Darwinism and anthropology led Hall to conclude that man had reached a higher level of evolution than woman and that a woman was 'less specialized and more generic, richer in intuition, and psychically nearer the child' (Hall, 1905, pp. 450, 497).

Although Thorndike held many of Hall's views on the nature of women and their education, his views were more generous toward their mental capacities. After testing thousands of boys and girls ranging from 9 to 20 years of age, Thorndike maintained 'the differences in sheer intellectual capacity are too small to be of any great practical importance to educational theory or practice' (Thorndike, 1906, p. 212). Even so, Thorndike held a theory that many educationists today would consider damaging to the status of women and unfair to men as well. Although he believed there were no important differences in the *average* abilities of men and women, Thorndike reported that men attain higher and also lower levels of ability than women do.

> In intellectual traits at least the male sex is the more variable group: the very highest and very lowest marks in mixed college class will commonly be given to men ... Of the thousand most eminent intellects of history, ninety seven per cent are men, the variability which causes the monopoly of genius causing also the existence of twice as many male as female idiots! (Thorndike, 1906, p. 212).

Thus Thorndike believed 'that of the hundred most gifted individuals in this country not two would be women...' (Thorndike, 1906, p. 213). It seems probable that today most, if not all, sociologists and educational psychologists would reject this theory of Thorndike and, instead, would look at an accumulation of social disadvantages for women to account for the differences in accomplishments between men and women. Jonathan R. Cole and Stephen Cole, brothers and recognized sociologists specializing in the study of social stratification in science, describe how accumulative advantages and disadvantages arise.

> By virtue of being in top graduate departments and interacting with influential and brilliant scientists, some scientists have a social advantage in the process of stratification. Once position has been established in this initial phase, the probabilities may no longer be the same for two scientists of equal abilities. The one who is strategically located in the stratification system may have a series of accumulating advantages over the one who is not a member of the elite corps (Cole and Cole, 1973, pp. 74–5).

Furthermore, J. Cole (1979) relates these accumulative disadvantages to women scientists.

7

Potentially, this process can influence the careers of women scientists. If for one reason or another they do not attend superior training centers, do not apprentice for master scientists, do not have facilities to carry out their research ideas, their chances for recognition and esteem are diminished (p. 8).

J. Cole further believes that it is '. . . the cultural forces that lead women to select themselves out of science careers. It should be remembered that the obstacles that confront women may have an additive or possibly a multiplicative effect that cumulates over time' (Cole, 1979, p. 284).

Availability of Elementary and Secondary Education to Women

As might be expected, the early English colonists based their attitudes toward the status and education of women on the traditions of their mother country. Goodsell described the situation: 'In the American colonies married women had no legal status, having surrendered their legal personality to their husbands at marriage. In the words of the old English common law, "husband and wife are one, and the husband is the one"' (Goodsell, 1931, p. 1). Colonists believed 'that woman's sphere was in the home, bearing and rearing a "quiver full" of children and carrying on a varied round of domestic industries without which the colonists could not have survived' (Goodsell, 1931, p. 2).

Whereas boys were encouraged to attend grammar school, high school, and college, most colonists looked with disfavor on education for girls. Many believed that women were intellectually inferior and, thus, incapable of intellectual pursuits. In a 1778 letter Abigail Adams told her husband, John Adams, then serving at the Continental Congress, '. . . but in this country you need not be told how much the female education is neglected, nor how fashionable it has been to ridicule female learning' (C.F. Adams, 1876, in Woody, 1929, p. 501). Because of the efforts of Abigail Adams, and others who believed that an educated woman made a more fit wife and mother, over the next seventy-five years an elementary education was gradually accepted as proper for girls in the United States.

By the early 1800s, women had gained access to a public high school education as well. In the late 1700s seminaries, a type of private high school for girls, sprang up chiefly in the East and South where girls were seldom allowed to attend public high schools with boys. The better seminaries were established by notable women whose education had been promoted by their families. Usually, however, these schools were not free, and girls from families of little or no wealth seldom received more than a meager education in a public elementary school. Many girls and women remained illiterate.

Availability of College Education to Women

Although many of the better women's seminaries offered courses equivalent to those in junior colleges, the seminary directors themselves considered the use of the term 'college' to describe their schools a presumptuous error. In fact, Emma Willard, a notable leader in the establishment of better seminaries for women, was hesitant to use the term: 'When presenting her "plan to improve female education" to the New York State Legislature in 1819, Willard purposely refrained from using the term "college" for fear of ridicule' (Newcomer, 1959, p. 11).

We must note that higher education for men in the United States began in the early colonial days with the founding of Harvard College in 1636, followed by William and Mary (1693), Yale (1701), Princeton (1746), and Columbia (1754). It was not until 1837, however, 200 years after the opening of Harvard, that formal higher education became available to women in the United States when Oberlin admitted four women. Even so, Oberlin kept the female department separate and did not allow a woman to receive a degree until the late 1840s. At that time, according to Boas, 'it was customary to deplore the mere suggestion of degrees for women as ostentatious aping of man. A woman with a degree would be unsexed, since by divine will woman was assigned to domestic duties' (Boas, 1935, p. 11).

As men of wealth gained an interest in women's education due to the influence of educated women within their own families, funds were obtained to establish women's colleges. The first of these was Vassar College, founded in 1865, followed by Smith, Wellesley, Bryn Mawr, and others. It is interesting to note that the first women's college in England, Girton in Cambridge, opened in 1869 — four years after Vassar. Mozans describes the reaction to the founding of Girton and Newnham, another English women's college:

> When the students of Girton and Newnham in 1897, after passing the Cambridge examinations — many of them with the highest honors — applied for degree, 'the undergraduate world [of men] was stirred to a fine frenzy of wrath against all womankind,' and an astonished world saw re-enacted scenes scarcely less disgraceful than those which characterized the

riotous demonstrations which, seventeen years before, had greeted seven young women at the portals of the University of Edinburgh (Mozans, 1913, pp. 100–1).

Such riots are all too reminiscent of the mid-1900s when the blacks sought entrance to the universities of the southern United States. Thus, it seems that although women struggled to gain access to education in America, our country was far more generous toward women's education in the later 1800s than was England. The English situation was not representative, however, of all European countries. Even before the early 1800s, women of the United States who wished to receive a higher education and who had willing and financially able families often traveled to the great universities of Germany.

Despite the establishment of women's colleges in America, the struggle for equal education was far from over. 'The new name "female college" caused consternation in the hearts of some and ridicule in others. Ridicule was the chief weapon used against it' (Woody, 1929, p. 151). Thomas Woody states further,

> Another [objection] was stressed which, had it proved valid, would have brought the college movement [for women] to an early end. Women, it was confidently asserted, simply could not do college work; they did not have minds like those of men. These sex differences in mind were said to be an insuperable barrier, against which no propaganda for the equality of women could be effective (Woody, 1929, p. 154).

Despite such objections, women did receive support and affirmation, principally from clergy and educated laymen of wealth and, to a lesser degree, from academic men in positions of leadership. Without these endorsements, the funding of women's colleges might well have been delayed for years, perhaps into the present century. Even today, the lack of general support from academic male leaders portends a bit of irony and bitterness in the minds of academic women. For example, Charles William Eliot, President of Harvard College from 1869 to 1909, stated during the 1870s, 'now, women differ more from men than men differ from each other; there is a pervading difference which extends to their minds quite as much as their bodies' (Woody, 1929, p. 155). Perhaps such statements allow us to understand better why, in 1913, John A. Zahm, under his pseudonym of H. K. Mozans, AM, PhD, added to the main title of his book the subtitle of *Woman's Long Struggle for Things of the Mind*.

Coeducation: Availability of Equal Education to Women

A major reason for the rise of coeducation was economy. By the late 1800s, education for women was established as a necessity in the minds of most political and academic leaders, whether or not they, as individuals, agreed. Economic situations, particularly in the young states of the Midwest and West, did not allow sufficient educational financing to establish separate facilities for boys and girls. In addition, education provided in the girls' schools and women's colleges was often considered inferior to that of the schools of boys and men. Concerning women's colleges, Tarbell declared in 1884: 'A diploma from Michigan University [open to women since its founding] is of much more value to a lady than one from any of the colleges for women' (Woody, 1929, p. 263). In a minority report on coeducation at Williams college, John Bascom declared: 'the graduates [of Vassar] . . . are not prepared to take charge even of our high schools. They cannot fit young men for college' (Bascom, 1908, p. 444). The women's schools did not agree with such statements, and Vassar officials replied to Bascom that they did not even offer a teacher-training program as a part of their curriculum (Woody, 1929).

At the same time, many considered the education provided by lower schools for girls of poor quality: 'When public high schools segregated boys and girls, the girls' schools were likely to be inferior' (Newcomer, 1959, p. 35). Commenting on coeducation in the high schools, Comstock states:

> Baltimore was inclined to look askance ... Learning was commendable, of course, for its young men, but for women? It just wasn't being done ... Prior to 1888, only negro [sic] girls of Baltimore would have been able to pass college-entrance exams because of the fact that colored high schools were coeducational and gave fair preparation, while 'segregation of the sexes' was practiced in white high schools, and the institutions for girls were of incredibly low academic level (Comstock, 1930, p. 36).

Other cities of the East and South maintained separate high schools because of 'traditions, buildings, impropriety, vicious influence of the boys, size of schools, and the variant character of those attending...' (Woody, 1929, p. 228). During the early twentieth century, psychologist G. Stanley Hall wrote: 'Coeducation in the middle teens tends to sexual precocity. This is very bad; it is one of the subtlest dangers that can befall civilization' (Earnest, 1953, pp. 196–7). In spite of such objections, by 1900 coeducation in public elementary schools was almost universal (Woody, 1929). Approximately 98 per cent of the public high schools in 1900 were coeducational, and by 1920 over 50 per cent of the parochial schools admitted both boys and girls (Woody, 1929).

As with coeducation in elementary and secondary schools, coeducation in colleges and universities also had its start in the Midwest. Oberlin College broke with tradition in 1837, long before girls' colleges were established in the East. Other midwestern colleges, including Albion in Michigan (1850), Antioch in Ohio (1852), and Earlham in Indiana (1859), were coeducational from their inceptions. Soon, state universities of the Midwest followed the example of private schools. The University of Iowa granted a bachelor's degree to a woman in 1863. Both the University of Wisconsin and the University of Michigan were opened to women by 1870. By 1880 more than 50 per cent of the colleges in the United States allowed women to enroll at their institutions. Men's colleges and universities in eastern states were more reluctant to admit women. They changed their policies, however, when offered large sums of money for the addition of departments for women. William C. Russell, Vice-president of Cornell, apparently considered a commingling of the sexes a true abomination: 'When I have heard a lady student calling one young man into a room, shutting the door, kissing him it has embittered months of existence' (Rudolph, 1962, p. 327). Nevertheless, in 1872 Cornell University accepted $250,000 from Henry W. Sage to build the Sage College for Women as a part of Cornell (Woody, 1929). Both Johns Hopkins and the University of Rochester also were promised special endowments if they admitted women, although Johns Hopkins did not accept these terms until 1907. In like manner, Sophie Newcomb Memorial College for Women was established by Tulane University upon an endowment from Mrs Josephine Newcomb of New York.

Although tradition hindered the older eastern universities from opening their doors on a coeducational basis, these universities found a compromise midway between coeducation and separate colleges by the establishment of coordinate colleges. Both Sage and Sophie Newcomb were coordinate to men's colleges. Radcliffe became coordinate to Harvard and Barnard to Columbia. Whether the system of coordinate colleges for women established an equal education for both sexes has long been debated. If the facilities of each college are truly open to both men and women, the system may well furnish an adequate program for all students. Apparently such a situation has not always been the case:

The first Radcliffe students had to obtain books from the [Harvard] library by messenger after the library closed in the evening, and the books were returned by messenger when the library opened in the morning. Whether the students stayed up all night to read them is not recorded. Library facilities [of Radcliffe] have greatly improved over the years, but the Radcliffe women are still excluded from the Harvard undergraduate men's library. The explanation offered by the librarian, as late as the 1940s, was that the building had many alcoves and policing would be too expensive (Newcomer, 1959, p. 198).

Indeed, some persons have deemed the establishment of coordinate colleges for women an act of subterfuge by men's colleges as a means of avoiding coeducation. Perhaps an article in the *New York Times Magazine* in 1949 was indicative of the thinking of many people at that time. The article was entitled 'Harvard Goes Coed, but Incognito' (Lewis, 1949, p. 38). Because of the expense of financing separate colleges, the number of coeducational institutions increased steadily during the first half of this century. Table 1.1 shows the number of colleges open to men and women from 1870 to 1957.

Table 1.1   United States Colleges Open to Men and Women, 1870–1957[a]

Year	Number of institutions	Percentage of institutions		
		Men only	Women only	Coeducational
1870	582	59	12	29
1890	1082	37	20	43
1910	1083	27	15	58
1930	1322	15	16	69
1957	1326	13	13	74

Source: Newcomer, (1959), p. 37, by permission.
Note: a Data include all institutions of higher education, except for 1957 which is limited to four-year degree-granting institutions.

Availability of Graduate Education to Women

Women gained formal entrance to graduate education more easily than to the lower levels of schooling, perhaps because many doctoral recipients enter the teaching field and women were already established as teachers. In addition, women already had proved themselves capable of completing the baccalaureate program.

The first doctoral programs in American institutions were little more than our present master's degree, and it was not until the founding of Johns Hopkins in 1876 that graduate education in the United States really began (Feldman, 1974). Other strong programs were established at Clark University and the University of Chicago. These three programs were the models for graduate degrees initiated later at Columbia, Yale, Harvard, and Brown. Of these early programs, all except Johns Hopkins admitted women when their graduate schools opened. The Graduate School of Johns Hopkins University, however, barred women until 1907, although women were still denied entrance to their undergraduate school. In 1907 the President of Johns Hopkins issued the following report: 'Women who have taken the baccalaureate degree at institutions of good standing [are to be] admitted to graduate courses provided there is no objection on the part of the instructor concerned' (Woody, 1929, p. 337). In reality, then, the Johns Hopkins policy presented two barriers that women were forced to overcome in order to gain admission to one of the finest graduate schools in the United States. First, they must obtain a baccalaureate from an institution considered by Johns Hopkins to be of good standing; and, second, they must find an instructor, most or all of them men, who would accept a woman in his class. Fortunately, women of the Midwest were not faced with similar formal obstacles in either undergraduate or graduate schools. Informal barriers, however, must have played an important role in women's choice of graduate schools for, even today, greater percentages of graduate women are still found in the medium-quality and low-quality colleges than in the universities or high-quality colleges (Feldman, 1974) (see Table 1.2).

Table 1.2   Distribution of Graduate Students at United States Institutions by Sex and Institution Type, 1969[a]

Type of institution	Percentage male	Percentage female	Projected total[b]
High-quality universities	74.1	25.9	172,306
Medium-quality universities	71.1	28.9	259,236
Low-quality universities	74.7	25.3	222,089
High-quality colleges	73.8	26.2	60,757
Medium-quality colleges	56.7	43.3	120,682
Low-quality colleges	58.7	41.3	171,764

Source: From Carnegie Commission on Higher Education in Feldman (1974), by permission.
Notes: a Includes graduate and professional-school students.
        b Weighted data, based on sample of 32,963 students.

Availability of Professional Training to Women

Women's first professional careers were in elementary school teaching. If women undertook any studies beyond high school, they received their training in normal colleges where only one year of attendance was considered sufficient for a beginning teacher. Because of the rapid development of public grammar schools and the need for teachers, women met little opposition to entering the field. Like dressmaking, teaching was considered an appropriate position for a lady. Because teaching young children was allocated to women, this level of teaching was relegated to a lower status. Such stratification has often been observed in those areas identified as woman's work, for example, nurse, telephone operator, secretary, and clerk. Saul Feldman states:

> Like female-dominated occupations, female-dominated academic disciplines are low in prestige, low in economic rewards, and low in power. Moreover, they have other characteristics that set them apart from male-dominated fields. Female-dominated fields are in the humanities with great emphasis on teaching, while male-dominated fields are more mathematical, with greater emphasis on research (Feldman, 1974, p. 46).

Table 1.3 shows the percentages of men and women in public school teaching from 1870 to 1970. As indicated, the percentage of women in public school teaching has remained well above the percentage of men.

Table 1.3   *United States Public Elementary and Secondary School Faculty by Sex, 1870–1970*

	1870	1880	1890	1900	1910	1920	1930	1940	1950	1960	1970
Women (thousands)	123	164	238	296	413	565	703	681	719	985	1440
Men (thousands)	78	123	126	127	110	93	140	195	195	402	691
Women (percentage)	61.2	57.2	65.5	70.1	78.9	85.9	83.4	77.8	78.7	71.0	67.6

Source: From National Center for Education Statistics (1980).

Although women have long been accepted as teachers in elementary and secondary schools, their appointment to faculties of colleges and universities has progressed more slowly. Table 1.4 shows the number of men and women holding faculty positions in higher education from 1870 to 1970. By 1890 the number of women faculty reached approximately 25 per cent and remained at about that level through 1970.

Table 1.4   Faculty in United States Institutions of Higher Learning by Sex, 1870–1970[a]

	1870	1880	1890	1900	1910	1920	1930	1940	1950	1960	1970
Women	666	4,194	3,105	4,717	7,348	12,808	22,369	40,601	60,533	83,781	206,000
Men	4,887	7,328	12,704	19,151	29,132	35,807	60,017	106,328	186,189	296,773	619,000
Women (percentage)	11.9	36.4	24.4	19.8	20.1	26.3	27.2	27.6	24.5	22.0	24.9

Source: From National Center for Education Statistics (1980).
Note: a Numbers are estimated for 1870, 1880, 1890, and 1970.

Other than in teaching, women have met severe obstacles when attempting to enter training programs in professional fields such as medicine, law, and engineering. The medical profession provides a good example of professional barriers for women. In 1848 Elizabeth Blackwell became the first woman to enter a medical school in the United States. After great efforts, involving studies in both Europe and the United States, Blackwell gained admission to Geneva Medical School in New York. Mozans offers an account of Miss Blackwell's efforts: 'She was told ... that it was highly improper for a woman to study medicine and that no decent woman would think of becoming a medical practitioner. As to a *lady* studying or practicing surgery that, of course, was out of the question' (Mozans, 1913, p. 300). Even her formal petition for admission was treated without respect. 'The circumstances of her admission were strange: the faculty not wanting to take responsibility for her rejection had turned the matter over to the students — who in an uproarious general assembly — voted an unanimous "yes" as a joke' (Lopate, 1968, p. 4).

Harriett Hunt had similar experiences in her attempt to enter Harvard Medical School. Her first application in 1847 was turned down. 'Three years later the request was repeated, and acted upon favorably; but due to the fact that three Negroes had just been admitted and the addition of a woman to the student body seemed likely to result in great discontent on the part of students, the faculty requested the candidate to withdraw her application' (Woody, 1929, p. 352). As it happened, Harvard Medical School did not again admit a woman until 1945 — fewer than forty-five years ago and 100 years after Hunt's acceptance and rejection.

In response to women's demands for admission to medical school, and because some medical men objected to serving in the capacity of midwife, women's medical colleges were established in several eastern states. These schools were generally recognized as inferior to those for men, the primary curriculum consisting of obstetrics and child care. In 1848 a medical doctor, Samuel Gregory, expressed the opinion of several of his colleagues in a publication attacking the idea of men serving as midwives. Gregory's title provides the main idea of the treatize: *Mid-wifery Exposed and Corrected; or the Employment of Men to attend women in childbirth, shown to be a modern invention, unnecessary, unnatural and injurious to the physical welfare of the community, and pernicious in its influence on Professional and Public Morality* (Woody, 1929, p. 342). Once again, those occupations considered appropriate for women were afforded lower status and were deemed inappropriate for men.

In contrast to the eastern states, the situation for midwestern women in medicine was quite different. In 1870 the University of Michigan Department of Medicine and Surgery became coeducational, followed by a number of other schools in that region. Twenty years later, Johns Hopkins Medical School was opened to women as the result of a $350,000 gift from Dr Elizabeth Garrett Anderson, Dr Anderson stipulated that the gift was contingent upon the admission of women to the school. John Hopkins School of Medicine opened on 2 October 1893 with sixteen students, three of whom were women (Woody, 1929). 'The medical school [of Johns Hopkins] became the first in America "of a genuine university type" to open on a coeducational basis' (Lopate, 1968, p. 15).

In Europe women were more readily accepted in medicine. As early as 1870 medical schools in Switzerland opened their doors to women and, shortly thereafter, universities in Germany followed a similar pattern. Consequently, many women in the United States traveled to Europe to receive a medical education. 'As a result of these opportunities, there were 2,432 American women doctors registered in 1880; in 1890, there were 4,557; and by 1900, the number had jumped to 7,387' (Lopate, 1968, p. 14).

Some of the other professions for women have followed a pattern similar to that for medicine. Table 1.5 provides further information

Table 1.5   *Percentages of Women in Selected Professions in the United States, 1910–50*

Fields	1910	1920	1930	1940	1950
Public school and higher education faculties	75.1	82.3	78.4	70.5	67.2
Journalists	12.2	16.8	23.0	25.0	32.0
Physicians	5.1	5.0	4.4	4.7	6.1
Dentists	3.1	3.3	1.8	1.5	2.8
Clergy	0.6	1.4	2.2	2.4	4.1
Lawyers	0.5	1.4	2.1	2.5	3.5
Engineers	0.01	0.03	0.05	0.34	1.24

Sources: Data drawn from United States Bureau (1960) and Wolfle (1954).

concerning the number of women in selected professions during the period from 1910 to 1950. The table indicates that women teachers and professors greatly outnumbered women in all other careers combined. The second greatest number of women was found in journalism, although this group comprised only one-fifth to one-third of the first group throughout the entire period.

The Role and Status of Women in the Sciences

As stated at the beginning of this chapter, one cannot expect to enter a profession before receiving the appropriate training for the selected field. The discussion so far has been concerned with the history of women's access to a full education. We have seen that American women were unable to gain access to a graduate education and professional training within the United States until the late 1800s. As a consequence, few women were able to contribute to the sciences before the beginning of this century. In reality, except for the social sciences, the percentage of women doctorates in the sciences has remained amazingly low, even through 1980, as shown in Table 1.6. The underlying reasons for this and other situations for women will be discussed in later chapters.

Since 1900 a relatively small number of American women have earned a minimum of recognition in sciences, although only a few are widely recognized. In 1913 Mozans presented a surprisingly long list of the names of women who had contributed to science, including women in mathematics, astronomy, physics, chemistry, natural science, archaeology, medicine, and surgery. In the natural sciences alone, he described the work of twenty-four American women contributors and, from his accounts, it appears that all of those women were worthy of his descriptions.

Today, we find none of those names in the books on the history of biology, except occasionally that of twelfth-century St Hildegard, the learned Abbess of the Benedictine Convent at Bingen on the Rhine. A review of books describing the history of science reveals that the names of few or no women are included. Charles J. Singer has undoubtedly produced the greatest number of college texts on the history of science, including those on the history of medicine, history and methods of science, technology and history, and the history of anatomy from the Greeks to Harvey. Singer's book, *A History of Biology*, has been a standard text since it was first published in 1931 and revised in 1955. Even today, the book is considered a classic reference for college courses on the history of biology. Throughout all of his books Singer

Table 1.6   *Science and Engineering Doctorates Granted in the United States to Women by Field, 1920–80*

Field	1920–29		1930–39		1940–49		1950–59		1960–69		1970–79		1980	
	No.	%	No.	%	No.	%	No.	%	No.	%	No.	%	No.	%
Physical sciences[a]	247	7.6	442	6.6	406	5.0	685	3.7	1577	4.6	3981	8.8	502	13.9
Engineering	2	0.9	6	0.7	7	0.5	20	0.3	77	0.4	427	1.4	90	3.8
Life sciences[b]	378	15.9	765	15.1	738	12.7	1318	9.1	3078	11.6	8908	22.2	1342	33.7
Social sciences[c]	325	17.1	562	15.8	580	14.5	1510	11.0	3604	14.3	14628	32.4	2165	52.9
All fields	952	12.2	1775	11.0	1731	8.9	3533	6.7	8336	12.6	27944	17.4	4099	29.1

Sources: Data drawn from NRC (1979–81).
Notes: a   Physical sciences: mathematics, astronomy, physics, chemistry, earth science and computer sciences for 1970–80.
   b   Life sciences: biological, agricultural, medical.
   c   Social sciences: anthropology, sociology, economics, political science/public administration, psychology.

mentions no women scientists except Hildegard at Bingen, who he said 'produced elaborate mystical schemes based on the doctrine of the macrocosm and microcosm' (Singer, 1941, p. 153).

More recent writers of the history of science have cited a few more women scientists. Moore (1961), a woman writer, names Rosalind Franklin, Marie A. Jacuss, Martha Chase, Marie Lavoisier (wife of Antoine), Marie L. Pasteur (wife of Louis), Marianna Greenberg-Manago and Priscilla Ortiz (assistants to Severo Ochoa), and Mary Louise Stephenson at Harvard University in the 1950s. Philip Goldstein (1965) names only Martha Chase, a geneticist who worked in 1952. Taylor (1963) mentions only Hildegard; and Allen (1975) names Martha Chase, Rosalind Franklin, Hilde Mangold (who worked with Spemann on embryological studies), and Nettie M. Steven, a cytologist at Bryn Mawr.

Yost (1959) has written biographies of eleven American women scientists (three of them born and trained in other countries): Gerty Cori (Austrian-born medical researcher and recipient of the Nobel Prize with her husband in 1947); Lise Meitner (Austrian-born physicist); Helen S. Hogg (astronomer); Elizabeth Shull Russell (zoologist-geneticist); Rachel Fuller Brown (micro-biologist); Chien Shung Wu (nuclear physicist born in China); Edith H. Quimby (physicist); Florence Van Straten (meteorologist); Jocelyn Crane (zoologist); Gladys E. Emerson (biochemist); and Dorothea Rudnich (embryologist). Although these women worked and gained recognition before 1950, their names do not appear in the more recent history books mentioned above.

Perhaps the best source for identification of outstanding American women in science is a four-volume publication from Radcliffe College. Volumes I through III *Notable American Women, 1607–1950*. (James, James and Boyer, (Eds), 1971) cover the period from 1607 through 1950, and Volume IV *Notable American Women: The Modern Period* (Sicherman and Green, Eds, 1980) includes women who died between 1951 and 1975. Women whose deaths occurred only recently, and whose work is thus unproven in view of time, were eliminated; thus such women as anthropologist Margaret Mead and others, whom we may consider eligible, are not included. The basic and very restrictive criteria for selection were 'the individual's influence on her time or field; the importance and significance of her achievement; the pioneering or innovative quality of her work; and the relevance of her career for the history of women' (Sicherman and Green, 1980, p. x). Of particular note is the fact that the books contain more names of women in areas other than the sciences.

According to the Radcliffe publications, the greatest number of notable women from 1607 to 1975 was in literature; 455 women are included in that category. The notable women in the arts ranked second in number, with the selection of 299 women; science ranked third with 198 women, and education was last with 147 women. Although many interpretations can be given to the ranking of the fields by numbers of women, it seems likely that the relatively low number of notable women in science is due to their late entry into the field. No doubt, women have a longer history in letters, the arts, and in teaching than they have in the sciences, a field that has always been dominated by men. Reasons given for the lowest number of notable women in education can vary, of course. Although we find many more women in teaching than in other fields, women are more apt to drop out of teaching either temporarily or permanently than in other areas, thus offering women less chance to gain recognition based on a long-term career. It seems reasonable to believe that women in the arts and letters are more able to pursue their talents in the home.

Even within the sciences, the names of many notable women of the Radcliffe publications are not nationally recognized. For example, five women in biology are listed for the period 1607–1950: Cornelia Maria Clap, Rosa S. Eigenman, Ida Henrietta Hyde, Mary Jane Rathbun, and Nettie M. Stevens. Of these names, only Nettie Stevens appears in the history books described earlier. For the period 1951–75, again five women are named in biology: Rachel L. Carson, Ethel B. Harvey, Libbie H. Hyman, Ann H. Morgan and Margaret Morse. Although at least two of these names are recognized nationally, none of the women is included in the history books described above. The reason may be that science-history texts are revised and updated only infrequently. Also in Volume IV four women are named in botany: Emma Luch Braun, Mary Agnes Chase, Alice Eastwood, and Margaret C. Ferguson. Two notable women are named in chemistry, four in geology, three in physics, and one in astronomy.

Based on the Radcliffe publications, a well-researched and valid source, relatively few notable women have worked in the sciences. Several reasons may explain these findings. First, of course, is that fewer women enter the sciences than other fields. The principal reason, cited by many authors, is that both men and women consider science to be a man's field — an area not meant for women. Such reasoning is reminiscent of the early thinking regarding education for women.

Many other barriers and constraints exist. Some of those will be discussed in following chapters. An important implication, however, can be cited here. The serious problems faced by women, blacks and other minorities have resulted in legislation and governmental programs. Two important pieces of legislation include the following provisos:

> Federal regulations and laws require that there be no dis-
> crimination in any conditions of employment including
> recruitment, hiring, layoff, discharge and recall, and in-service
> training; wages and salaries; sick leave time and pay, vacation
> time and pay, overtime work and pay; medical, hospital, life
> and accident insurance; and optional compulsory retirement
> (National Academy of Sciences, 1979, p. 113).

Executive Order 11242 as amended by Executive Order 11375

> prohibits discrimination in employment by all employers who
> hold federal contracts, and requires affirmative action programs
> by all federal contractors and subcontractors. Firms with con-
> tracts over $50,000 and with 50 or more employees must
> develop and implement written programs of affirmative action
> (National Academy of Sciences, 1979, p. 135).

A large proportion of federal grants is awarded in the sciences and, thus, the effects of the affirmative action are felt strongly in those areas. Although many consider the affirmative action policy an unfortunate and cumbersome program, others, including federal officials, consider it a necessary policy to ensure equal opportunities for women and racial minorities. In addition, it has been claimed that affirmative action has not proven effective because reported cases of discrimination are not investigated and pursued by governmental agencies. At least, however, the federal policies provide strong evidence that discrimination does, indeed, exist in academic and other institutions. The affirmative action policy was based on direct evidence, such as differences in salary, rank and tenure for academic men and women. The differences in rank, noted in Figure 1.1, serve as an example. Note that the data in Figure 1.1 are for 1977, nearly fifteen years after the first anti-discrimination legislation, the Equal Pay Act of 1963.

Figure 1.1 shows the faculty rank distribution of doctoral scientists and engineers in three categories of academic institutions, based on federal research and development expenditures of institutions. The data were provided by fourteen federal agencies responsible for more than 19 per cent of all federal obligations to universities and colleges. According to the figure, the differences in the percentages of men and women at different ranks remain approximately the same. In the professorial positions of all three groups of institutions, the greatest number of women held the rank of assistant professor, and the least number held the rank of full professor. The opposite was true for men;

Figure 1.1

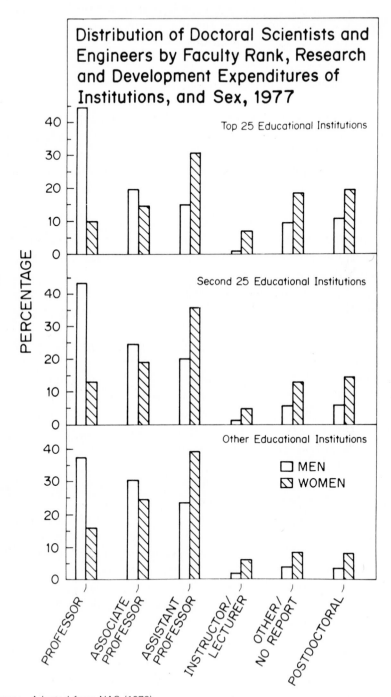

Source: Adapted from NAS (1979).

the greatest percentages of men were in the rank of full professor and the lowest percentages were at the rank of assistant professor. Therefore, women are concentrated in the non-tenured positions while men are concentrated in tenured positions.

Conclusion

In most situations the role of an individual determines the status of that person. In the case of the sciences, we must conclude that historically women have had only a minor role and, therefore, lower status than men. On the brighter side, the position of women in most of the sciences is slowly improving, as shown in the data of this and later chapters.

Because of the lack of availability of a complete education, women have arrived late to the sodality of science. With few exceptions, they are still learning how to feel at ease in the male-dominated institution. I have watched an intelligent, capable — and frightened — woman speaking before a science faculty consisting mostly of males, as a part of her application for a position in biology. On numerous occasions, I have observed experienced women in science who are timid and nervous when speaking out at a conference table surrounded mostly by men of science. On occasion, in my early career, I have been among such groups of women. It takes considerable spunk to be a woman in science.

With our relatively few years of access to equal education (about 100) and our fewer years of access to the higher levels of academic science (about twenty) we are still treading new ground. With more years in science and with the support of men in science, we will learn how to walk with full confidence in our abilities. The years of history do bring change, and women are gaining a greater respect. 'Woman's Place' in society is beginning to include the sciences.

I doubt that those of us who have felt the sting of discrimination toward women in science will be able to forget the bitter pain that comes with it. But today it seems we have reason to put the past out of mind and to look toward the future — which holds promise of a time when men and women will work together as equal partners, with confidence in each other. Society will then gain the full scientific talents of the other half of its people.

References

ALLEN, G. (1975) *Life Science in the 20th Century*, New York, John Wiley and Sons.

BASCOM, J. (1908) 'Coeducation', *Educational Review*, 36, p. 444.

BOAS, L.S. (1935) *Woman's Education Begins: The Rise of Women's Colleges*, Norton, MA., Wheaton College Press.

BOYD, W. and KING, E.J. (1975) *History of Western Civilization*, Totowa, NJ, Barnes and Noble.

COLE, J.R. (1979) *Fair Science: Women in the Scientific Community*, New York, The Free Press.

COLE, J.R. and COLE, S. (1973) *Social Stratification in Science*, Chicago, IL, University of Chicago Press.

COMSTOCK, A.L. (1930) *The American College Girl*, Boston, MA., L.C. Page and Co.

EARNEST, E. (1953) *Academic Procession*, Indianapolis, IN, Bobbs-Merrill Co.

FELDMAN, S. (1974) *Escape from the Doll's House*, New York, McGraw-Hill.

GOLDSTEIN, P. (1965) *Triumphs of Biology*, Garden City, NY, Doubleday and Co.

GOODSELL, W. (Ed.) (1931) *Pioneers of Women's Education in the United States*, New York, McGraw-Hill.

HALL, G.S. (1905) *Adolescence: Its Psychology and Its Relations to Physiology, Anthropology, Sociology, Crime, Religion and Education*, Vol. 2, New York, D. Appleton and Co., (reprinted by Arno Press, 1969).

JAMES, E.T., JAMES, J.W. an BOYER, P.S. (Eds.) (1971) *Notable American Women, 1607–1950*, Vol. I–III, Cambridge, MA., Belknap Press of Harvard University Press.

LEWIS, J.A. (1949) 'Harvard goes coed, but incognito', *New York Times Magazine*, 1 May, p. 38.

LOPATE, C. (1968) *Women in Medicine*, Baltimore, MD., The John Hopkins University Press.

MONROE, P. (1919) *A Textbook in the History of Education*, New York, Macmillan Co.

MOORE, R. (1961) *The Coil of Life*, New York, Alfred A. Knopf.

MOZANS, H.K. (1913) *Woman in Science, with an Introductory Chapter on Woman's Long Struggle for Things of the Mind*, New York, D. Appleton and Co.

MYRDAL, G. (1944) *An American Dilemma*, New York, Harper and Row.

NATIONAL ACADEMY OF SCIENCES (NAS) (1979) *Climbing the Academic Ladder: Doctoral Women Scientists in Academe*, Washington, DC, National Academy of Sciences.

NATIONAL CENTER FOR EDUCATION STATISTICS (1980) *Digest of Educational Statistics*, Washington, DC, US Government Printing Office.

NATIONAL RESEARCH COUNCIL (NRC) (1979, 1980, 1981) *Summary Reports of Doctoral Recipients from United States Universities*, Washington, DC,

National Academy of Sciences.

NEWCOMER, M. (1959) *A Century of Higher Education for American Women*, New York, Harper and Brothers.

RUDOLPH, F. (1962) *The American College and University: A History*, New York, Random House.

SELLER, M. (1981) 'G. Stanley Hall and Edward Thorndike on the education of women: Theory and policy in the Progressive Era', *Education Studies*, 11, p. 366.

SICHERMAN, B. and GREEN, C.H. (Eds) (1980) *Notable American Women: The Modern Period*, Cambridge, MA., The Belknap Press of Harvard University.

SINGER, C.J. (1941) *History of Science to the 19th Century*, London, Oxford University Press.

SINGER, C.J. (1955) *A History of Biology*, New York, H. Schuman.

TAYLOR, G.R. (1963) *The Science of Life*, London, Thames and Hudson.

THORNDIKE, E.L. (1906) 'Sex in education', *The Bookman*, 23, p. 212.

WOLFLE, D. (1954) *America's Sources of Specialized Talent*, New York, Harper and Brothers.

WOODY, T. (1929) *A History of Women's Education in the United States*, Vol. II, New York, The Science Press.

YOST, E. (1959) *Women of Modern Science*, New York, Dodd, Mead and Company.

ZUCKERMAN, H. and COLE, J.R. (1975) 'Women in American science', *Minerva*, 13, pp. 82–102.

2   Factors Affecting Female Achievement and Interest in Science and in Scientific Careers

Marsha Lakes Matyas
Purdue University

Research has consistently shown that, in general, girls do not achieve as well in science classes as do boys. Between ages nine and fourteen, girls' science achievement declines and their interest in science wanes (NAEP, 1978; Hardin and Dede, 1978). During high school girls do not elect to take science and mathematics courses as often as do their male peers (Dearman and Plisko, 1981; NSF, 1982); and, among college-bound senior high school students taking the Scholastic Aptitude Tests (SAT) in 1980, males outscored females by eight points on the verbal portion and forty-eight points on the mathematical portion. In college fewer girls choose science, especially the physical sciences, as their major area of study. On the other hand, the percentage of young women choosing social science as their field of study is twice the percentage of young men, and three times as many women as men select education as a college major (Butler and Marzone, 1980). Although equal percentages of men and women choose biological sciences as a field of study, the percentage of men entering physical science is twice that of women, entering technical majors (e.g., electronics, mechanics, data processing) is 3.5 times that of women, and entering engineering is 9.5 times the percentage of women (Butler and Marzone, 1980).

These statistics should not be interpreted as an indication that women have not been interested in science and in scientific careers. Historically, women have contributed in botany, astronomy, anatomy, bacteriology, anthropology, psychology, and nutrition and, recently, opportunities have opened for them in other scientific fields. The data, however, indicate that factors still exist which significantly affect young women's science education as well as entrance and retention in a scientific career. In order to increase the number of women in science, these factors must be exposed and examined. A considerable body of work is in progress and, in general, researchers have isolated three groups of factors: educational, sociocultural, and personal. In this chapter all three types will be examined.

Educational Factors

To examine educational factors affecting girls' avoidance of science, one logically studies formal science classes, for it is expected that most students receive their first formal science instruction within a class. Florence Howe (1978) has described the critical impact of school learning on a child's future interests and career choice: 'What you learn in school is not a joking matter. It forms an invisible network of belief — interfaced by the networks of church and family and now the media — that may blind you or may free you to see' (p. 21). Some believe that differential experiences within science and mathematics classes have not 'freed' women to perceive future scientific careers (Skolnick, Langbort and Day, 1982; Kahle and Lakes, 1983). Recent data from the 1976–77 National Assessment of Educational Progress (NAEP) provide strong support for the claim that boys and girls do not receive the same science education within the critical environment of the classroom.

Class Experiences

In 1976–77 NAEP conducted its third survey of science. Using national samples of nine, thirteen, and 17-year-olds, it assessed both science achievement levels and science attitudes. The student sample was balanced according to race and community type and is generalizable to the national population. The results showed that, as early as age thirteen, girls' science achievement was significantly lower than that of boys. In addition, the responses to attitudinal items indicated that girls, compared with boys of the same age, held less positive attitudes toward science and had participated in far fewer science activities (Kahle and Lakes, 1983) Differences between boys and girls in attitudes toward and achievement in science are not restricted to the United States. A recent multi-national study explored the relationship between science attitudes and science achievement in nineteen countries. The results were described by Allison Kelly (1981), who stated that '... pupils with favorable attitudes toward science tended to achieve better in science than pupils with less favorable attitudes. Attitudes toward science were significantly related to achievement in science even when ability ... was taken into account' (p. 36).

In order to understand the cause of achievement and attitudinal differences, responses to two types of NAEP questions were examined. One type of question assessed the number of actual science experiences encountered by a student; the second type assessed the student's wish to participate in these same activities regardless of actual participation opportunities. Responses to this second type of question indicate whether girls' reported lack of science experiences was due to lack of interest or dearth of opportunity. Responses comparing girls' desires for typical classroom science experiences (e.g., 'Would you like to see a sprouting seed?') versus their actual experiences ('Have you seen for real a sprouting seed?') revealed some surprising results (Figure 2.1). At age 9, although girls expressed interest in many science activities, the actual number of science activities they had participated in was significantly less than the number boys had experienced. For example, the NAEP survey included questions on a variety of scientific instruments, phenomena, and experiences (Figures 2.1–2.2). Girls were asked whether they would like to observe scientific phenomena (birds hatching and seeds sprouting, etc.), use scientific equipment (scales, telescopes, thermometers, and compasses) and work with experimental materials (magnets, electricity, and plants). Girls consistently reported fewer experiences with these scientific materials than did boys of the same age. However, other responses, in general, indicated that girls as well as boys wished to have these opportunities (Kahle and Lakes, 1983). Other responses by 13 and 17-year-olds indicated that the disparity in science experiences between boys and girls increased with age. In addition, responses to science attitude questions indicated that girls' desires to participate in science activities diminished between ages 9 and 13. This decline parallels a decline in science achievement levels and in science experiences between 9, 13, and 17 years of age. According to the NAEP data, by the time students enter high school girls, compared with boys, have had fewer science experiences with instruments and materials and score lower on science and mathematical achievement tests.

Mathematics Curriculum

In addition to fewer basic science experiences, many researchers suggest that the lack of mathematical training for girls in elementary and secondary schools is critical. A substantial body of research has investigated factors affecting girls' lower achievement levels in mathematics and lower enrollment rates in advanced high school math courses. Much

Figure 2.2

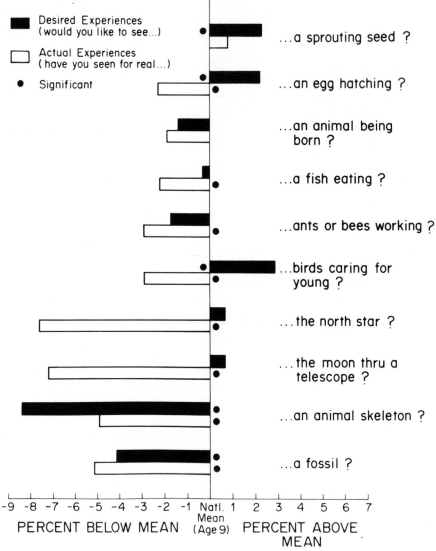

Female Differences From National Mean On Items
Concerning Desired Versus Actual Experiences Of
Scientific Observations, Age 9.

Source: Data drawn from Kahle and Lakes (1983).

Figure 2.1

Female Differences From National Mean On Items Concerning Desired Versus Actual Experiences In The Use Of Science Instruments, Age 9.

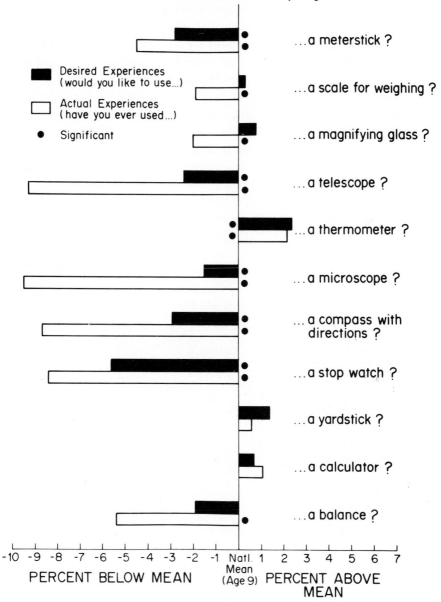

Source: Data drawn from Kahle and Lakes (1983).

of this work was inspired by early studies which indicated a large disparity between the percentages of males and females entering college with four years of high school mathematics (Sells, 1973). Researchers have estimated that high school graduates with less than a full college preparative series of mathematics courses may be filtered out of three-quarters of all college majors (Tobin in Iker, 1980). Since high school mathematics is a requirement for many occupations and fields of study (Table 2.1), mathematics has often been called the 'critical filter' in the training of future scientists and engineers.

Maccoby and Jacklin (1974) found that during elementary school both boys and girls enjoy mathematics. Nevertheless, by high school graduation, girls' SAT-Math scores are lower than boys' by almost fifty points. This difference does not appear to be due to differences in the math sequence taken but may result from attrition from that sequence. Recent data indicate that although comparable percentages of boys and

Table 2.1   High School and College Mathematics Required for Admission and Graduation, by Degree Program, Purdue University, 1983

School (degree program)	Required semesters	
	Admission	Graduation
SCIENCE (Biology, Chemistry, Computer Science, Geoscience, Mathematics, Physics, Statistics)	6	11
MANAGEMENT (Accounting, Business Law, Small Business Management, Economics, Finance, Industrial Relations, Investments, Marketing, Organizational Behavior)	6	14−17
PHARMACY (Community Practice, Hospital Pharmacy, Long-Term Care, Nuclear, Wholesale, Industrial, Government)	6	6
VETERINARY MEDICINE (Veterinarian, Veterinary Technology)	6	5
ENGINEERING (Aeronautical, Food, Forest, Chemical, Civil, Land Surveying, Construction, Electrical, Computer, Industrial, Mechanical, Nuclear)	6	17−21
NURSING (Registered Nurse, Bachelor's Degree)	4	0
HUMANITIES, SOCIAL SCIENCE, AND EDUCATION (Audiology and Speech, Communication, Creative Arts, English, History, Foreign Language, Philosophy, Political Science, Psychology, Sociology, Criminology, Social Work)	4	6
AGRICULTURE (Economics, Engineering, Finance, Sales and Marketing, Agronomy, Animal Sciences, Foods and Business Management, Food Science, Forestry, Horticulture, Landscape Architecture, Natural Resources Management, Wildlife Management)	4	8
TECHNOLOGY (Aviation, Building Construction, Computer, Electrical Engineering, Industrial Illustration, Mechanical Engineering, Supervision)	4	5−11
CONSUMER AND FAMILY SCIENCES (Nursery School or Day-Care Teaching, Consumer Sciences, Retailing, Food Science, Nutrition Science, Restaurant/Hotel/Institution Management, Vocational Home Economics)	2	3−6

Source: Data drawn from individual school bulletins, Purdue University, 1983.

girls (46.4 and 43.1 per cent respectively) enroll in college preparatory mathematics sequences in high school (Dearman and Plisko, 1981), on the average girls, compared with boys, still enter college with one-third year less high school mathematics (NSF, 1982; Chipman and Thomas, 1980). Girls' higher attrition rates from college preparatory math sequences cannot be attributed to poor grades. Remick and Miller (1978) found that Asian American and Caucasian American girls who continued beyond two years of college preparatory math were superior students, while their male colleagues in advanced courses were frequently average students.

Several explanations for the noted differences in enrollment patterns and achievement levels between girls and boys in math courses have been offered. Benbow and Stanley (1980, 1983) at The Johns Hopkins University suggest that boys perform better than girls on math achievement tests because they have greater aptitude for math, not because they enroll in more math courses. Additional studies, however, indicate otherwise. Sherman (1981) performed a longitudinal study on high school students to determine what factors were important in predicting whether students enroll in future mathematics courses. Her analysis (Table 2.2) indicates the following factors are most important for girls: (1) spatial visualization ability; (2) Quick Word Test performance; (3) perceived usefulness of mathematics; and (4) confidence in learning mathematics. The most important factor among girls in this study was spatial ability; that is, the ability to visualize objects in their spatial orientation and to rotate them within their field in one's imagination. Spatial ability has frequently been related to successful learning of mathematics. Previous studies have indicated that females, in general, have poorer spatial abilities than do males (Maccoby and Jacklin, 1974;

Table 2.2   *Rank Order of Importance of Variables Used to Predict Mathematics Enrollment among Secondary School Students by Sex, 1981*

Variables	Females	Males
Spatial visualization	1	11
Quick Word Test	2	5
Usefulness of mathematics	3	9.5
Confidence in learning mathematics	4	1
Mathematics achievement	5.5	2
Father's encouragement	5.5	8
Effectance motivation in math (enjoyment)	7	4
Attitude toward success in math	8.5	9.5
Math as a male domain	8.5	3
Teacher's encouragement	10	7
Mother's encouragement	11	6

Source: From Sherman (1981).

Treagust, 1980). However, Fennema and Sherman (1977) and deWolf (1981) found that when the number of space-related courses taken by students was considered, differences in spatial visualization abilities and mathematics achievement scores disappeared. Recently, Linn's (1982) meta-analysis of sex differences in spatial ability research revealed no significant differences betwen males and females before, during, or after puberty. Furthermore, Skolnick, Langbort and Day (1982) maintain that girls can improve their spatial abilities by relevant exercises and experiences and possibly increase their interest and achievement in math-science courses as well. Figure 2.3 provides an example of such an exercise. Of the three other factors cited by Sherman (1981), only one, the Quick Word Test, is a measure of ability. The Quick Word Test is described simply as a vocabulary test of verbal skill and general ability. The other two factors deal with girls' attitudes toward and perceptions of mathematics. Girls' perceptions of the future usefulness of mathematics as instrumental in their decision to take advanced courses has been cited not only by Sherman (1981) but also by other researchers (Iker, 1980; Fennema and Sherman, 1977). The same group of researchers also found that girls have less confidence in their ability to learn mathematics and do not perceive positive parental attitudes toward them as math learners. Girls, therefore, may not lack the necessary abilities for achievement in mathematics, although they do seem to lack the prerequisite positive attitudes and personal confidence.

The relationship between mathematics coursework and achievement and the possibility of a future science career seems clear. If girls take fewer high school math courses and have lower achievement levels in them, they limit their selection of scientific or technical majors in college as well as their probable success should they elect such a major. Research shows that professionals successful in math-related careers average at the 90th percentile level on SAT-Math tests (Chipman and Thomas, 1980). Those attaining these elite scores are usually males as are those students who have taken more than four years of mathematics in high school (Dearman and Plisko, 1981). Accordingly, if girls do not overcome a reticence to enroll in mathematics courses, the female pool of potential professional scientists and engineers will not increase effectively.

Extracurricular Activities

Disparities between the science education of girls and boys do not end at the classroom door; for girls report fewer science experiences both

Figure 2.3.

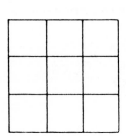

Can you find the 5 hidden
squares in this figure?

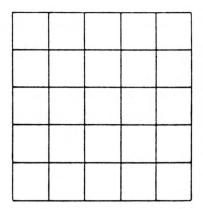

Can you find the 30 hidden
squares in this figure?

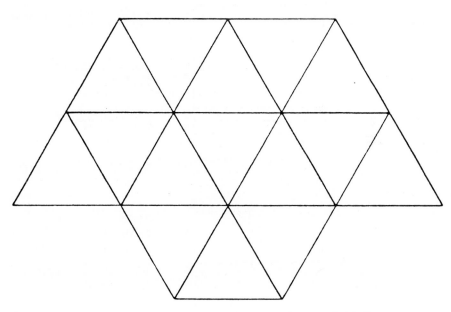

Can you find the 15 small triangles in this figure? Can you find 6 larger triangles? How many small diamond shapes can you find? Large diamond shapes? Hexagons? Trapezoids?

Source: From Skolnick, Langbort and Day (1982).

within and outside the classroom. According to Figure 2.4, responses to NAEP survey items showed that girls, ages thirteen and seventeen, participated in extracurricular science activities significantly fewer times than did boys. These activities included reading science articles and books, watching television shows on scientific topics, and doing science

Figure 2.4.

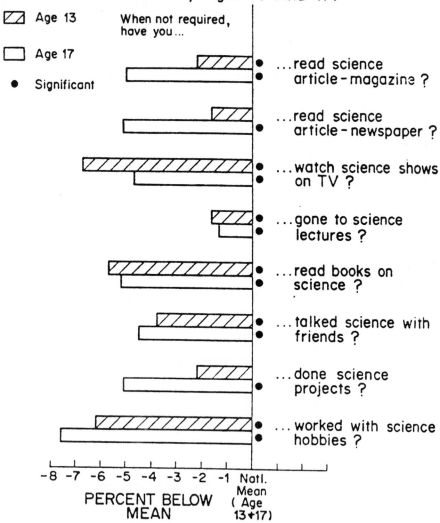

Female Differences From National Mean On Items Concerning Extracurricular, Non-required Science Activities, Ages 13 And 17.

Source: *Journal of Research in Science Teaching*, Jane Butler Kahle and Marsha K. Lakes, Copyright © 1983 by National Association for Research in Science Teaching, and John Wiley & Sons, Publishers. Reprinted by permission.

projects and hobbies. When field trip opportunities were surveyed, girls in all three age groups reported visiting far fewer places than did boys. Although 9-year-old girls expressed more interest than boys in participating in many field trips, by ages thirteen and seventeen fewer girls than boys had visited twelve out of fourteen field sites listed (Kahle and Lakes, 1983).

Even when children are at play, their experiences may provide unequal preparation for later science instruction. Male and female children are given different toys to play with and are encouraged by parents, teachers, and peers to engage in sex-appropriate play. Boys' toys and games tend to emphasize relationships between objects, manipulation of objects in space, grouping of objects, and taking apart and rebuilding of objects, while girls' activities are more closely associated with verbal, interpersonal, and fine-motor skills (Skolnick *et al.*, 1982). The play activities of boys, therefore, are more likely to provide practice at spatial-visualization tasks which are useful later in both science and mathematics courses.

These differences in types of play are common and appear to have long-term effects. In the NAEP survey, 13 and 17-year-old girls were asked how often they had done electrical or mechanical tasks (traditionally masculine tasks) and how often they had worked with an unhealthy plant or animal (traditionally feminine tasks) (Figure 2.5). Girls ranked far below boys in the number of times they had performed 'masculine tasks', yet above boys in number of times they had per-

Figure 2.5.

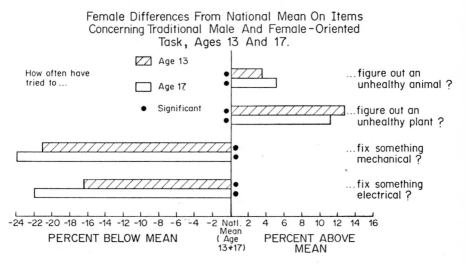

Source: Data drawn from Kahle and Lakes (1983).

formed 'feminine tasks'. These findings support those of Torrance who found that third grade girls were

> ... conditioned to accept toys as they are and not manipulate or change them ... By fifth grade, girls were quite reluctant to work with science toys at all and frequently protested 'I'm a girl, I'm not supposed to know anything about things like that'. Boys, even in these early grades, were about twice as good as girls at explaining ideas about toys (Torrance, 1962, p. 112).

The relationship between play and experiences and science classwork is clearly explained by Samuel (in Kelly, 1981):

> Boys are often encouraged to play with mechanical, electrical or construction toys and to help with tasks around the home involving tools, but girls are less likely to have this background experience. Thus, the girls are doing something new and unfamiliar in science laboratory classes, and it is, perhaps, not surprising that they often look for reassurance and encouragement, even though they have been given and have understood the directions (p. 248).

Samuel's explanation can be easily demonstrated by means of a simple analogy. Envision the thoughts and feelings of an adolescent boy asked to enter the kitchen, recipes and definition list in hand, and to prepare a full meal on which he will consequently be graded. Realize that he is in competition with female peers who, though they also have never done this particular task, have considerably greater facility with the equipment required. Perhaps by this analogy we can understand the apprehension of the adolescent girl deciding whether or not to take high school physics. In fact, a recent study performed in Nigeria provides strong evidence that sex stereotyping of tasks significantly influences performance (Ehindero, 1982). Although boys and girls perform equally well on gender-neutral Piagetian tasks, when mathematical word problems of equal difficulty but which deal with typically male or typically female situations are presented, boys perform significantly poorer on the feminine situation problems and girls perform significantly poorer on the masculine situation problems. Since the only differences in the problems are the content areas, extracurricular activities must play a role in children's familiarity with various content areas and, consequently, with their performances. The lack of familiarity with tools and techniques useful in science, many of which are available through extracurricular experiences, may be a contributing factor in girls' low enrollment levels and high attrition rates from science courses and perhaps in their lower achievement levels in science.

Socio-Cultural and Personal Factors

Research studies have explored a variety of social and personal factors which limit science as a career choice for girls. Since it is difficult to separate society's influence from personal choice, these two types of factors will be discussed together.

Sex-Role Stereotyping

Sex-role stereotyping has been cited as one of the major reasons for women's avoidance of science careers; that is, girls view science careers as masculine and, therefore, avoid them. Vockell and Lobonc (1981) tested these assumptions and found that high school girls rate science careers as masculine, especially physical science careers. Sex-role stereotyping of careers has been found as early as kindergarten (Vockell and Lobonc, 1981). In addition, the stereotyped characteristics associated with women are generally not those commonly associated with scientists. According to Broverman, Vogel, Broverman, Clarkson and Rosenkrantz (1972), women are associated with a 'warmth-expressiveness' cluster of attributes such as gentleness, quietness, tenderness, emotionality, passivity, dependence, and subjectivity. Men, on the other hand, are associated with characteristics such as aggressiveness, dominance, rationality, independence, calmness, un-emotionality, and objectivity (Broverman *et al.*, 1972). These traits are readily associated with the stereotypic view of scientists. A longitudinal study by Chambers (1983) asked 4807 children, grades K to five, to draw a picture of a scientist. Of the 4807 pictures drawn, only twenty-eight were of women, all drawn by girls. Clearly, children's stereotypic image of a scientist is masculine. Girls who are interested in science careers, therefore, must break the stereotypic mold of sex-appropriate careers, as well as accept that they will be associated with stereotypically-masculine attributes.

Not surprisingly, sex-role stereotyping of science careers is less pronounced among girls who attend single sex schools. Dale (1974) has found that girls in single sex schools have higher preferences for science and math courses than do girls in coeducational schools. This preference difference cannot be totally attributed to higher socio-economic status among girls in single sex schools. While holding socio-economic class factors constant, Dale has found that the student's choice of subject was still biased. Arithmetic and physics were favored among girls in single sex schools, while in coeducational schools girls chose French, sewing, and cooking. Perhaps girls in single sex schools do not feel some of the social pressures which affect girls enrolled in science and math classes in coeducational schools. A. Kelly (1981) made similar observations, finding that girls in single sex schools have better attitudes toward science than do their counterparts in coeducational classes.

With the current public emphasis on the feminist movement and on equal job opportunities for women, one would anticipate that stereotyping of occupations would decline. In fact, a recent study by Hensley and Borges (1981) found that females (age 7–8 and college age) did not sex-stereotype occupations but that males of the same age groups did. The same study also found that children of working mothers stereotyped occupations to a greater extent than did children of non-working mothers. It may be that children with working mothers have a more realistic view of the jobs to which women have ready access and, since over 50 per cent of children have mothers who are currently employed (Cocks, 1982), a large proportion of young girls may be confused by conflicting information. The information they are receiving from their mothers' experiences in the real world of employment opportunities contrasts with the information they may receive at school or through the media which indicates that professional careers in traditionally masculine areas are now open to young women. Such conflicting information leaves young women in a 'triple bind':

> [T]he traditional vision of the full time wife and mother conflicts with economic realities which dictate that most women must work; the newer vision of the career women conflicts with child rearing, which is still seen mainly as women's responsibility; and the new ethic of equality inspires girls to be more independent and competent than they suspect is really acceptable and more than they have been taught to feel. To reconcile old and new demands and their own feelings, girls would have to become superwomen (Skolnick *et al.*, 1982, p. 39).

Such conflicts are real and immediate for high school girls and may quench a girl's interest in a professional career. One 11th grade girl, when asked what she what she would like to do as an adult, stated that she would like a professional career, in this case, as a lawyer:

> As far as going to school, I can go to about any school I want to, but the thing is I don't know if I am going to go out and become a

lawyer after law school. It's like if I become a lawyer, it's a full-time operation and maybe I'll have a husband and I'll want to have kids. I would want to spend time with them and I don't know if I can be a full-time lawyer and a full-time lover, and I don't want to take anything away from my kids or take anything away from my occupation. It bothers me so much ... It's just that — I don't know — I want to be somebody that people write down in history, somebody that is not forgotten. I don't want to be just another skeleton in the ground. I think I will become a housewife and it bothers me because I don't know what to do (Skolnick *et al.*, 1982, p. 37).

These conflicts, resulting from social pressures, are experienced by many young women making professional career choices, and the social pressures are even greater for girls interested in science. Girls choosing to continue science and mathematics studies during high school may be viewed as non-conformists at a developmental period when conformity is highly valued by peers. Girls taking science courses describe themselves as '... less feminine, less attractive, less popular, and less sociable. That is, they appear to see themselves as less socially attractive than their peers' (Smithers and Collins in Kelly, 1981, p. 166). The seriousness of this social pressure is suggested by Fox (in Iker, 1980) who states that many gifted girls do not enter accelerated math courses because of negative social consequences, especially peer rejection. Horner (1972) and Stein and Bailey (1973) report that girls have lower motivation to achieve in traditionally male areas because of the perceived consequences. Finally, Ormerod (1975) summarizes this situation, stating that '... at an age when they are becoming acutely aware of the other sex, in co-education boys and girls are expressing preferences and, when possible, choices in such a way as to reaffirm their perceived sex role' (p. 265). Unfortunately, the socialized female sex role does not currently include scientific aspirations.

Role Models

If girls do not perceive science, math, and technological careers as appropriate for their sex, steps must be taken to change this perception. Emphasis has been placed on the use of role models to encourage girls' participation in science. Hardin and Dede (1978) point out that there is a dearth of female role models in scientific careers. In addition, many of these role models have not achieved success. Recent surveys indicate that women with advanced degrees do not obtain tenure as early and, at every degree level and age, are paid less than men (Vetter, 1981).

Research on the effects of role models on student behaviors has produced conflicting results. Some studies have found role models to be an important influence on the achievement and career decisions of female students (O'Donnell and Anderson, 1978; Seater and Ridgeway, 1976; Stake and Granger, 1978). Other studies, however, found that role models did not have a significant effect (Basow and Howe, 1980; Vockell and Lobonc, 1981). In addition, Kelly (1981) has found that, although the number of female role models varies from country to country, the difference in science achievement between girls and boys in various countries remains constant.

Before any effect of role models can be substantiated, researchers may need to delineate how role modeling actually works. Brush (1979) has found that the similarity between a student's self-image and her/his image of a scientist is a good predictor of whether that student chooses to take science classes. If a student attributes the same personal characteristic to her/himself as s/he does to a scientist, s/he is more likely to take optional science classes. The critical factor for role models, therefore, may be to emphasize the similarities between themselves and students. As stated by Ebbertt (in Kelly, 1981), 'If females in science careers are seen to require such characteristics as capability, logicality, and exactitude, there may be considerable self-selection away from science subjects by girls who do not see themselves as possessing these traits...' (p. 121).

One of the first science role models girls encounter is their science teacher. Many investigators agree that the importance of the teacher in developing a girl's attitude toward science cannot be overemphasized. Female scientists surveyed by Remick and Miller (1978) reported that the 'encouragement of a single high school teacher was the deciding factor in their choice of a career in science. (Higher school counselors, on the other hand, are uniformly reported as negative influences.)' (p. 282) Stake and Granger (1978) measured teacher influence on science career commitment and found that same-sex teachers perceived as an attractive individual by the student had a greater positive influence on science career commitment than did opposite-sex teachers. The highest science career commitment was found among students who had varied and important same-sex teacher contacts such as participation in science research projects under the direction of a same-sex role model. Unfortunately, only 24 per cent of all high school science teachers nationally are female (NSF, 1982), therefore, girls have fewer opportunities for this important same-sex teacher contact.

Other researchers have tried specifically to discern teacher behaviors which differentially affect boys and girls. Results indicate that boys receive more direct questions from their teachers than do girls, that boys are praised more frequently than are girls for correct answers, and overall that boys have more interactions with teachers than do girls (Brophy and Good, 1970). Although a greater amount of interaction with boys is concerned with criticism and disapproval, this negative feedback is generally directed toward disciplinary aspects rather than toward academic/work-related aspects of boys' behavior (Brophy and Good, 1970). Girls, on the other hand, receive more criticism of their academic performances than of their classroom actions. Negative academic interactions with teachers may be a significant reason for girls' lack of self-confidence and expectancy for success in academic settings (Fennema and Sherman, 1977).

Solutions

The factors affecting girls' levels of achievement and interest in science are many and diverse. Unlike blatant sex discrimination, these differences are subtle and, taken individually, appear almost insignificant. Their collective effect, however, exerts a powerful force upon young women to think long and hard before committing themselves to a scientific career. Not only must they make important decisions about the high academic standards demanded by science, but they must also decide to face the social and interpersonal conflicts which a science career currently places on women. If girls do not receive an equal science education at the elementary school level and then receive little encouragement during high school, there is little chance that they will become scientists. It will require the combined effort of teachers, parents, and counselors to break this pattern and to offer female students the chance to excel in science, mathematics, and engineering.

Because of the importance of teacher/student interactions, it is imperative that science teachers do not unwittingly convey perceptions of science as a masculine endeavor. Bowyer (in Trowbridge, Bybee and Sund, 1981), states that boys in school are 'valued for thinking logically, independently, with self-confidence, and an appropriate degree of risk taking.' Girls, however, are 'valued for their emotional expressiveness, sensitivity to others, dependency, and subjective thinking' (p. 97). Teachers' value judgments such as these do not increase girls' science potential and must be consciously avoided.

Some researchers have suggested that girls and boys may require different teaching methods for optimal achievement in science classes (Ormerod, 1975; Treagust, 1980). There may be simpler, more direct solutions to the problem, however. For example, girls' extracurricular science activities might be increased by offering more in-class activities. Classroom data indicate that for grades K-3, only seventeen minutes per day and during grades 4–6 only twenty-eight minutes per day are spent in science instruction (Weiss, 1978). In addition, 36 per cent of all elementary science classes are conducted in rooms with no science facilities whatsoever. School boards and administrators, therefore, need to mandate more time to be spent each day on science activities and more funding for science equipment.

This lack of classroom science activities may also be due to inadequate science training among elementary school teachers. Only 22 per cent of elementary school teachers in the same survey indicated that they felt 'very well qualified' to teach science, and 16 per cent indicated they were not well qualified to teach science (Weiss, 1978). With this in mind, the number of science activities for all students might be increased by improving the science preparation of elementary school teachers. In addition, materials are now available to help teachers at both the elementary and junior high school levels teach children basic skills in science, mathematics, graphing, and spatial visualization (Skolnick *et al.*, 1982). These materials can provide girls with the practice needed to catch up and keep up with their male peers in science and mathematics.

Undoubtedly, a key factor in changing girls' attitudes will be science teachers and counselors and their attitudes. As stated by Skolnick *et al.* (1982), 'Teachers' expectations are communicated to children in myriad ways, not only through what they say explicitly but also through what they do not say, what they do, and whom they call on. Indirect or covert messages constitute a hidden curriculum which is sometimes more powerful than the lessons in the textbooks...' (p. 17). If teachers in both elementary and high schools can convey positive attitudes toward scientific and mathematical studies and can encourage girls to pursue science course work and careers, then real changes in female achievement in and attrition from science courses might occur.

High school counselors have been cited as a negative factor in girls' choice of science as a career (Remick and Miller, 1978). Counselors must convey to students the knowledge that class and curriculum choices early in high school can eliminate science career choices later on. Girls must be encouraged not only to pursue but also to excel in mathematics; their confidence in their math skills must be bolstered, and their participation in spatial visualization activities should be stressed. Counselors must emphasize to young women the wide range of scientific occupations available to them and encourage them to keep their options open by pursuing science and mathematics electives during high school.

Finally, the role of parents in developing positive attitudes toward science cannot be ignored. Parental influence on a girl's potential as a scientist begins in the preschool years. Through toys, games, and play, parents can encourage their daughters' inquisitiveness and development of spatial visualization and problem-solving skills (Skolnick *et al.*, 1982). During later childhood and adolescence, parents can exert a great influence on choice of extracurricular activities for their children and can affect both the number and kind of science activities girls experience outside school. As previously discussed, parental attitudes toward girls' science classwork affect girls' choices of science classes, their confidence in math classes, and their perception of science as masculine. In addition, lack of parental encouragement operates as a factor in the high attrition rate of girls from science majors in college (Graham, 1978). Finally, parents must take an active interest in the science education their children are receiving.

Summary

In summary, several factors significantly contribute to lower science and mathematics achievement levels of girls as well as their higher attrition rates from scientific courses and careers. A lack of science-based experimental and extracurricular activities in the elementary school years followed by less than a full college preparatory series of mathematics and science courses places girls at a disadvantage when selecting a college major and ultimately a career. In addition, various socio-cultural factors including sex-role stereotyping, peer pressure, and lack of or ineffectual role models discourage girls from science classes and careers. Interactions with teachers, parents, and counselors may fail to provide the kind of encouragement necessary to prevent or to overcome these socio-cultural factors.

Finally, it should be noted that the intent of any educational program should not be to force girls into a career unsuited to their particular talents and interests, but, as stated by Kaminiski and Erickson (1979), 'This is not to argue that all females need to be pushed into science careers. Rather, like high school males, more females (particularly those with higher ability) need to leave a wider variety of options open to themselves for later, more informed career decisions'

(p. 15). The technological society in which we live cannot afford to lose the scientific brainpower of over one-half of its population. Girls still should be free to see themselves as scientists and engineers and to see science as a viable option by the time they reach college. It is critical that girls do not close the door to scientific success at the level of the primary or secondary school.

References

BASOW, S.A. and HOWE, K.G. (1980) 'Role-model influence: Effects of sex and sex-role attitude in college students', *Psychology of Women Quarterly*, 4, 4, pp. 558–72.

BENBOW, C.P. and STANLEY, J.C. (1980) 'Sex differences in mathematical ability: Fact or artifact?' *Science*, 210, pp. 1262–4.

BENBOW, C.P. and STANLEY, J.C. (1983) 'Sex differences in mathematical reasoning ability: More facts', *Science*, 222, pp. 1029–31.

BROPHY, J.E., and GOOD, T.L. (1970) 'Teachers' communication of differential expectations for children's classroom performance: Some behavioral data,' *Journal of Educational Psychology*, 61, 5, pp. 365–74.

BROVERMAN, I.K., VOGEL, S.R., BROVERMAN, D.M., CLARKSON, F.E. and ROSENKRANTZ, P.S. (1972) 'Sex-role stereotypes: A current appraisal', *Journal of Social Issues*, 28, 2, pp. 59–78.

BRUSH, L.R. (1979) 'Avoidance of science and stereotypes of scientists', *Journal of Research in Science Teaching*, 16, 3, pp. 237–41.

BUTLER, M. and MARZONE, J. (1980) *Education: The Critical Filter. A Statistical Report on the Status of Female Students in Post-Secondary Education*, Vol. 2, San Francisco, CA., Women's Educational Equity Communications Network Far West Laboratory for Educational Research and Development.

CHAMBERS, D.W. (1983) 'Stereotypic images of the scientist: The draw-a-scientist test,' *Science Education*, 67, pp. 255–65.

CHIPMAN, S.F. and THOMAS, V.G. (1980) *Women's Participation in Mathematics: Outlining the Problem*, Washington, DC, Report to the National Institute of Education, Teaching and Learning Division.

COCKS, J. (1982) 'How long till equality?' *Time*, 12 July, pp. 20–9.

DALE, R.R. (1974) *Mixed or Single Schools*, Vol. 3, London, Routledge and Kegan Paul.

DEARMAN, N.B. and PLISKO, V.W. (1981) *The Condition of Education*, Washington, DC, National Center for Education Statistics.

DEWOLF, V.A. (1981) 'High school mathematics preparation and sex differences in quantitative abilities,' *Psychology of Women Quarterly*, 5, 4, pp. 555–67.

EHINDERO, O.J. (1982) 'Correlates of sex-related differences in logical reasoning,' *Journal of Research in Science Teaching*, 19, pp. 553–7.

FENNEMA, E. and SHERMAN, J. (1977) 'Sex-related differences in mathematics achievement, spatial visualization and affective factors,' *American Educational Research Journal*, 14, 1, pp. 51–71.

GRAHAM, M.F. (1978) 'Sex differences in science attrition', Doctoral dissertation, State University of New York at Stony Brook, 1978, *Dissertation Abstracts International*, 39, 2570–B (University Microfilms No. 78–21, 847).

HARDIN, J. and DEDE, C.J. (1978) 'Discrimination against women in science education,' *The Science Teacher*, 40, pp. 18–21.

HENSLEY, K.K. and BORGES, M.A. (1981) 'Sex role stereotyping and sex role norms: A comparison of elementary and college age students,' *Psychology of Women Quarterly*, 5, 4, pp. 543–54.

HORNER, M.S. (1972) 'Toward an understanding of achievement-related conflicts in women,' *Journal of Social Issues*, 28, pp. 157–75.

HOWE, F. (1971) 'Sexual stereotypes start early,' *Saturday Review*, 16 October, pp. 76–94.

HOWE, F. (1978) 'Myths of Coeducation,' Paper presented at Wooster College, Wooster, OH, November.

IKER, S. (1980) 'A math answer for women,' *MOSAIC*, 11, pp. 39–45.

KAHLE, J.B. and LAKES, M.K. (1983) 'The myth of equality in science classrooms,' *Journal of Research in Science Teaching*, 20, pp. 131–40.

KAMINSKI, D.M. and ERICKSON, E. (1979) 'The magnitude of sex role influence on entry into science careers,' Paper presented at the meeting of the American Sociological Association, Boston, August 1979 (ERIC Document Reproduction Service No. ED 184855).

KELLY, A. (1981) *The Missing Half*, Manchester, England, Manchester University Press.

LINN, M. (1982) 'Gender differences in spatial ability; meta-analysis,' Paper presented at Purdue University, November.

MACCOBY, E.M. and JACKLIN, C.N. (1974) *The Psychology of Sex Differences*, Stanford, CA., Stanford University Press.

NATIONAL ASSESSMENT OF EDUCATIONAL PROGRESS (NAEP) (1978) *Science Achievement in the Schools* (Science Report No. 08-S-01), Denver, CO, Education Commission of the States, December.

NATIONAL SCIENCE FOUNDATION (NSF) (1982) *Science and Engineering Education: Data and Information* (NSF 82–30), Washington, DC, National Science Foundation.

O'DONNELL, J.A. and ANDERSON, D.G. (1978) 'Factors influencing choice of major and career of capable women,' *Vocational Guidance Quarterly*, 26, pp. 215–21.

ORMEROD, M.B. (1975) 'Subject preference and choice in co-educational and single-sex secondary schools,' *British Journal of Educational Psychology*, 45, pp. 257–67.

REMICK, H. and MILLER, K. (1978) 'Participation rates in high school mathematics and science courses,' *The Physics Teacher*, May, pp. 280–2.

SEATER, B.B. and RIDGEWAY, C.L. (1976) 'Role models, significant others, and the importance of male influence on college women,' *Sociological Symposium*, 15, pp. 49–64.

SELLS, L.W. (1973) 'High school mathematics as the critical filter in the job market,' Unpublished manuscript, University of California, Berkeley.

SHERMAN, J. (1981) 'Girls' and boys' enrollments in theoretical math courses: A longitudinal study,' *Psychology of Women Quarterly*, 5, 5, pp. 681–9.

SKOLNICK, J., LANGBORT, C. and DAY, L. (1982) *How to Encourage Girls in Math & Science*, Englewood Cliffs, NJ, Prentice-Hall.

STAKE, J.E. and GRANGER, C.R. (1978) 'Same-sex and opposite-sex teacher model influences on science career commitments among high school students,' *Journal of Education Psychology*, 70, pp. 180–6.

STEIN, A.A. and BAILEY, M.M. (1973) 'The socialization of achievement orientation in females, *Psychological Bulletin*, 80, pp. 345–66.

TORRANCE, E.P. (1962) *Guiding Creative Talent*, Englewood Cliffs, NJ, Prentice-Hall.

TREAGUST, D.F. (1980) 'Gender-related differences of adolescents in spatial representational thought,' *Journal of Research in Science Teaching*, 17, pp. 91–7.

TROWBRIDGE, L.W., BYBEE, R.W. and SUND, R.B. (1981) *Becoming a Secondary School Teacher*, Columbus, OH, Charles E. Merrill.

VETTER, B.M. (1981) 'Women scientists and engineers: Trends in participation,' *Science*, 214, pp. 1313–21.

VOCKELL, E.L. and LOBONC, S. (1981) 'Sex-role stereotyping by high school females in science,' *Journal of Research in Science Teaching*, 18, pp. 209–19.

WEISS, I.R. (1978) *Report of the 1977 National Survey of Science, Mathematics and Social Studies Education* (SE–78–72), Washington, DC, U.S. Government Printing Office.

3   Retention of Girls in Science: Case Studies of Secondary Teachers

Jane Butler Kahle
Professor of Biological Sciences and Education
Purdue University

As described in the previous chapter, some obstacles to girls and women in science are found in our schools and classrooms. Yet, my observations have been that some teachers, perhaps using unique instructional materials or techniques, are inordinately successful in encouraging girls in school to become women in science. In order to quantify those observations, I began to keep records when I was asked to evaluate a teacher or a program. I found several commonalities and developed some scales in order to quantify my observations. Verification of my casual observations was the next step, and the national concern with science and mathematics education provided the opportunity. The National Science Board's prestigious Committee on Precollege Education in Mathematics, Science, and Technology asked the National Association of Biology Teachers' Committee on the Role and Status of Women in Biology Education to assess factors influencing the retention of women in science.

This chapter describes our nine-month project, conducted from Maine to California.[1] Committee members, supplemented by other concerned researchers, sought to observe, describe, and analyze teaching strategies and teacher attitudes which successfully encouraged girls in science. Biology, taken by over 80 per cent of high school students, was the course selected for observation; for if girls are turned off to science in biology, they effectively close the doors to scientific or technological careers. Two types of information were gathered: first, qualitative assessments, which formed the basis of individual, observational case studies; and, second, quantitative assessments, which provided the data for an overall summary.

Two types of people have contributed greatly to the information included in this chapter: Case Study Researchers,[2] the people who conducted the studies and described their observations; and Case Study Teachers,[3] the classroom instructors who were observed and who assisted by distributing and collecting surveys, by being interviewed, and by arranging for the researcher to interact with administrators, parents, and students. Researchers were sought who could provide geographic, racial, and socio-economic representation in the various case studies. Each researcher was free to select a case study teacher for his/her report. The basic criterion was that the teacher selected had to have a proven record of success with young women in science. The distribution of the case study researchers resulted in the diversity of sites, shown in Table 3.1. Although it was hoped that certain standardized data could be collected, the primary aim of the study was the thoughtful observation and analysis of teacher behavior and student/teacher interactions. The intent of the overall project was to identify instructional strategies or teaching behaviors among the teachers, from rural Texas to urban Chicago, which could be adopted by other teachers to improve the retention and achievement of girls in science classes and the entrance and success of women in science careers.

Table 3.1　*Number of Schools in Basic Groups*

Geographic area	Community type	Racial/ethnic group
1 East	3 Urban	4 White, Non-Hispanic
3 Midwest	2 Suburban	2 Black
2 South	3 Small town/rural	2 Hispanic
1 Rocky Mountain		
1 Far West		

Note: One school was dropped from the data analyses because surveys were not completed. It was in the Far West area and was an urban school with a predominantly Hispanic population.

Case Studies

Throughout our work we have asked, individually and collectively, what makes these teachers exceptional? How do they succeed, not only in encouraging girls, but in inspiring both boys and girls in science? What commonalities are found in these classrooms from Maine to California, from center city to rural community, from modern edifice to deteriorating facade? What theme unites their work and our study? The answers have been obtained from hours of transcribed interviews, from dozens of former student notes and messages, from carefully articulated reports of trained observers, from responses to thousands of survey items, and from a critical review of the literature. Although commonalities will be discussed among teachers and across student groups, the purpose of our study was to observe in diverse communities. Therefore, there are few similarities among schools or communities. The hope was that eight diverse situations would provide a composite picture as well as a collective pool of data, in which commonalities could be found and from which generalizations could be made. This chapter, then, provides both a qualitative and quantitative description of teachers who make a difference.

Communities and Schools

All socio-economic levels were represented in the overall sample of students and in the sample of schools. The urban schools in two diverse metropolitan areas as well as several rural schools described at least part of their students as disadvantaged. In contrast, another school was in an affluent white suburb, and one enrolled middle-class and upper-middle-class blacks. In some cases, the general socio-economic level of students within a school was atypical of the community in general; the central city high school in Colorado, the laboratory school in Louisiana, and the inner city school in Chicago were examples of this situation. In other instances, the school population reflected the general socio-economic level of the community; for example, in Indiana, Maine, and Missouri, the schools were microcosms of their communities. Although political and religious information was reported sporadically, there was every reason to believe that all views were expressed approximately pro-portionally to their national representation. Together the communities and schools formed a composite picture of public high schools in the United States.

Classrooms and Instruction

Although the physical condition of the eight high schools varied greatly, all the biology rooms observed were filled with posters, pictures, models, live specimens, equipment, and projects. They were visually stimulating. One commonality among these eight teachers, who had been successful in encouraging girls in science, was an attractive, well-equipped and maintained classroom. Each case study researcher attributed these pleasant learning places to the energy, creativity, and initiative of the individual teacher. In diverse schools and communities, these teachers had been successful in creating optimal learning environments. The extent of their success may be found by comparing their responses to items on a survey concerning facilities to those of a national sample (Weiss, 1978).[4] Although teachers in both the case study and the national samples responded that improvement was needed in building/classroom facilities (28.6 per cent and 34 per cent respectively), space for classroom preparation (28.6 per cent and 28 per cent respectively), space for small group work (42.9 per cent and 44 per cent respectively), and availability of laboratory assistants or paraprofessionals (71.4 per cent and 62 per cent respectively), the case study teachers compared to the national survey teachers did not report a need for more equipment (14.3 per cent vs 35 per cent respectively), supplies (0 per cent vs 21 per cent), money for daily supplies (14.3 per cent vs 47 per cent), or storage space (14.3 per cent vs 39 per cent). The ambience of their classrooms, pleasant, cheerful, and well-stocked, was the first commonality identified among the teachers in these divergent schools.

Many of the observed teachers bemoaned the quality of the curricular materials, particularly the textbooks, available. One suggested that she had gone along with the other teachers in selecting a traditional text, while another one defended her style of 'teaching from the text'. All of them responded that they used more than one published text (compared to 52 per cent of the national sample who used multiple texts) and six of the seven biology teachers reported that they frequently used text replacements or supplements.[5] All texts in use were analyzed for sexism in language, illustrations, citations, and references. Those analyses suggested that although progress had been made, it was limited. Women, for example, were pictured in non-traditional careers and were represented in approximately 50 per cent of the illustrations. However, their meaningful contributions to science were seldom cited or referenced.

In addition, teacher-developed instructional materials were examined for any sexist characteristics. Almost all used both pronouns or the plural pronoun; approximately equal numbers of scientists, researchers, etc. were referred to as men or as women. In one lesson concerning superstitions about reproduction and birth, items showing both male and female bias were included. In answers to surveys taken prior to the study, all case study teachers stated an awareness of sexism in science. For example, 71 per cent of these teachers stated that they included information about the important contributions of women scientists in their class discussions and that they tried to correct the conception that science is an exclusively male domain. Seventy-one per cent of them had invited female scientists to their classes to discuss science careers with their students. Generally, another commonality among these teachers was the complete absence of sexist language, materials, or humor in their instructional materials.

As a group, the case study teachers taught in a particular way. When compared with the national sample, described by Weiss (1978), they reported using laboratory and discussion activities much more frequently. Over 80 per cent of the case study teachers used laboratory materials in their classes at least once a week; less than half of the national survey teachers used hands-on materials that often. Dramatic differences are shown in Table 3.2 in the use of science materials by these two groups of science instructors. All of the case study teachers indicated that microscopes, models, balances, living plants, and living animals were essential for teaching their science classes and a large majority of these teachers used these materials ten or more days. One-third or more of the national survey teachers responded that microscopes, living plants, and living animals were unnecessary for instructing their classes. Furthermore, all of the case study teachers used microscopes ten or more days each year, while only one-half of the national survey teachers used microscopes that often.

In addition, a majority of the case study teachers used filmstrips,

Table 3.2.   Use of Audio-Visual Equipment and Science Materials by Frequency and Availability

Audio-visual equipment	Used once per month or more		Percentage of teachers Needed but not available		Not needed	
	NABT sample	National sample	NABT sample	National sample	NABT sample	National sample
Films	71.4	55	0	9	0	5
Filmstrips	100	48	0	8	0	8
Film loops	57.1	8	14.3	22	0	38
Slides	71.4	10	14.3	20	0	32
Overheads	71.4	38	0	4	28.6	19
Videotape	0	10	14.3	16	0	54

Science materials	Used more than ten days		Needed but not available		Not needed	
Calculators	28.6	26	14.3	14	14.3	47
Microscopes	100	50	0	1	0	33
Models	85.7	44	0	12	0	15
Balance	71.4	57	14.3	1	0	9
Living plants	71.4	38	0	4	0	39
Living animals	71.4	28	0	7	0	43

film loops, and slides at least once a month; less than one-half of the national survey teachers used those media as often. Over one-half of the national sample indicated that videotapes were not needed for their teaching; although most case study teachers did not use videotapes often (85.7 per cent responded they used this item 'less than once a month'), all of these teachers indicated that videotapes were necessary for their instruction.

In addition, all of them responded that they used weekly quizzes or tests. In comparison, only 37 per cent of the national sample responded that they evaluated students at least once a week. The case study teachers invited in guest speakers and took their students on field trips more often than the national sample. Furthermore, students of the case study teachers were more frequently assigned independent projects, library research, and televised instruction. In contrast to the national sample, these teachers less often lectured or performed teacher demonstrations.

All of these responses suggest good science teaching as another commonality among these teachers. In fact, we began to wonder if there were any unique teaching behaviors contributing to their success with girls. We found unique behaviors as we observed their interactions with students, which will be described later. However, it is important to note that laboratory-based science teaching has been found to be an especially effective strategy for interesting girls in science (Harding, 1983). Over and over, girls responded 'The labs', to the question, 'What do you like best about your high school biology class?' Perhaps it was expressed best by a 15-year-old, black girl in the deep south, who said, 'I enjoyed working with microscopes. We had a cow heart and we opened it up. [We] looked in the microscope at the different parts of the inside of the heart and I enjoyed that.' Instructional techniques that involve students also may encourage and excite young women to study science. As a minority girl in a large city school stated, '[Our teacher] always has discussions. We always ask questions, and we learn the most from discussions.'

Teachers

The case study teachers had taught an average of 18.4 years and all of them held college degrees beyond the bachelor degree level. Five of the seven held at least one biology degree. Science teachers in the national survey, on the other hand, had taught an average of 11.8 years and only 54 per cent held advanced degress. Eighty-six per cent of the case study teachers were women; nationally, women compose 24 per cent of all science teachers. Both groups of teachers had approximately the same number of students per class; the averages were 25.2 students per class for case study teachers and 22.8 for national survey teachers. While the majority of teachers in both groups reported their classes were composed mainly of students with average abilities or with a wide range of ability levels, more case study teachers than national survey teachers taught high ability students. However, none of the case study teachers was teaching classes composed primarily of low ability students.

These instructors taught between two and six hours of biology classes a day and spent four or more hours a week preparing biology lessons. Four of the teachers sponsored a science club at their high school. In general, teachers thought their science programs were well supported by their school communities. Responses to items querying sources of support rated parental support the highest. It was followed by support from other teachers, principals, superintendents, and school boards, in that order. Six of the teachers reported that they were more enthusiastic about teaching now than when they began their careers. In addition, their answers to items in a science attitude inventory indicated that they held very positive attitudes toward science as a discipline.

The case study teachers were active professionals. All but one had attended at least one science-related professional meeting within the last ten years. Eighty-six per cent had made presentations at local science teacher meetings or at in-service teacher education functions. Most of them had been involved in science-related activities outside their school. For example, several had coordinated science workshops and science fairs, one was on the local park board, and one had been on the staff of a college marine biology institute. Their hobbies ranged from soapbox racing and hot air ballooning to reading and gardening. Several indicated that they enjoyed photography and had science-related hobbies such as bird-watching and wildlife exploring.

The case study teachers were special in two other aspects of teaching. They provided career information and related biology to everyday life. Although all students liked those aspects of their biology classes, girls, especially, mentioned them. For example, girls attending an affluent, suburban school commented, 'She gives us up-to-date information and relates it to how we are living today. She does not give us old stuff from the textbook . . . If we want to go into a science career, she tells you what classes you should take for a particular career.'

When survey responses were tabulated for all case study students, both boys and girls were positive about the instructional techniques of

Jane Butler Kahle

their teachers. As Table 3.3 shows, these teachers were uniformly fair in their treatment and expectations of both boys and girls. In fact, this unisex treatment was another commonality found. Unfortunately, most teachers still hold, consciously or unconsciously, sex- stereotypes which affect their classroom behaviors. The importance of teacher behavior and instructional style cannot be underestimated. Jan Harding (1983) suggests that they may be more influential in encouraging girls in science than the presence of a same-sex role model as a science teacher.

Table 3.3. Male and Female Students' Perceptions of Their Case Study Teacher

| Does your biology teacher... | Students who agree | |
	Percentage of Males	Percentage of Females
encourage you to be creative, original?	58.2	66.8
differentiate between jobs for males and for females?	27.0	23.3
frequently talk with you individually?	57.4	54.5
encourage education and/or training beyond high school?	67.1	76.5*
describe science course work as difficult?	28.9	21.5
give advice on future plans?	38.7	37.9
encourage mathematics courses?	50.3	44.0
encourage optional choices for post-high school?	47.5	42.2
differentiate between courses in which males and females can be successful?	27.1	14.0*
encourage basic skills?	70.5	72.4
treat you childishly?	20.1	12.5*
seldom take your opinions seriously?	18.0	18.5

Key: * Denotes significance at the .10 level.

Descriptions of Current Students

Students who were currently enrolled in biology courses taught by the case study teachers were asked to complete several demographic surveys, attitude scales, and cognitive ability tests. Their responses were voluntary and not all students chose to return them. However, the majority did and their answers paint a generalized picture, if not a detailed portrait, of a diverse, national sample of students. In addition to questions concerned with demographics (grade, gender, race, etc.), previous academic experiences, and extracurricular activities, students responded to items about their future career plans, including any probability of science careers, as well as their opinions concerning women's roles and scientific abilities. Furthermore, each student received a spatial visualization test, a cognitive style test, a locus of

56

control test, a science attribution scale, a science attitudes scale, and a science anxiety scale. These tests were selected and used because scores on each of them have revealed gender differences in previous research. It was hypothesized that there would be no differences between the scores of male and female students for the variables of science attitudes, science anxiety, and participation in extracurricular science activities. In other words, the case study teachers would have had a positive influence on the science attitudes, the levels of science anxiety, and the number of science extracurricular activities of girls enrolled in their classes.

In all, 205 girls (58.2 per cent) and 147 boys (41.8 per cent) from seven high schools completed the questionnaires and surveys. The students were primarily 9th and 10th graders (87 per cent), and the sample was predominantly white (73.9 per cent) with some blacks (18.9 per cent), Hispanics (3.7 per cent), and Asian/Pacific Islanders (1.4 per cent) represented. There were no gender differences in racial distribution but, as indicated in Table 3.4, the schools varied considerably in their racial composition.

Table 3.4   Distribution of Students by Race and School

School	American Black	Hispanic	White, Not Hispanic	Asian/ Pacific	Other
			(percentages)		
Suburban Missouri	1.0	—	95.0	3.0	1.0
Rural Indiana	—	1.5	95.5	—	3.0
Urban Colorado	2.3	2.3	90.9	2.3	2.3
Urban Texas	13.6	40.9	45.5	—	—
Urban Illinois	87.0	4.3	4.3	—	4.3
Suburban Louisiana	95.3	2.3	—	—	2.3
Rural Maine	—	—	96.1	2.0	2.0

Students identified their academic abilities in a fairly typical fashion, and self-estimates of grades did not differ between the boys and girls in the sample. Students also were asked to estimate their abilities in relation to those of an average person of their own age. Boys estimated their abilities considerably higher than girls did in athletics, math, mechanics, science, problem-solving, and ambition. Girls, on the other hand, ranked themselves approximately as high as boys only in academic, speaking, and social abilities; girls did not rank themselves higher than boys in any given category. The student sample, therefore, had very traditional and sex-stereotyped views of individual abilities.

However, when actual enrollments were assessed, few differences were found in the percentages of boys and girls taking advanced or honors courses in math, English, foreign languages, or social studies.

Perhaps more important than the lack of gender enrollment differences in honors/advanced courses was the lack of differences between boys and girls in the number of courses taken in algebra, plane geometry, trigonometry, college algebra, senior math, calculus, biology, chemistry, and physics.

When surveyed about future educational plans, a large percentage of both boys (85.7 per cent) and girls (76.6 per cent) planned to attend college after high school. Their educational aspirations probably reflected the educational levels of the students' parents. For example, 32.2 per cent of their fathers and 35.8 per cent of their mothers had attended one to three years of college or had a bachelor's degree. Over 22 per cent of fathers and 11.6 per cent of mothers held advanced or professional degrees. Overall, 74.9 per cent of fathers and 66.4 per cent of mothers had had some kind of post-high school training or education.

Some items assessed student interests in and aptitudes for a scientific career; others probed for the factors behind student career choices. Although large percentages of both male and female students in this study (79.7 per cent and 55.1 per cent, respectively) had considered science careers, students — especially female students — still viewed science and engineering as difficult areas and as predominantly masculine endeavors. When students were asked whether they could become scientists, only 5 per cent of females and 12.3 per cent of males indicated that they wanted to become scientists and that there were no major obstacles in their paths. However, 40 per cent of males and 48 per cent of females stated that they did not wish to pursue scientific careers due to inadequate grades, excessive educational requirements, or lack of required courses.

The case study students were asked to indicate with whom they had talked about jobs, work, or careers. Proportionately more females than males had talked with family members (97 per cent versus 91 per cent respectively). Over 90 per cent of both boys and girls had discussed careers with friends and nearly 60 per cent had discussed careers with teachers. Furthermore, students indicated that the case study teacher, in particular, had encouraged students to consider education and/or training beyond high school (76.5 of females, 67.1 of males), had given students advice on what to do after high school (37.9 per cent of females, 38.7 per cent of males), and had encouraged students to explore many choices for post-high school plans (42.2 per cent of females, 47.5 per cent of males). There were no gender differences in students' perceptions of career counseling from their case study teachers.

What about the high school counselor? Most students were surveyed during the late spring of the 10th grade; therefore, most would have decided on either an academic, vocational, or general course of study. Probably, most of them were actively involved in choosing courses for the following year. Yet, over 35 per cent of girls and 40 per cent of boys had not discussed post-high school training or education with a counselor within the last year. Furthermore, over 40 per cent of girls and 55 per cent of boys had not discussed jobs or occupations with a counselor within the last year. There was one gender difference; girls had discussed jobs/occupations with counselors somewhat more frequently than boys had. In summary, these students had found family members, teachers, and friends more important sources of career information and advice than were high school counselors.

As noted previously, all students in the observed classes were actively involved in learning. However, each case study teacher practiced what Shirley Malcolm (1983) calls 'directed intervention'. That is, girls as well as boys could not sit passively in the back of these rooms. Girls were called upon to recite, were requested to assist in demonstrations, were selected to be group leaders, and were expected to perform experiments. They could simply not get by taking notes as boys dissected, titrated, measured, etc. The effect of this instructional strategy showed when the responses of these students were compared with those from the 1976–77 National Assessment of Educational Progress' (NAEP) survey of science.[6] Table 3.5 illustrates percentages responding to items which showed active participation in science classes. Overwhelmingly, young women in the case study classrooms have had more opportunities to use scientific apparatus, to conduct science experiments, and to participate in scientific field trips.

However, gender differences were found in our sample for those activities which dealt with traditionally masculine areas such as electricity, mechanics, and astronomy. In addition, male students of the case study teachers reported more science hobbies, watched more science TV shows, and read more science books than did their female peers. These findings agreed with those of the 1976–77 NAEP survey, reported and discussed in Chapter 2. However, one important gender difference, reported in 1976–77, was not found in the current study; that is, girls and boys did not significantly differ in number of science projects completed.

Our survey, in contrast to the National Assessment one, also included items on co-curricular activities. Responses indicated that there were no differences between boys' and girls' participation in science clubs, science fairs, and math/computer clubs. However, significant gender differences were found in participation in chess club, chorus/choir, thespians/drama club, varsity/intramural sports. In all of

Table 3.5   Percentages of NAEP and NABT Students Responding Positively and Presence of
            Sex Differences in Extracurricular Science Activities

QUESTION Have you ever ...	Percentage responding positively		Significant sex difference*	
	NAEP** sample	NABT*** sample	NAEP** sample	NABT*** sample
experimented with erosion?	42.9	38.7	Yes	No
used a meter stick?	78.8	93.8	Yes	No
used a barometer?	48.5	57.1	Yes	No
used a computer?	36.2	83.1	Yes	No
used a graduated cylinder?	63.6	79.4	Yes	No
visited a sewage plant?	25.8	19.8	Yes	No
visited a weather station?	24.3	33.9	Yes	No
visited a research laboratory?	31.9	33.2	Yes	No
made a piece of science equipment?	53.1	51.1	Yes	No
made something from junk?	81.4	70.8	Yes	No
collected leaves/flowers?	83.3	95.1	Yes	No
found a fossil?	60.0	64.0	Yes	No
seen an animal skeleton?	87.7	86.7	Yes	No
seen an eclipse of the moon or sun?	78.7	79.7	Yes	No
seen the moon through a telescope?	56.8	52.9	Yes	No
seen a solar heat collector?	19.9	43.9	Yes	No

Notes: *Significance levels are not included because the data treatment in each case was not
            identical. The comparisons, therefore, are only estimates. Percentages of males were
            higher than females in each case where a significant sex difference was found.
            **17-year-olds.
            ***Present students of case study teachers, predominantly 15-year-olds.

those activities, participation was based on traditional sex-role stereotypes. It is, therefore, even more important that differences were
not found between percentages of boys and girls participating in science
clubs, science fairs, or math/computer clubs.

Perhaps, as the result of more experiences, more career information, and more extracurricular science activities, girls demonstrated
more positive attitudes toward science classes and science careers than
they did in the 1977 assessment. As shown in Table 3.6, proportionately
more students in the NABT sample felt 'curious', 'confident', and
'successful' in their science classes than did students in the NAEP
sample. According to other responses, the case study students also
enjoyed their science classes more than did students in the NAEP
sample. None of the gender differences in attitudes, typically found
among children 13 and older, was found. Girls enrolled in classes taught
by the case study teachers held science attitudes equally as positive as
those of their male peers.

Generally, students, girls as well as boys, of the case study teachers
were actively involved in science. They performed experiments in their

Table 3.6   Student Attitudes Concerning Science Classes, by Sex and Sample Population

How often have science classes made you feel:	NAEP sample Percentage responding			NABT sample Percentage responding		
	Total	Male	Female	Total	Male	Female
curious?*	50.7	53.4	48.1	85.3	84.2	86.1
stupid?**	60.8	69.5	52.3	45.8	40.4	49.7
confident?*	21.5	26.8	16.4	59.9	59.6	60.2
successful?*	28.2	32.4	24.1	67.9	73.7	63.5
How often do you like to go to science classes?*	37.3	42.8	31.9	70.2	74.5	67.2

Notes: *Response = 'Often' or 'Sometimes'.
 **Response = 'Seldom' or 'Never'
In all cases, a significant sex difference was present in the NAEP sample but was not present in the NABT case study sample.

classes; they investigated opportunities in the field; they participated in science and math clubs, and they conducted special projects. The attitudes of girls toward science were positively affected by these myriad opportunities. In contrast with both the results reported in the 1976–77 and 1981–82 National Assessments of Science, these young women were confident, curious, and successful in their science classes.

The effect of the teachers also was noted in the responses of students to instruments assessing science anxiety and attribution, cognitive style, spatial ability, and locus of control. Responses to a scale concerning science anxiety (Alvaro, 1978) were particularly interesting. Math anxiety and, to a lesser extent, science anxiety have been suggested as major detriments to girls achieving well in science (Smail, 1983). Others have maintained that experience ameliorates anxiety and that girls particularly must work with scientific materials (Malcolm, 1983; Kahle, 1983). Whether male or female, responses showed that experience alleviated anxiety. Selected responses in Table 3.7 show that, in general, girls were more anxious about tests and new experiences such as visiting a museum. However, students of both sexes demonstrated less anxiety if they were familiar with the task such as focusing a microscope (girls) or planning an electrical circuit (boys). The Science Attribution Scale used was a modified version of Fennema, Wolleat, and Pedro's Mathematics Attribution Scale (1979). The scale presented students with nine biology course situations in which the student was told that he/she had succeeded or failed. After each situation, the student was asked to agree or disagree with four different reasons for success or failure: ability, effort, task difficulty, or other environmental conditions (teacher, friends, luck, etc.). Scores were

Table 3.7   Percentages of Male and Female Students Indicating Anxiety about Science-Related and Non-Science-Related Activities

How much does it frighten you to:	Not at all		A little		A fair amount		Much		Very much	
	M	F	M	F	M	F	M	F	M	F
... study for final exam in English or history?*	32.2	23.8	28.0	27.1	23.7	16.0	10.2	18.2	5.9	14.9
... study for final exam in chemistry or physics?**	31.3	22.7	31.3	23.2	14.8	23.8	13.9	16.0	8.7	14.4
... visit the museum of science and industry?**	40.5	26.0	24.1	32.6	23.3	26.0	8.6	8.3	3.4	7.2
...focus a microscope?*	73.3	85.1	11.2	9.9	7.8	2.2	4.3	2.2	3.4	0.6
... plan an electrical circuit?**	55.9	30.8	26.3	33.5	15.3	19.8	1.7	11.0	0.8	4.9

Key: Significant differences between male and female responses
      * X^2 test, df = 4, p < .05
      ** X^2 test, df = 4, p > .10

tallied by the number of 'agree' or 'strongly agree' responses given.

Previous research with non-scientific tasks had found that males attributed success/failure significantly more to ability and effort than females did (Pasquella, Mednick and Murray, 1981). In the present study, however, no gender differences were found in attribution of success/failure in science to ability, effort, or environmental factors. A significant gender difference did occur, however, in attribution on success/failure in science to task difficulty/ease. Significantly more girls than boys attributed success/failure to the difficulty of the scientific task. Girls enrolled in case study teachers' biology classes held equally high opinions of their abilities, efforts, and the influence of environmental conditions in achieving scientific success. However, typically, girls more than boys attributed their degree of success in science to the difficulty of the task.

Students also completed a modified version of the Hidden Figures Test (HFT) to determine their mode of cognitive style (ETS, 1971). The HFT differentiates between persons with a field-independent and a field-dependent mode. Usually, field-independent persons are better at cognitive restructuring tasks, tend to think analytically, and are more autonomous in personal relations and work behaviors. Field-dependent persons, on the other hand, display social behaviors useful for interpersonal relationships, tend to have extended experience in working with others and gathering information from them, and are less autonomous (Witkin and Goodenough, 1981). Although gender differences have been reported with more males than females scoring on the field-independent side of the scale (Witkin and Goodenough, 1981), results from the present study do not concur with those findings. In this case, there were no differences related to subject's gender across schools or in any individual school.

Students of the case study teachers also were asked to complete a modified version of the Flags Test (Thurstone and Jeffrey, 1956) in order to measure spatial ability, the ability to visualize and rotate three-dimensional figures. Many researchers had suggested that gender differences in spatial ability contributed to math and science achievement differences in boys and girls. As discussed in Chapter 2, although Maccoby and Jacklin (1974) concluded that spatial ability was one of the few attributes for which gender differences were consistently found, Linn and Petersen (1983) did not reach that conclusion with their meta-analysis of studies since 1974. In the case study sample, boys scored significantly higher than girls on a measure of spatial ability, but further analyses showed that the gender difference was mainly due to a significant difference found in only two of the seven samples.

Locus of control is an expression of the extent to which individuals believe that they, rather than outside factors, control their actions and behaviors. Externally oriented individuals tend to attribute control to outside forces, while internally oriented people believe in their own control. Traditionally, women have demonstrated more external beliefs than men have on locus of control measures (Phares, 1976; Kahle, 1982). Furthermore, students with positive science attitudes and with intentions to pursue science careers generally are found on the internal side of the locus of control continuum (Kahle, 1982). With this in mind, case study students were asked to complete the Adult Nowicki-Strickland Scale, a modified version of an earlier instrument developed by Phares (1957). There were no gender differences in any of the seven sub-samples or in the total sample; and students generally scored at the internal end of the scale.

In summary, students in case study classrooms responded to a battery of personality measures. Their responses were compared to those of other samples in order to see if teacher behaviors and instructional techniques had affected student level of anxiety, attribution of success, belief in self-control, or mode of perception. Previous research had suggested that specific instructional strategies could influence mode of cognitive style and locus of control orientation (Kahle, 1983; Head, 1983). In addition, researchers had hypothesized that spatial abilities could be fostered by the use of specific curricular activities (Skolnick, Langbort and Day, 1982). Furthermore, it had been suggested that science anxiety could be ameliorated by certain teacher behaviors and student classroom experiences (Malcolm, 1983). Comparisons of the responses of students of case study teachers with those of comparable groups indicated that, although other factors might be partially responsible, those teachers had an effect. Girls in case study classes expressed the same personality modes as did boys. Since some of these traits (internal locus of control orientation, field-independent mode of cognitive style, high spatial ability, and low science anxiety) have been directly related to success in science courses and choice of science careers, the absence of gender differences was important.

Reflections of Former Students

Former students, who were science majors in college or who were pursuing science-related careers, were surveyed by mail. Although a bias was present in their selection (all were recommended by either a case study teacher or a counselor), their answers were completely confidential. Therefore, they could be as frank as they wished in responding to questions concerning their choice of science careers, their future plans, and their past incentives. They were asked to indicate how certain people, courses, and activities had influenced their decision to pursue and their persistence in pursuit of science careers. Among the types of people rated (parents, science teachers, math teachers, other teachers, counselors, etc.), high school biology teachers (in all cases the case study teacher) were ranked first.[7] In addition, unsolicited comments indicated the extent of the case study teacher's influence.

> My role model was my high school biology teacher. She helped me decide on a science career because she showed me the many different aspects of science and the many different opportunities science has to offer career-wise.

> He was (and is) an enthusiastic, challenging, and supportive teacher. He helped me see, in concrete terms (in concrete successes) that I could be successful in medical science. He is one of a handful of outstanding instructors I have had in college (Harvard) and high school.

> [My] biology teacher . . . taught me how exciting biology can be.

> I had a very good teacher who interested me in biology and made me want to show other children how interesting science can be.

> She gave me support and guidance in matters of everyday living
> as well as my career decision.

These students almost unanimously (94.7 per cent) felt that their high school biology teacher offered frequent opportunities for individual discussions and encouraged his/her students to consider further education. Furthermore, most indicated that their biology teachers encouraged them to be creative and original (84.2 per cent) and to explore many educational and career choices (73.7 per cent). None of the former students surveyed felt that their biology teachers treated students childishly or distinguished between educational opportunities for boys and girls. Several students described the biology teacher as a role model.

When asked whether any science courses had influenced their career decisions, former students indicated that high school biology and college biology courses were important.[8] Their comments about high school biology course(s) were revealing.

> The first experience I had with science as an exciting subject came in high school biology. Advanced biology was a difficult course but was good preparation for college level work. It was in high school that genetics was first mentioned. I thought it was a good area for me because I have always done well in math.

> I think that high school biology courses and my training in college certainly prepared me for my career in the research area. In my high school biology class I remember going on many field trips. The questioning and searching for information was certainly helpful to what I am doing today.

> High school biology helped me appreciate the richness and diversity of science.

> The [high school biology experiences] have taught me what hard work is necessary for obtaining goals.

Overall, the students indicated that they enjoyed their science courses. All respondents (100 per cent) indicated that they had enjoyed their biology courses, 84.2 per cent enjoyed chemistry courses, and 60–90 per cent liked various mathematics courses. Case study teachers had significantly influenced some former students' career choices.

The positive influence of the case study teachers on both their past and present students was another commonality found among them. Responses to innumerable survey items suggested that their common teaching behaviors and their use of similar instructional materials and techniques were instrumental in encouraging all students to continue their education. Many more students than usual selected advanced courses in science, which opened doors to future scientific careers. Over and over again students praised these teachers — their contagious enthusiasm, their high academic requirements, their personal concern. Since girls often do not receive such positive messages from science teachers (Smail, 1983), their influence on girls continuing in science was disproportionately effective.

Perspectives of Current and Former Students

Evidences of change have been described. Girls in these classrooms performed science experiments, enjoyed science activities, and demonstrated confidence in their scientific abilities. Consequently, many continued in science courses and selected scientific careers. But, did the positive role model of a biology teacher and a positive image of science change traditionally held sex-role stereotypes concerning women as scientists? Responses to items and written comments on both the past and present student surveys suggested some progress. Differences were seen between the responses of 15-year-olds (average age of current students) and 22-year-olds (average age of former students). For example, only 14 per cent of the 15-year-olds responded that women should work full-time without interruption for marriage or children; in contrast, 26 per cent of the older respondents considered full-time, uninterrupted work a viable option for women (themselves or their wives). Overwhelmingly, both groups of students planned to marry and thought that the most appropriate life-role for women was marriage and/or family combined with a career. Other questions were directed specifically toward the role of women in science careers. Current students were asked whether they approved of science careers for women. Although proportionately more girls than boys expressed approval, the percentages of both who approved of science careers for women were large, as shown in Table 3.8. However, the boys and girls differed considerably when questioned further on the issue of women in scientific careers. Table 3.9 presents student responses to a series of statements about women in scientific as well as other types of careers. In all but two cases, girls, compared with boys, expressed stronger beliefs in a woman's potential for success in a traditionally masculine career (astronautics, government, science).

In summary, both present and past students theoretically sup-

Table 3.8   Current Student Opinions Concerning Science Careers for Women

Opinion	Percentage responding		
	Total	Males	Females
Approve	77.2	69.1	82.9
Probably Approve	6.5	9.4	4.5
No Opinion	13.9	18.0	11.1
Probably Disapprove	0.9	0	1.5
Disapprove	1.5	3.6	0

Note: $X^2 = 17.05$, df $= 4$, p $= .0019$.

Table 3.9   Current Student Agreement with Statements Concerning Women in Science

Statement	Percentage of males responding		Percentage of females responding	
	Strongly Agree	Agree	Strongly Agree	Agree
Women are as interested in mathematics as are men.	37.6	53.2	48.0	44.0
Men don't like to work for women supervisors.	23.6	42.9	21.0	51.5
Women should stick to 'women's jobs'.*	7.4	20.0	3.6	4.1
Women have as much science ability as men do.*	38.8	49.6	63.2	33.3
Education is wasted on women since they usually get married and raise a family.*	5.9	11.0	3.1	2.6
Women have the ability and endurance to make successful space flights.*	19.3	56.4	44.2	49.7
According to the latest Census data, equal job opportunities have now been achieved.*	10.8	46.8	6.5	50.2
I strongly approve the election of women as governors.*	18.8	50.7	56.2	34.8
I approve of appointing a woman as chairperson of the Atomic Energy Commission.*	19.0	51.8	46.5	47.0
I would choose for myself the best qualified dentist available regardless of sex.*	53.2	36.2	71.4	20.6

Note: * Denotes significance at the .05 level or higher.

ported not only a woman's pursuit of a career, but also a woman's right to pursue a particular scientific career. Both groups expressed naive opinions about the possibility of interrupting a successful career without affecting it. Generally, 15-year-old boys, compared to girls, held more negative and more stereotypic views about the role of women in science-related careers. However, some girls in the case study classes expressed stereotypic views of science and of scientists. A privileged girl in a suburban high school said, 'Men are scientists. It is a masculine job career. Women don't go into it because being a scientist will make them look bad.' Her opinion was reiterated by a black girl in an inner-city school, who stated, 'If I married a scientist, he'd never have time to be home with his family. I think men scientists would have more time than women scientists. It depends on the woman. If she can do it, fine; but most women can't.' But, across the country, girls, at least those in the case study classrooms, were beginning to question the old, masculine views of science and scientists. Two interesting and revealing comments were:

> I don't know if it is women thinking scientists should be men, or men thinking scientists should be men.

> There are some women scientists; but men have been in it longer. Women can do the same job as men. They may have a different way of thinking and might improve science.

Former students, those who had passed through these classrooms, also held refreshing and less stereotypic views of scientists. They were asked to select from a variety of clustered characteristcs the groups which best described a 'typical scientist' and the ones which best described themselves. The results (Table 3.10) indicated that a student's self-image was very similar to his/her image of a scientist and that these students held broader, less–stereotypic views of scientists. For example, over a quarter responded that scientists were 'social, helping, guiding, and group-oriented'.

Table 3.10   Percentages of Students Selecting Groups Which Describe Themselves and Scientists

Characteristics	Groups which best describe ... *	
	Yourself	A typical scientist
Realistic, Technical, Mechanical, Outdoor	57.9	63.2
Investigative, Scientific, Inquiring, Analytical	78.9	84.2
Artistic, Musical, Self-Expressive, Independent	31.6	5.3
Social, Helping, Guiding, Group-Oriented	47.4	26.3
Enterprising, Profit-Oriented, Persuasive, Political	5.3	15.8
Conventional, Methodical, Organized, Detailed	57.9	68.4

Note: *Students were asked to choose three groups which best described themselves and scientists.

Conclusions and Recommendations

The number of commonalities found among the case study teachers was surprising, and a synthesis and analysis of their teaching behaviors, classroom climates, instructional materials, and academic preparations suggest ways to improve the retention rates and the achievement levels of girls in science. Before delineating factors which young women found especially encouraging, some general characteristics should be mentioned. Although exemplary teaching was not a criterion for selection, all of the case study teachers were outstanding classroom instructors. For example, the case study researcher in Colorado concluded,

> I think that rather than identifying a teacher who consciously encourages females in science, we have simply identified a very good teacher, whose talent, commitment, and rapport with her students combine to make the study of science an interesting and enjoyable endeavor. I am hard put to suggest any more direct cause and effect relationships, because the data will not support them, any more than the data will support more than a broad philosophic argument for the generalizability of [her] teaching approach to other classrooms.

His conclusion was repeated in most of the observational reports. As the researcher in Chicago stated,

> The case study teacher's experience, attitudes, and goals give her tremendous strength in motivating students to achieve. She is an exemplary teacher. Observing and talking with her, her colleagues, and her students, leaves one with the strong sense that there are no simple explanations for her success as a teacher. A major factor in her desire to motivate young people developed because she, herself, was frustrated in her search for loftier goals. She also is able to recognize the special needs of black inner-city students and address them in a sometimes humorous, always supportive way. She has a keen understanding of biological principles and a love for the field that is an important key to success in any subject. She is given recognition not because she seeks it, but because it is so well deserved.

Since these observations could not be generalized, we compared and contrasted the answers of the case study teachers to survey questions with responses provided by a national sample. We found that the case study teachers were all experienced teachers and active professionals. Proportionately more case study teachers than national survey teachers cited professional organization meetings and professional journals as important sources of information for curricular materials and new educational developments. The case study teachers were confident in their teaching abilities; proportionately fewer of these teachers than national survey teachers indicated that they needed assistance in various aspects of teaching such as obtaining information about instructional materials, using manipulative materials, or maintaining plants and animals. Although these teachers used many kinds of laboratory materials, none of them indicated that inadequate facilities were a serious problem or that improvement was needed in obtaining equipment or supplies. The successful case study teachers showed greater willingness than the national survey teachers to use varied methods of instruction, and they emphasized hands-on science experience for their students in teaching their courses. One general conclusion from the classroom observations, the past and present student surveys, the teacher reports, and all the analyses is that *good teachers make a difference*. Each teacher successful in encouraging girls as well as boys to continue in science courses and careers was also a successful teacher. For example, they were active professionally, were involved in science activities in their communities, were skilled in a variety of instructional techniques, and were informed about science careers and their educational requirements. In their own words, they were proud professionals. From rural Indiana to urban Louisiana they stated,

> Teaching is a profession. I can walk down the street and feel proud that I am a teacher. I think anything we can do as educators to put a feather in our cap; to say, 'hey, this is a proud profession,' is important. Let's build it up and speak positively about it.

> In the years I have been teaching, I have become, what I call, dedicated. I try to be professional, and I have influenced the lives of many young people. I have taught required courses and had the opportunity to touch every student who has been through the laboratory school for the last twenty-four years. I enjoy teaching.

Although at some point during the observational period, all teachers expressed a concern about sexism in science, the initial interviews and observations were structured to prevent the researcher from introducing any bias. However, by the end of the observational period, all teachers were aware of this special interest, and they, too, attempted to ascertain what they had done 'right'. As one teacher explained, 'If I have any secret it is that I try to be fair to all students. I don't care who their parents are, what they did last year, or whether they are boys or girls. I just try to treat them all alike.' Although some case study teachers expressed a lack of any special treatment, others admitted that they worked at encouraging girls in science. One teacher explained why she took special steps.

> I think it is ingrained in females that they don't have to take any more science. I work really hard ... getting girls into science. All the male [students] want to take AP chemistry. The teachers tell them that this is the really hard course; this is the course for the men. I think [the female students] get a little scared.

Case study teachers worked to correct any negative images of science as well as its masculine mystique. The extent of the problem is indicated in the following excerpt.

> The impressions students have of scientists are generally negative, although they recognize that scientists are probably doing what they want to do. They envisage scientists as men in long white coats looking through microscopes. They think more men than women are scientists, and two students would place more faith in the work of a male scientist than a female scientist. Two other students said they would trust the work of men and women equally, but then qualified that statement, 'I would trust [the work of men and women] the same if they have enough background to know what they are doing. I think women usually don't have enough time to work and to know as much as men.'

Although each teacher attempted to correct stereotyped views of science and scientists in his/her own way, some commonalities were found. For example, one observer wrote,

> All seating and lab work is completely irrespective of sex. The teacher attempts to be fair so that the first person who volunteers to be a lab captain is the person chosen. When the lab requires the use of heavy equipment the girls are not given special consideration. However, since the beginning of this study the teacher has been more alert to the possibility of any sex bias in her teaching.

Most case studies included comparable observations. Generally, these concerned active professionals were striving to encourage all students to reach their maximum potentials. As the observer in a magnet school in Chicago wrote,

> In addition to motivating students to strive for academic and professional excellence, [the case study teacher] seeks to change

their attitudes toward biology. Words such as 'nasty', 'ugly', and other such terms are unacceptable. She wants to give students an appreciation of things that are not familiar to them. They must become thinkers and listeners. Career awareness is another goal; she has invited speakers from a variety of scientific disciplines to address her classes. She has taken students on field trips to museums, to Argonne National Laboratory, and to nature preserves and zoos. Students prepare 'career profiles' — oral and written reports on various scientific professions.

In addition to their generally high professionalism and concern for all students, these teachers displayed other commonalities. Certain teaching behaviors and instructional techniques were observed in all classrooms. In addition, analyses of both current and former student responses to a variety of surveys and measures indicated factors which positively influenced the retention of girls in science courses.

What were these commonalities?

1   Whether the teacher taught behind locked doors in an out-of-date, traditional laboratory with bolted chairs and tables or in a modular, open-concept arrangement with flexible seating and stations, their classrooms were attractive, well-equipped and maintained. All noted that they did not need equipment and supplies or money for further purchases. In addition, all had adequate storage space.

2   All used non-sexist teacher-developed instructional materials to supplement the basic text. As one researcher noted,

> There is no overt discussion of sexism that might be inherent in any of the instructional materials used, as none of the materials seem to present that problem. Five tests were provided for analysis. There appeared to be no problem with sexist language; scientific contributions were treated as neutral relative to gender.

Interestingly, no observer reported a single use of sexist humor by the case study teachers.

3   All the observed teachers were aware of sexism in science. Although they maintained that they did not treat boys and girls differently, they brought women scientists into their classes and they included a range of non-sexist career information. As one observer suggested,

Perhaps the equitable treatment of male and female students is itself special, given what has been learned about the generally inequitable treatment of female students in the science classroom. Perhaps the simple lack of preferential treatment for males has resulted in a situation where the female students feel comfortable and are confident in their ability to contribute at an equal level with their male colleagues. Certainly, there is not enough data to support that hypothesis, attractive as it might be.

4   The teachers, perhaps unknowingly, presented what Harding (1983) and Smail (1983) call 'girl friendly science'. One observer wrote about this phenomenon in the following way.

> Although she argues that one does not need special activities to interest girls in science, it is possible that for the less-motivated girl certain labs and/or research projects are more appealing. For non-science-oriented girls, experiments such as audio-tutorial units on bacteriology have considerable appeal. Nutrition and diets appeal to many girls. A unit on 'Complementary Proteins: A simulation' has appealed to many girls. Similarly, 'Dissection of an Orange,' is very popular with many students. The teacher feels that the girls' interests are as varied as those of the boys. Last year a girl designed and built a windmill for a local garage and another girl spent hours assisting a vocational teacher who is building an airplane.

As noted, teachers used more laboratories, discussions and tests than is commonly found.

5   The case study teachers all had solid, academic preparations for teaching. It should be noted that most had degrees in their subject areas and that all had continued their formal educations. All were more enthusiastic about teaching now than when they began to teach.

6   These teachers were respected, generally recognized, and supported within their communities. In addition, all but one mentioned that they received strong support from the parents of their students.

7   These teachers participate in and encourage their students to enjoy science beyond the schoolhouse door. As a result, one finds equal numbers of girls and boys preparing science projects and joining science, math, and computer clubs.

8   The case study teachers, individually and collectively, were unique in their emphasis on careers and further education. Although all students benefited from that interest, girls seemed to notice it and respond to it more than boys did.

9   According to their students, the instructional techniques of the case study teachers encouraged creativity, further education, and basic skill development. Again, girls noted these characteristics more often than boys did.

10   Both current and former students noted the positive attitudes as well as encouragement as unique personal characteristics and teaching behaviors of the case study teachers.

These ten special teaching behaviors and instructional strategies resulted in proportionately more girls in their classes continuing in math and science courses in both high school and college. Generally, the behaviors identified in Figure 3.1 characterize teachers who are successful in encouraging girls to pursue science.

Figure 3.1   Teaching Behaviors and Techniques Effective for Retaining Women in Science

Do	Don't
use laboratory and discussion activities	use sexist humor
provide career information	use sex-stereotyped examples
directly involve girls in science activities	distribute sexist classroom materials
provide informal academic counseling	allow boys to dominate discussions or activities
demonstrate unisex treatment in science classrooms	allow girls to passively resist

In conclusion, Cecily Connan Selby has suggested that excellent science teaching must be innovative and exciting. She says, 'Science must be presented as not only basic but beautiful, as those of us whose lives and professions have been touched by this beauty are so proud and privileged to know' (Selby, 1982). The case study teachers demonstrate those feelings about science. Perhaps, because science is presented as beautiful, they are able to capture and intrigue the girls in their classrooms.

Notes

1 This project was supported by a grant from the National Science Foundation to the National Association of Biology Teachers (NABT). Any opinions, findings, conclusions, and recommendations expressed herein are those of the contributors and do not reflect the views of the National Science Foundation or NABT.
2 JANE ABBOTT, JANE BUTLER KAHLE, JOSEPH D. McINERNEY, ANN HALEY-OLIPHANT, JULIA RIGGS, EXYIE RYDER, ELIZABETH STAGE, and FRANCES VANDERVOORT were the case study researchers.
3 Since some teachers desired anonymity, their names are not provided. The authors and researchers are grateful for both their cooperation and their contributions.
4 Although the results are not directly comparable due to the difference in sample size between the national and case study samples (586 teachers vs 7 teachers, respectively), rough comparisons can be drawn. It should be noted, however, that 14.3 per cent of case study teachers represent one teacher; and 28.6 per cent represent two teachers. Tabular data, therefore, should be interpreted with this in mind.
5 The eighth teacher taught high school algebra, therefore her responses are not included in the analyses concerning science teaching and science classrooms.
6 Periodically NAEP assesses 9, 13, and 17-year-old students in specific subject areas. Chapter 2 briefly describes its sampling techniques.
7 On a 1–5 scale (1 = very important to 5 = not applicable), the following pertinent average ratings were found: high school biology teacher (1.74), fathers (1.95), mothers (2.32) high school counselors (3.58).
8 On a 1–5 scale (1 = very important), high school biology courses were rated 1.56, while college biology courses received a 2.00 ratings.

References

ALVARO, R.M. (1978) 'The effectiveness of a science therapy program upon science anxious undergraduates', Unpublished doctoral dissertation, Loyola University, Chicago.
EDUCATIONAL TESTING SERVICE (ETS) (1971) *Manual for French Kit Tests*, Princeton, NJ, Educational Testing Service.
FENNEMA, E., WOLLEAT, P. and PEDRO, J.D. (1979) 'Mathematics attribution scale: An instrument designed to measure students' attributions of the causes of their successes and failures in mathematics', *JSAS Catalog of Selected Documents in Psychology*, 9, 26 (Ms. No. 1873).
HARDING, J. (1983) *Switched Off: The Science Education of Girls*, Schools Council Programme 3, York, England, Longman Resources Unit.
HEAD, J. (1983) 'Sex differences in adolescent personality development and the

implications for science education', *Contributions to the Second GASAT Conference*, Oslo, Norway, University of Oslo, Institute of Physics, pp. 53–61.

KAHLE, J.B. (1982) *Double Dilemma: Minorities and Women in Science Education*, West Lafayette, IN, Purdue Research Foundation.

KAHLE, J.B. (1983) 'Disadvantaged majority: Science education for women', Association for the Education of Teachers in Science, Outstanding Paper for 1983. Burlington, NC, Carolina Biological Supply Company.

LINN, M.C. and PETERSEN, A.C. (1983) 'Emergence and characterization of gender differences in spatial ability: A meta-analysis', Unpublished manuscript, University of California, Berkeley, CA.

MACCOBY, E.E. and JACKLIN, C.N. (1974) *The Psychology of Sex Differences*, Stanford, CA, Stanford University Press.

MALCOLM, S.M. (1983) 'An assessment of programs that facilitate increased access and achievement of female and minorities in K-12 mathematics and science education', Washington, DC, American Association for the Advancement of Science, Office of Opportunities in Science, 31 July.

PASQUELLA, M.J. MEDNICK, M.T.S. and MURRAY, S.R. (1981) 'Casual attributions for achievement outcomes: Sex-role identity, sex, and outcome comparisons', *Psychology of Women Quarterly*, 54, pp. 586–90.

PHARES, E.J. (1957) 'Expectancy changes in skill and change situations', *Journal of Abnormal Social Psychology*, 54, pp. 339–42.

PHARES, E.J. (1976) *Locus of Control in Personality*, Morristown, NJ, General Learning Press.

SELBY, C.C. (1982) 'Turning people on to science', *Physics Today*, July, p. 26.

SKOLNICK, J., LANGBORT, C. and DAY, L. (1982) *How to Encourage Girls in Math and Science*, Englewood Cliffs, NJ, Prentice-Hall.

SMAIL, B. (1983) 'Getting science right for girls', *Contributions to the Second GASAT Conference*, Oslo, Norway, University of Oslo, Institute of Physics, pp. 30–40.

THURSTONE, T.G. and JEFFREY, T.E. (1956) *Flags: A Test of Space Thinking*, Chicago, IL, Industrial Relations Center.

WEISS, I.R. (1978) *Report of the 1977 National Survey of Science, Mathematics, and Social Studies Education* (SE 78–72), Washington, DC, National Science Foundation.

WITKIN, H.A. and GOODENOUGH, D.R. (1981) *Cognitive Styles: Essence and Origins*, New York, International Universities Press.

4 Obstacles and Constraints on Women in Science: Preparation and Participation in the Scientific Community

Marsha Lakes Matyas
Purdue University

Although we have seen that educational, socio-cultural, and personal factors all affect the selection of science by women, young women are choosing to enter the sciences in increasing numbers. Many are found in graduate school, where the current status of female graduate students in science may be viewed with cautious optimism. Although the status of women is far from equal to that of male graduate students, inequities are diminishing. As Figure 4.1 shows, increasing proportions of women have been enrolling in science and engineering graduate programs. According to data collected by the Science Manpower Commission of AAAS and the National Academy of Science, in 1979 women comprised 43 per cent of all graduate students enrolled in science and engineering, and 31.8 per cent of all full-time doctoral science students (Vetter, 1981). Between 1970 and 1981 the percentage of all doctorate degrees earned by women increased from 13 per cent to 31.5 per cent and, in science and engineering, from 9.1 per cent to 23.4 per cent. Proportionally, the largest increases were in the life sciences and in engineering. In addition, increasing proportions of undergraduate women were planning graduate studies in science (Vetter, 1981). Although the qualifications of women for graduate school admissions historically had been equal to or better than their male counterparts' (Feldman, 1974), many undergraduate women may have been discouraged from entering graduate school in science because of negative perceptions of subsequent personal and professional advancement.

Figure 4.1

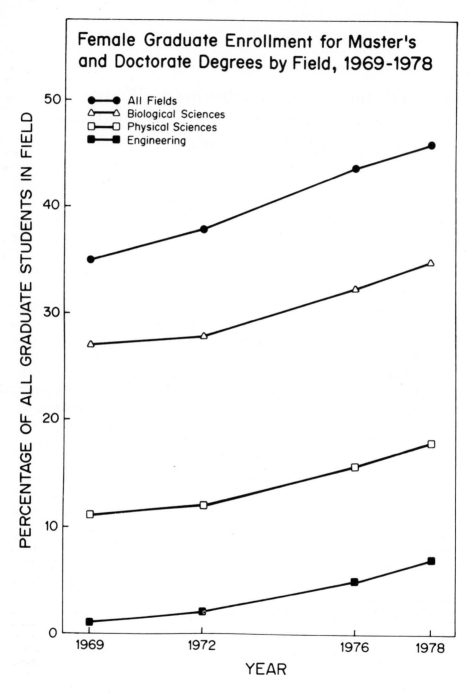

Female Graduate Enrollment for Master's and Doctorate Degrees by Field, 1969-1978

Source: Data drawn from NSF (1982b).

Graduate Education in Science

Science has long been considered a masculine field and, although progress has been made in the last two decades, it is still viewed as such in the ranks of higher education.

> Higher education cannot magically create equality ... Higher education, however, is just as guilty as other aspects of education in perpetuating the belief that women are naturally suited for some fields and men are naturally suited for others (Feldman, 1974, p. 138).

According to Feldman, scientific disciplines viewed as masculine included engineering, physics, geology, chemistry, mathematics, and biochemistry. 'Neutral' sciences included bacteriology, physiology, zoology, and botany. According to his data, only liberal arts, social sciences, and nursing were considered feminine disciplines (Feldman, 1974).

Current data indicate that Feldman's categories are still generally valid. For example, Table 4.1 shows that among 1981 doctoral recipients, the male/female ratios in 'masculine' areas (excluding biochemistry) range from almost 6:1 to 25:1. Ratios in neutral areas are approximately 3:1, while ratios in feminine areas are less than 2:1. Biochemistry, therefore, appears to be changing from a 'masculine' to a 'neutral' area. Furthermore, as Figure 4.2 indicates, the male/female

Table 4.1. Doctoral Degree Recipients by Field and Sex, 1981, and Masculine/Feminine Rating, 1974

Field	Number receiving PhD in 1981			Description of field in 1974 by Feldman
	Males	Females	Ratio M/F	
Engineering	2,429	99	24.54	Masculine
Physics	942	73	12.90	Masculine
Earth Science (including Geology)	526	56	9.39	Masculine
Chemistry	1,376	235	5.86	Masculine
Mathematics	616	112	5.50	Masculine
Biochemistry	455	189	2.41	Masculine
Microbiology/Bacteriology	260	103	2.43	Neutral
Physiology	304	91	3.34	Neutral
Zoology	150	47	3.19	Neutral
Botany	105	42	2.50	Neutral
Liberal Arts (Humanities)	2,198	1,547	1.42	Feminine
Social Sciences	4,190	2,315	1.81	Feminine
Nursing	3	84	0.04	Feminine

Source: From NRC (1982) and Feldman (1974).

Figure 4.2

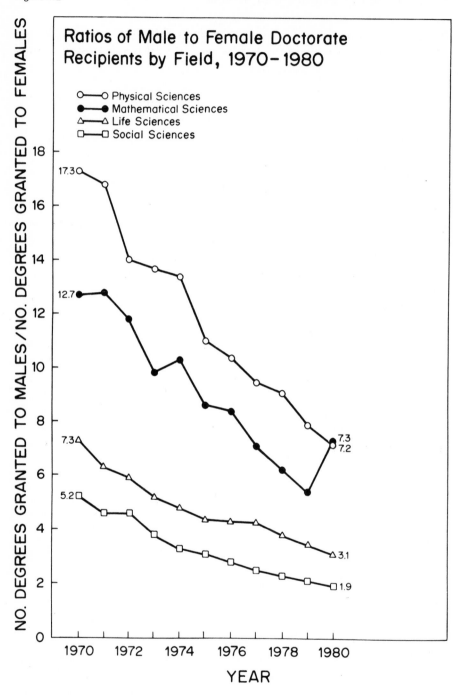

doctorate ratio has declined since 1970 not only in the social sciences but also in the mathematical, life, and physical sciences.

Although the ratio of men to women entering graduate school in science remains disproportionately high, women earn equal or better undergraduate grade point averages (Feldman, 1974), receive good recommendations (Stake, Walker and Speno, 1981), and earn equitable Graduate Record Examination scores. Therefore, additional factors must influence women to decide against graduate school in science or in engineering. High verbal and mathematics achievement scores, level of parental education, number of science courses taken, high level of work orientation, and low level of family orientation all appear to be associated with female entry into male-dominated fields (Peng and Jaffe, 1979). In addition, undergraduate women who had a female faculty role model expressed higher degree expectations and were more likely to plan graduate studies (Seater and Ridgeway, 1976). However, it would be naive to assume that women are not affected by the experiences they anticipate as a women graduate student in a 'man's field'. Today it may be that these anticipated socio-cultural barriers are more important than traditional academic barriers in deterring women from graduate studies in science.

Barriers to Women: Academic

After entering graduate study in science, women have a higher attrition rate from their programs than men do. This has often been attributed to either a woman's lack of commitment to work or to a withdrawal from studies for childbearing and/or childrearing. These commonly acknowledged reasons may be incorrect, since several alternative factors have been identified which seriously affect both the retention and performance of women graduate students in science. First, women graduate students, whether they are serious about their science studies or not, frequently are viewed as undedicated by faculty and fellow students (Tidball in Speizer, 1981; Feldman, 1974). Studies also indicate that many faculty members less frequently reinforce female students' work than male students' work. Furthermore, male faculty perceive female, in comparison to male, students as less serious and less capable (Project on the Status and Education of Women, 1982). However, when women themselves are questioned about career primacy, that is, subordinating all aspects of life to one's work, women do not appear less dedicated than men. In botany, women were more career oriented than their male counterparts and in chemistry, bacteriology, and physiology, women and men were equally career oriented (Feldman, 1974).

It might be tempting to advise women entering male-dominated studies to simply ignore faculty and students who consider women less capable and undedicated, yet for the graduate student this may be a difficult task.

> Even though only 20 per cent to 25 per cent of the faculty and graduate students in American higher education believe that women are not as dedicated as men, we cannot simply dismiss as meaningless the attitude of small minority. Individuals with this attitude may have a key role in the careers of female students, and the belief that women lack dedication affects how they are educated (Feldman, 1974, p. 103).

If they are perceived as less dedicated, women students may be treated differently than men students by their professors, who play a key role in a graduate student's education. Professors instruct not only in the formal classroom setting, but also during informal discussions both in and out of the laboratory setting. The relationship between graduate student and major professor is particularly critical. As stated by Feldman (1974),

> A close, working relationship with a professor should facilitate research and aid the building of a professional self-image. Few men or women claim that they have no contact with professors outside the classroom, but women are much less likely to have the benefits of a close, working relationship (p. 119).

This situation has changed little in the last decade; female graduate students are still not well accepted as professional colleagues by faculty (Project, 1982).

A close working relationship appears to be especially important for women who, during the course of their education, may have been the victims of blatant sexism or, even more commonly, of 'micro-inequities'. Micro-inequities are 'small differential behaviors that often occur in the course of everyday interchanges' (Project, 1982, p. 5). These exchanges indicate to women that they are in some way different or inferior. Taken individually, 'micro-inequities' seem trivial yet, during the lifetime of a female student, they can create an atmosphere of self-doubt and unequal opportunity. Understandably, a professor/student relationship in which a female student is subtly made aware of her 'inabilities' is detrimental to both her self-image and her career motivation. Research indicates that among graduate women a productive professor/student working relationship is positively correlated with positive self-image, higher career goals, more publications, and lower attrition rates (Feldman, 1974). Recently, research has explored the benefits and disadvantages of having a same-sex or opposite-sex sponsor or mentor. Graduate students with advisors of the same sex, compared with those with opposite-sex advisors, published significantly more research (Goldstein in Speizer, 1981). In addition, female faculty advisors of women graduate students provided positive role models by showing how they balanced their personal lives with their professional careers (Mokros, Erkut and Spichiger, 1981). Professor/student relationships also play a role in the financial status of graduate students. Although male and female graduate students receive equitable amounts of financial assistance and equal proportions of male and female graduate students receive teaching fellowships, men receive twice as many research fellowships as women do (NRC, 1982). As Figure 4.3 shows, the primary source of graduate income for 45 per cent of women doctorates was personal funds, while 18.5 per cent received teaching assistantships. However, among men doctoral students, only 30 per cent relied primarily on personal funds, while 22 per cent received research assistantships and 18.7 per cent held teaching assistantships (NRC,

Figure 4.3

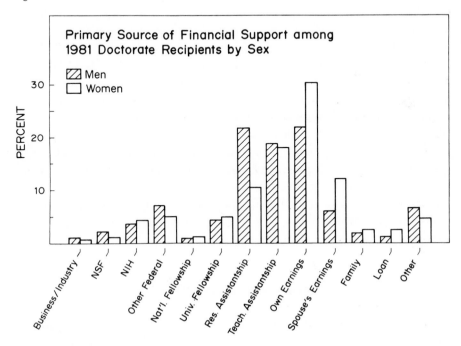

Source: Adapted from NRC (1982)

1982). More often women must divert time and energy from research and writing to teaching in order to obtain financial support. In addition to these burdens, research fellowships are viewed as higher status appointments than teaching fellowships are. Frequently, major professors, usually male, decide the type of award. Their attitudes concerning the seriousness of women students may cause them to place female graduate students in positions of lower status with less time available for research and writing, the primary goals of graduate education in science.

The fact that both faculty and students perceive women graduate students as less dedicated, and women graduate students more frequently are assigned to lower status fellowships does not go unnoticed by the women graduate students. Although female compared to male graduate students have higher entrance GPAs and equal numbers of publications, they are less likely to rate themselves as among the best students in their classes or as a 'scholar' and 'scientist' (Feldman, 1974). Furthermore, negative self-image, which may be reinforced by 'micro-inequities' and/or blatant sexism, may cause female graduate students to contribute less in class, to avoid seeking help outside class, and to lower their career aspirations. In addition, such factors would undermine self-confidence of women hoping to excel in science (Project, 1982).

Women graduate students are not the only ones affected by negative collegial relationships; classroom and/or research group inequities toward women may be detrimental to male graduate students as well. Negative attitudes toward women in science, especially by professors, may prevent male graduate students from perceiving women as peers, from collaborating with them, and, eventually, from relating to women as equal workers and family members (Project, 1982). Science classes and research groups are weakened by the limited participation of women, and society loses potential professionals as well. With the current trend toward decreased loans for graduate students, it will be increasingly difficult to find financial support for graduate work (Gray, 1982). Women, who traditionally have had fewer avenues of support, may bear the brunt of this lack of funds and have even less access to graduate education in science.

Barriers to Women: Family Responsibilities

Although labor force statistics indicate that the working wife and/or mother has become the expected, rather than the exception, in our culture (Cocks, 1982), little has been done to ease the strain of dual home and career roles for women. During the graduate years this strain may be unbearable. As Feldman (1974) states,

> ... the least successful female students are those who attempt to combine the student and spouse roles ... For men, on the other hand, marriage has an entirely different impact and is complementary to the student role. Married men have someone to care for their needs ... Losing this support through divorce has a negative effect on men's performance in graduate school (p. 125).

Female compared to male graduate students are more family oriented, are more likely to be enrolled part-time, and are more constrained by their spouse's role (Feldman, 1974). Unfortunately, research also shows that marital disruption (divorce or separation) among women with six or more years of college is considerably higher than it is among women with four years of college (19 per cent compared to 10 per cent), men with six years of college (12 per cent), or men with four years of college (11 per cent) (Houseknecht and Spanier, 1980). Therefore, while marriage tends to decrease tension for men graduate students, strains and conflicts are increased for married women graduate students. Indeed, female graduate students often state that emotional strain might cause them to leave graduate school (Feldman, 1974).

The preceding discussion of the home/career role conflict has described the situation in terms of traditional sex roles for both husband and wife. Flexibility in traditional roles may reduce role conflict and strain for women. Quality day care centers may be necessary to prevent interruptions of women's studies. Avoiding interruption is a critical factor in the development of a successful career. Research indicates that receipt of the doctorate at a later age, whatever the reason, is detrimental to status attainment and research productivity (Perun, 1982). Optimally, then, both husband and wife should pursue their graduate studies simultaneously and avoid delay of admission or completion of graduate studies by either one. Flexibility in household roles, especially when raising a family, is critical to the dual success of graduate student couples. As stated recently,

> It may have seemed funny and a little silly when feminists started talking about men sharing housework and wives began insisting to husbands that homemaking was a tough job all its own. But the joke may seem strained indeed to whoever is left in the kitchen and, guaranteed, there will be more diapers and dishes in Dad's future (Cocks, 1982, p. 24).

This will certainly hold true for dual career couples both of whom want successful careers as well as a family.

In summary, although women enter graduate school with higher grade point indices, good publication records, and strong career commitments, both faculty and peers perceive them as less dedicated and less capable. In addition, female graduate students are subjected to both blatant sexism and 'micro-inequities'. Consequently, graduate women often develop low self-images and may be less confident than their male counterparts. In addition, married graduate women must deal with additional strains due to role conflicts between home and career.

Participation in the Sciences: The Career Period

Although the situation for graduate women is serious, career women scientists in academia or in industry face even greater obstacles. Claims of advancement have been made, yet the facts deny them:

> ... in both sectors, women and men are distributed differently both in terms of rank or grade level and in terms of work activities; women with identical education and work experience as men earn less and have less expectation of advancement. That this situation, a reflection of the general historical patterns of employment, should still remain for older employees is perhaps no surprise: the very fact that they were disadvantaged in employment over a long period may now make them less experienced and knowledgeable and, therefore, less qualified. That newly trained women scientists face a very similar future despite nearly a decade of equal-opportunity mandate is cause for grave concern (NRC, 1980, p. 39).

The preceding quote may seem harsh and critical of the significant advancements which have been made by women in higher education and industry, yet studies continue to show serious inequities. Although there has been a rapid increase in highly-trained women scientists, an increase in affirmative action regulations, and a change in social attitudes on the role of women, the resulting increase in women scientists in academia, industry, and government has been slow to materialize.

Female Labor Force

An overview of the status of the general female labor force is needed in order to place the status of women in science in perspective. In 1979 women constituted 40 per cent of the national labor force (US Department of Labor, 1980), but their distribution in that labor force was inequitable and the inequalities were shown to be continuing over time. For example, from 1940 to 1970 occupational segregation indices point out that, while occupational segregation by race decreased substantially, occupational segregation by sex remained at a consistently high rate, that is, the majority of employed women remained confined to a narrow group of jobs (Treiman and Hartmann, 1981). Average salaries also show major inequalities. In 1978 the average salary for a woman with four years of college was less than that of a white male with an eighth grade education (Treiman and Hartmann, 1981). Even with five or more years of college, women earn less, on the average, than white males who have graduated high school (Treiman and Hartmann, 1981).

Women Scientists

It might be expected that among doctorates sex differences in salaries, promotions, and hiring would be smaller due to equally extensive training and rigorous testing of both men and women. Unfortunately, this expectation is not fulfilled. In 1981 the unemployment rate of women in the doctoral science labor force was three to four times higher than that of males with equivalent experience (Vetter, 1981). Although differences in entrance salaries have decreased, the average female doctoral scientist in 1979 received a salary $6800 less than that of her male counterpart (NSF, 1982a). Figure 4.4 indicates that the median annual salary difference between male and female doctorates in biology and chemistry with two to five years' experience is over $1500. Even larger differences are found among doctorates with twenty-one to twenty-five years' experience. Salary differences can be explained if women applying for faculty or industrial positions are less qualified, and they can be rationalized if women academians are less productive than their male colleagues. The first assumption is unjustified; according to the National Academy of Sciences, based on ' ... academic records, elapsed time from B.A. to Ph.D., and ranking of graduate departments attended, women scientists and engineers on the average are at least equal to men in quality at receipt of the doctorate' (NRC, 1980, p. 19). There is, however, evidence to indicate that female scientists are less

Figure 4.4

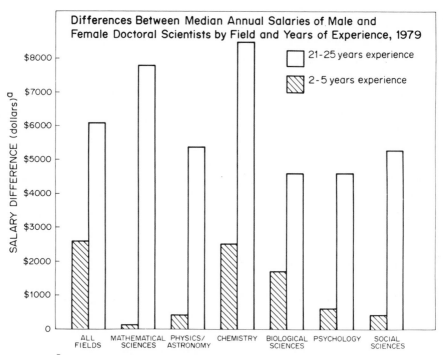

Differences Between Median Annual Salaries of Male and Female Doctoral Scientists by Field and Years of Experience, 1979

[a]MALE SALARIES ARE GREATER THAN FEMALE SALARIES IN ALL CASES.

Source: From NSF (1982b)

productive in publishing their research; this research will be discussed later in the chapter. The lag in salary increments for women scientists is, of course, concommitant with a lag in promotions and in granting of tenure. Although 12.5 per cent of all doctoral science and engineering positions at educational institutions are held by women, only 35 per cent of those women hold tenure, compared to 63 per cent of males (NSF, 1982b). As indicated in Table 4.2, women doctorates at all levels of experience are less likely to be tenured and, among recent doctorates, more women than men are employed in non-tenure track positions. Furthermore, a study of matched pairs of male and female doctorates found women at every experience level concentrated in lower rank positions (NRC, 1981).

Finally, it must be noted that women's contributions to science have been nearly unrecognized; proportionately, they have received far fewer awards (Rossiter, 1982). For example, there have been only five female Nobel science laureates among 345 winners and only forty-six

Table 4.2. Tenure Status among Matched Pairs of Doctorates, by Sex and Year of Doctorate Receipt, 1981

Year of doctorate	Percentage tenured		Percentage tenure track[a]		Percentage non-tenure track[a]	
	Men	Women	Men	Women	Men	Women
1940–59	98	89				
1960–69	91	83				
1970–74	52	35				
1975–78	15	9	70	66	15	25

Source: From NRC (1981).
Note: a Data not available for doctorates earned 1940–74.

women have been elected to the National Academy of Sciences, with 78 per cent of those recognitions occurring within the last twelve years.

Factors Affecting the Current Status of Women Scientists

Science has always been considered a meritocracy; that is, a system in which reward follows performance. Research in the history of science has supported this assumption (Cole, 1981). However, Rossiter (1982) discusses many methodological flaws in such research; for example, men studied only male scientists. For female scientists, either science is not equally meritocratic, or female scientists are influenced by other factors which hinder their success and/or performance. Several such factors are frequently cited, and each will be examined.

Teaching versus Research

The relationship between teaching and research and its effect on career status is critical. The impact of this relationship has been described in the following way:

> Exciting fields appear to be oriented toward science, not toward teaching. And for their research and scientific efforts, incumbents of exciting fields are better paid than are persons in the less exciting fields (Feldman, 1974, p. 49).

Fields such as comparative anatomy or botany with strong teaching orientations offer less power, fewer privileges, and lower prestige. Consequently, those who enter the doctoral work force with a strong teaching orientation are faced with lower salary, lower status, and fewer opportunities for advancement. In addition, teaching at the faculty level diverts time and energy from research and, thus, from the publication productivity which typically leads to advancement. Furthermore, persons holding positions such as lecturer/instructor are seldom allowed to seek outside research support, thus precluding any method of establishing a record of research or publication.

Traditionally, more women than men doctorates have expressed strong teaching orientations, and academic appointments reflect those orientations. Although women held only 10 per cent of the nation's full professorships in 1980, they held 50 per cent of the lecturer/instructor positions (Magarrell, 1980). Traditionally, women have been employed more frequently in junior colleges than in four-year institutions with opportunities for research (Feldman, 1974). Even when women are employed in four-year institutions, heavy teaching commitments may preclude research activities. For example, participants in a 1978 NIE project at Purdue University designed to teach advanced research skills to women faculty from southern minority institutions were all full-time faculty, yet only one participant had published more than one professional paper. On the average, the faculty participants had 4.3 different class preparations each semester requiring excessive teaching preparations and leaving little time for research activities (Kahle, 1982).

This situation may be changing. Among matched pairs of men and women who earned doctorates from 1975 to 1978, 73 per cent of women compared to 67 per cent of men spent more than half of their time teaching (NRC, 1981). This difference is due to sex differences in teaching loads at four-year colleges, not at research universities (NRC, 1981). Women who obtain positions at research universities may be increasingly aware that teaching may be less highly rewarded than research in terms of status and salary. Therefore, the majority of their time is devoted to research.

Postdoctoral Experience

Reskin states that it has been assumed that a postdoctoral fellowship positively affects a scientist's later career due to opportunities for development of professional contacts, acquisitions of research skills, and prestigious recognition of the postdoctoral fellowship. For female scientists, however, postdoctoral fellowships do not appear to significantly enhance their receipt of tenure. In a 1976 study of doctoral chemists, the receipt of and prestige of a postdoctoral fellowship were significant predictors of a male chemist's first job and subsequent tenure. However, they did not predict tenure or job success for women chemists. In fact, the prestige of a woman chemist's postdoctoral fellowship was significantly and negatively related to type of entry level position (Reskin, 1976). Although 66 per cent of the 1972 female doctorates who had postdoctoral experience were employed in 1979, only 14 per cent, compared to 33 per cent of men, had received tenure (Vetter, 1981). Finally, between 1973 and 1979 the number of female graduate students taking postdoctoral appointments more than doubled (NSF, 1982b). However, unless the situation described by Reskin changes, this postdoctoral experience will do little to improve the status of women scientists in academia.

Research Productivity

As stated earlier, when compared to men, female scientists have fewer research publications. Research by Widom and Burke (1978) indicates that female faculty, in general, are more likely to edit books and journals while male faculty write books and journal articles. Furthermore, they found that, in contrast to male scientists, female scientists do not accurately appraise their own publication productivity; that is, women tend to overestimate or underestimate their productivity. The ability to estimate relative productivity is especially important for women faculty, because women faculty often receive salary increments proportional to publication performance, while their male colleagues more often are rewarded for years of experience and department-related activities (Ferber, Loeb and Lowry, 1978).

Collegial Relationships

Women scientists' difficulties in estimating research productivity may stem from limited access to the information network of their scientific cohorts. Although they have gained entrance to academia, women may still find themselves victims of either blatant sexism or poorly disguised chauvinism. As a result of these attitudes, women often lack the intellectual stimulation and encouragement afforded by professional camaraderie. Reskin (1978) suggests that scientists

> ... adapt conventional sex roles to the scientific setting to create a hybrid of gender and collegial roles that systematically introduces sex-role differentiation into the scientific community ...

If male and female scientific co-workers do not both choose to ignore the status discrepancy introduced by gender, they cannot interact as full colleagues. Alternatively, they may minimize their interaction, thereby isolating female scientists, or they may draw on nonscientific role relationships that are consistent with their gender statuses but inconsistent, to varying degrees, with the scientific role. Either result reduces the likelihood that women will be fully integrated into collegial relations (pp. 10, 29).

Reskin also stresses the importance of collegial relationships, stating that scientific colleagues fulfill the following functions. They

1   identify references or results which may have been overlooked,
2   share and evaluate each other's results,
3   provide technical assistance, instruction, collaboration, advice and encouragement,
4   function as potential competitors, thus providing impetus for research and publication,
5   act as a reference group for evaluation of one's own performance, and
6   provide social companionship.

It has been suggested by several researchers that women are not accepted as full members of the scientific community (Cole, 1981; Reskin, 1978; Liss, 1975; Laws, 1975; Young, MacKenzie and Sherif, 1980). If this is the case, then women scientists are being denied access to the benefits of collegial relationships with the consequence that their research and careers must ultimately suffer.

Tokenism

In 1975 Judith Laws described a unique form of collegial relationship which she called tokenism.

Tokenism is likely to be found wherever a dominant group is under pressure to share privilege, power, or other desirable commodities with a group which is excluded. Tokenism is the means by which the dominant group advertises a promise of mobility between the dominant and excluded classes ... The token does not become assimilated into the dominant group but is destined for permanent marginality ... The institution of tokenism has advantages both for the dominant group and for the individual who is chosen to serve as token. These advantages obtain, however, only when the defining constraints are respected: the flow of outsiders into the dominant group must be restricted numerically, and they must not change the system they enter (Laws, 1975, p. 51).

Although Laws offered no empirical evidence, a subsequent study by Young, MacKenzie and Sherif (1980) found that 'token' women (according to Laws' definition) in academia tend to minimize the discrepancies which exist between the status of male and female academics. In addition, 'token' women were more likely than 'non-token' women to have received tenure. If further studies confirm these findings, then 'token' women in academia may themselves comprise a barrier to the development of equal scientific meritocracy and full scientific citizenship for women.

Marriage and Family

From 1960 to 1980 the percentage of working married women increased from 32 to 51. During that same period, a major turnaround occurred: 'The number of children with mothers who work (31.8 million) has become, for the first time, larger than the number of children with mothers at home (26.3 million)' (Cocks, 1982, p. 23). Consequently, the working mother has become the standard, rather than the exception, in the United States. What are the consequences of employment for the working mother/wife and particularly for women scientists? Marriage and family are frequently cited as key factors which impede the careers of women scientists. It has been assumed that the roles of wife and/or mother require too much of a scientist's time, resulting in less time for competitive research and publication. Studies on the effects of marriage and family on careers, however, do not corroborate such claims. The previously mentioned study of matched pairs indicates that marital status and presence of children had no effect on the promotion of junior faculty women or on the attainment of senior faculty rank (NRC, 1981). Furthermore, studies on productivity and status attainment by faculty women indicate that the timing of marriage, child-bearing, and family responsibilities has no significant effect on women's professional attainment (Perun, 1982). Neither does marriage appear to be a factor in determining whether women doctorates remain employed (Vetter, 1981; NRC, 1981). Furthermore, married women scientists, including those with children, display significantly greater research productivity than do unmarried women scientists (Cole, 1981). Finally, research indicates that women scientists are not less productive than male scientists before and during the child-bearing years (Ferber *et al.*, 1978).

Are there any proven negative effects of marriage on professional attainment? Perhaps one of the strongest effects is the constraint on mobility that marriage imposes on professional women. Married women in academia are twice as likely as similarly employed males to reside in a large urban area, presumably so that both husband and wife can find employment (Marwell, Rosenfeld and Spilerman, 1979). In addition, women doctorates are twice as likely as their male counterparts to remain in the same community when switching from one job to another (Marwell *et al.*, 1979).

Constraints on mobility decrease the number of opportunities women have to secure new positions. With respect to labor supply, the concentration of married women scientists in urban areas results in a disproportionate oversupply of women doctorates in urban labor markets and a disproportionate undersupply in smaller labor markets. There are fewer opportunities for women to advance by switching positions, a key factor in academic success. For example, female, compared with male, assistant professors who changed employers between 1975 and 1979 failed to improve their national status (NRC, 1981). As stated by Marwell *et al.* (1979), 'Job switching is the rule in academic careers and it pays off in upward mobility ... [it] requires flexibility to make geographic moves, especially early in the course of one's career' (p. 1226).

Unfortunately, flexibility is a luxury not often enjoyed by two career couples. Women who hold postdoctoral appointments tend to publish more books than articles during this time (Astin, 1973). They also remain at their postdoctoral appointments for longer periods of time (Marwell *et al.*, 1979). It may be that married women find postdoctoral appointments and publishing books a convenient way to remain professionally active while remaining in the same geographic location as their spouse.

Occasionally, a married woman scientist becomes a 'fringe benefit' to her husband's career, particularly when the two are in the same field. Often, of course, such a situation is beneficial for both the husband and wife. At other times, however, the wife may be regarded as 'part-time help' to fill in when needed, often to the detriment of the woman's professional development and career. Frequently, in such part-time situations, the wife is not eligible for promotion and tenure considerations. Women in these situations often do not protest because of university politics that might adversely affect both careers or family finances. The allocation of credit for joint work often is unequal, with the husband receiving the greater proportion of credit (Reskin, 1978; Rossiter, 1982).

As the dual career marriage has become prevalent in our culture, the two-career family has also become common. Although day care centers provide a partial answer for women scientists with young children, by no means do they relieve all the responsibilities of parenting. If the mother is held responsible for all such duties, her work as a scientist will undoubtedly suffer. Interviews with women faculty indicate that they continue to hold primary responsibility for the maintenance and development of the home (Liss, 1975; Bryson, Bryson, Licht and Licht, 1976). Some women have opted to work part-time during these years, and some have chosen to interrupt their careers for a time.

The woman who chooses to remain at home to care for young children faces self-generated obstacles when she attempts to re-enter her professional field. New research techniques and findings accumulate during a leave of absence, making subsequent applications for grant monies more difficult. The situation may become acute for the woman with three or more children who is, therefore, absent from her profession for eight to ten years. Although women face similar circumstances in all disciplines, the situation is especially critical in the sciences where research may change radically each year. A woman scientist with a very young family may have little time to read scientific journals and little opportunity for conversations with others in her field. Time and finances may negate any opportunities for her to attend professional conferences. Evening and weekend laboratory courses and facilities are scarce, if available at all. Therefore, she cannot continue her science studies and research during hours when her spouse is available to care for the children. In fact, women scientists who have three or more children display significantly lower research productivity than married women scientists with fewer than three children (Cole, 1981).

It appears, therefore, that the solutions to the problems of re-entry of women scientists will require cooperation and compromise on the part of both the spouse and the institution. It is a tragic situation when universities and colleges lose the benefits of competent, often talented, women by failing to provide alternative ways for them to continue their careers.

In conclusion, marriage and family do place certain constraints on both men and women in dual career families. The fact that a woman scientist is married does not appear to affect her productivity as a scientist, but does affect her flexibility to move to new and better job opportunities. Childrearing may slow down or interrupt a female scientist's career, if she is primarily responsible for child care. Changes which may alleviate this situation include the increasing number of institutions hiring both husband and wife, the increasing number of quality day care centers, and the decreasing discrepancy between husbands' and wives' household workloads. Among dual career couples, women worked in the home 1.2–2.8 hours per day more than men in the 1960s, yet they averaged only twelve minutes per day more than men by the mid-1970s (Pleck and Rustad, 1981). The situation of the scientist/wife/mother is by no means hopeless but requires cooperation from both spouse and institution.

Personality and Socio-Cultural Factors

The shortage of successful female scientists has been attributed not only to external factors such as type of position, faculty attitudes and family commitments, but also to internal factors such as negative self-image and low self-confidence. Vivian Gornik describes the situation in the following manner:

> What did it mean to be one, or a few, among the many? What if a woman in science feels she's got to prove herself many times more than a man does; that her work is more often challenged and less often supported; that she can't get grants, equipment, promotions and tenure as easily as her male counterparts do; that she works under the peculiar strain of an excluding hierarchy of working colleagues that is always operative and always denied. What is life in science like for such a person? What happens to her nerve, her self-confidence, her ability to believe in the evidence of her own intelligence, her capacity for creative thought? (Gornik, 1981, p. 12).

Gornik's concern for the female scientist's self-confidence is well-founded. In attribution studies of equally successful men and women, it has been found that men attribute their success to ability (a stable factor) and tend to predict future success for themselves. Women, on the other hand, attribute their successes to effort (a factor which changes over time) and make lower predictions for future success (Erkut, 1979). Women, therefore, attribute their success not to ability, but to effort, and consequently their self-confidence is lower. Some studies have investigated whether women in male-dominated fields are motivated to avoid success due to a perceived role conflict between career role and the more traditional female role (Lockheed, 1975; Horner, 1972). After subjects read descriptions of women working in masculine areas, they were asked to complete stories about the women. Results indicated that, although women were seen as facing tremendous odds in the pursuit of a 'masculine' career, role conflict and a resulting motive to avoid success depended upon the environment in which the women worked or studied. If women were depicted as an accepted part of the environment, no role conflict was described (Lockheed, 1975). An environment of acceptance and encouragement may be critical for women scientists. In the 'masculine' field of engineering, research has already shown this to be the case: while male engineering students stated that extrinsic rewards were their prime motivators for remaining in the engineering field, female students indicated that encouragement and support from others were key motivators for their continued study (Davis, 1978).

Women scientists' undergraduate qualifications, their graduate qualifications, and their apparent scientific potential do not seem to account for their lower success rates in obtaining tenure, earning salary increases, and raising their research productivity. Future research, therefore, must investigate more thoroughly and empirically the personal and socio-cultural factors, including collegial relationships, which affect the success of women scientists.

Summary

Although the number of undergraduate women in science is increasing, the number of women entering science graduate programs has not kept pace. Science is still perceived as a masculine endeavor, and even highly-qualified female graduate students in science must face faculty and fellow students who doubt their dedication and ability. In addition, they are often forced to develop their research and professional attitudes without benefit of close professor/student relationships or financial support for research. Negative self-images and conflicts in the wife/mother/student roles can rob women graduate students of experiences and growth critical to the development of a successful career in science.

After receipt of the doctorate, women scientists face lower salaries, fewer promotions, lower status positions, and fewer opportunities for tenured positions than males have. Although such inequities frequently have been attributed to women's interruptions of scientific careers for marriage and childbirth, research indicates that lower research productivity, underdeveloped collegial relationships, accepting a token role in the scientific community, and lack of job mobility are more likely to affect their overall achievements and subsequent status.

This situation is changing for the better, but progress continues very slowly. Undergraduate women in science are by no means blind to the situation they will face as graduate students and this fact may cause a trend which affirmative action programs may not be able to change.

> Unless the pool of available Ph.D. women scientists increases significantly, the number employed in academe will not increase, and the pool of available Ph.D. women will not continue to increase unless higher education makes a more conscious effort not just to increase their numbers according to affirmative action goals, but to provide them with visible, respectable and prestigious permanent positions on the tenured faculty, or at least an equal opportunity to attain these positions (Rose, Nyre, Menninger and Foster, 1978).

Progress such as that described above will not be achieved merely by increasing the number of women graduate students in science or even the number and status of women science faculty. It will require science to become a true meritocracy.

> If there has been movement toward greater application of meritocratic principles over the past twenty-five or thirty years, it has taken the form of reducing the level of formal status inequality between men and women scientists. What has not been achieved to any significant degree is full citizenship for women in science (Cole, 1981, p. 389).

Women scientists must become active members of the network of communicating and collaborating scientists before they can make equal contributions to their fields. A view from the periphery will no longer suffice; women scientists must demand the full citizenship which they have earned through years of dedicated study and research.

References

ASTIN, H. (1973) 'Career profiles of women doctorates', in ROSSI, A.S. and CALDERWOOD, A. (Eds.), *Academic Women on the Move*, New York, Russell Sage.

BRYSON, R.B., BRYSON, J.B., LICHT, M.H. and LICHT, B.G. (1976) 'The professional pair: Husband and wife psychologists', *American Psychologist*, 31, pp. 10–16.

Cocks, J. (1982) 'How long till equality?' *Time*, 12 July, pp. 20–9.

Cole, J.R. (1981) 'Women in science', *American Scientist*, 69, pp. 385–91.

Davis, S.O. (1978) 'Beyond tokenism', *New Engineer*, 7, 2, pp. 22–9.

Erkut, S. (1979) 'Expectancy Attribution and Academic Achievement: Exploring the Implications of Sex-Role Orientation' (Center for Research on Women, Working Paper No. 27), Unpublished manuscript, Wellesley College, Wellesley, MA.

Feldman, S.D. (1974) *Escape from the Doll's House*, New York, McGraw-Hill.

Ferber, M.A., Loeb, J.W. and Lowry, H.M. (1978) 'The economic status of women faculty: A reappraisal', *Journal of Human Resources*, 13, 3, pp. 385–401.

Gornik, V. (1981) 'A mind of her own', *In These Times*, 4–10 November, pp. 12–15.

Gray, P.E. (1982) 'Support of graduate education', *Science*, 216, p. 129.

Horner, M.S. (1972) 'Toward an understanding of achievement-related conflicts in women', *Journal of Social Issues*, 28, 2, pp. 157–75.

Houseknecht, S.K. and Spanier, G.B. (1980) 'Marital disruption and higher education among women in the United States', *The Sociological Quarterly*, 21, pp. 375–89.

Kahle, J.B. (1982) *Double Dilemma: Minorities and Women in Science Education*. West Lafayette, IN, Purdue Research Foundation.

Laws, J.L. (1975) 'The psychology of tokenism: An analysis', *Sex Roles*, 1, 1, .pp. 51–67.

Liss, L. (1975) 'Why academic women do not revolt', *Sex Roles*, 1, 3, pp. 209–23.

Lockheed, M.E. (1975) 'Female motive to avoid success', *Sex Roles*, 1, 1, pp. 41–50.

Magarrell, J. (1980) 'More women on faculties: Pay still lags', *Chronicle of Higher Education*, 21, p. 8.

Marwell, G., Rosenfeld, R. and Spilerman, S. (1979) 'Geographic constraints on women's careers in academia', *Science*, 205, pp. 1225–31.

Mokros, J.R., Erkut, S. and Spichiger, L. (1981) 'Mentoring and being mentored: Sex related patterns among college professors' (Center for Research on Women, Working Paper No. 68), Unpublished manuscript, Wellesley College, Wellesley, MA.

National Research Council (NRC) (1980) *Women Scientists in Industry and Government: How Much Progress in the 1970's?* Washington, DC, National Academy of Sciences.

National Research Council (NRC) (1981) *Career Outcomes in a Matched Sample of Men and Women Ph.D.'s*, Washington, DC, National Academy Press.

National Research Council (NRC) (1982) *Summary Report 1981 Doctorate Recipients from United States Universities*, Washington, DC, National Academy Press.

National Science Foundation (NSF) (1982a) *Science and Engineering Educa-*

tion: Data and Information (NSF 82–30), Washington, DC, National Science Foundation.

NATIONAL SCIENCE FOUNDATION (NSF) (1982b) *Women and Minorities in Science and Engineering* (NSF 82–302), Washington, DC, National Science Foundation.

PENG, S.S. and JAFFE, J. (1979) 'Women who enter male-dominated fields of study in higher education', *American Educational Research Journal*, 16, 3, pp. 285–93.

PERUN, P.J. (1982) 'Academic women, productivity, and status attainment: A life course model' (Center for Research on Women, Working Paper No. 29), Unpublished Manuscript, Wellesley College, Wellesley, MA.

PLECK, J.H. and RUSTAD, M. (1981) 'Husbands' and wives' time in family work and paid work in the 1975–76 study of time use' (Center for Research on Women, Working Paper No. 63), Unpublished manuscript, Wellesley College, Wellesley, Mass.

PROJECT ON THE STATUS AND EDUCATION OF WOMEN (1982) *The Classroom Climate: A Chilly One for Women?* Washington, DC, Association of American Colleges.

RESKIN, B.F. (1976) 'Sex differences in status attainment in science: The case of the postdoctoral fellowship', *American Sociological Review*, 41, pp. 597–612.

RESKIN, B.F. (1978) 'Sex differentiation and the social organization of science', *Sociological Inquiry*, 48, pp. 6–37.

ROSE, C., NYRE, G.F., MENNINGER, S.A. and FOSTER, P. (1978) 'Responsiveness vs. resources: The implementation and impact of affirmative action programs for women scientists in post secondary education', Paper presented at the Association of Institutional Research Annual Forum, Houston, TX, 21–6 May.

ROSSITER, M.W. (1982) *Women Scientists in America: Struggles and Strategies to 1940*, Baltimore, MD, Johns Hopkins University Press.

SEATER, B.B. and RIDGEWAY, C.L. (1976) 'Role models, significant others, and the importance of male influence on college women', *Sociological Symposium*, 15, pp. 49–64.

SPEIZER, J.J. (1981) 'Role models, mentors, and sponsors: The elusive concepts', *Signs: Journal of Women in Culture and Society*, 6, 4, pp. 692–712.

STAKE, J., WALKER, E.F., and SPENO, M.V. (1981) 'The relationship of sex and academic performance to quality of recommendations for graduate school', *Psychology of Women Quarterly*, 5, 4, pp. 515–22.

TREIMAN, D.J. and HARTMANN, H.I. (1981) *Women, Work, and Wages: Equal Pay for Jobs of Equal Value*, Washington, DC, National Academy Press.

US DEPARTMENT of LABOR (1980) *Twenty Facts on Women Workers*, Washington, DC, US Department of Labor Women's Bureau.

VETTER, B.M. (1981) 'Women scientists and engineers: Trends in participation', *Science*, 214, pp. 1313–21.

WIDOM, C.S. and BURKE, B.W. (1978) 'Performance, attitudes, and professional socialization of women in academia', *Sex Roles*, 4, 4, pp. 549–62.

YOUNG, C.J., MACKENZIE, D.L. and SHERIF, C.W. (1980) 'In search of token
women in academia', *Psychology of Women Quarterly*, 4, 4, pp. 508–25.

5   Minority Women: Conquering Both Sexism and Racism

Mildred Collins and Marsha Lakes Matyas
Stillman College and Purdue University

More and more, young Black women are starting to think about their future as Black women in the United States. They are not accepting societal interpretations of their roles. In the process of thinking things through they are being realistic about the roles that they will embrace. Black women will still have to work, but they want to work at jobs that are more challenging and that more fully use their strengths and talents. They want quality education and training to develop their abilities and interests. They want education that respects cultural differences and that educates for liberation and survival (Hart, 1977, p. 2).

The above quotation by Donna Hart indicates that black women in the United States consider education important and view it as a key to opening doors which, in the past, have been closed to both black men and women. It also emphasizes that black women will no longer tolerate an education which only has surface, not substantive, value. Historically supportive of education, black women have become painfully aware that 'equal opportunity' education may open few doors: 'Despite the faith of black women in the education system as a means for social and economic advancement, equal education has not assured them equal access to opportunity . . . ' (Hart, 1977, p. 2). This situation is true for both black working women in the general population as well as for those who work in educational institutions.

Current Status

As Table 5.1 shows, the number of minority women holding the doctorate degree in the United States is extremely small. Therefore,

Table 5.1.   Female Doctorates in Science and Engineering by Race and Field, 1982

| | Frequency | | | |
Field	Black Americans	Mexican Americans	Native Americans	Puerto Ricans
Physics/Astronomy	7	1	0	—
Biology/Life Sciences	295	48	32	32
Chemistry	38	9	5	5
Engineering	5	6	6	6

Source: Data drawn from NSF (1982b).

statistics seldom are computed separately for different minority groups and often are not computed for minority women at all. However, some research has been reported on black women scientists; therefore, this chapter will concentrate on that specific group.

In 1979, 53 per cent of black women were members of the US labor force, comprising nearly half of all black workers (US Department of

Figure 5.1

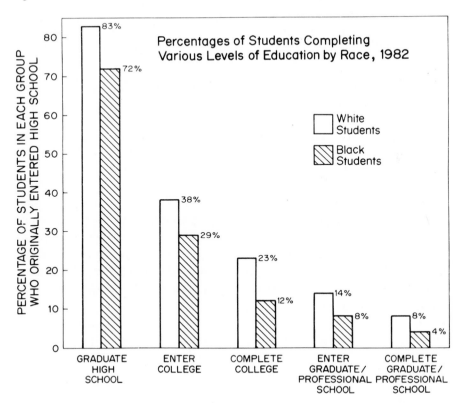

Source: Adapted from Ford Foundation's Committee on the Higher Education of Minorities (1982).

Labor, 1980). Twenty-five per cent of those black women workers provided the primary income for their families, and, on the average, the black woman worker earned one-third of the total family income (US Department of Labor, 1980). However, black women, compared with white men, white women, and black men, have the highest unemployment rate and the lowest median salary level (US Department of Labor, 1980).

As Figure 5.1 shows, 72 per cent of the blacks who enter high school graduate from it. However, only 29 per cent enter college, and only 12 per cent complete college. Furthermore, only 8 per cent of black high school graduates enter graduate school, where the attrition rate for blacks is 50 per cent. As a black student's academic career continues, the chances for success narrow, perhaps due to the greater number of obstacles faced by the average black student. The achievement/attrition statistics are even worse for minority women, undoubtedly due to the additional burdens faced by women in academe. In order to isolate some of the unique factors affecting the education and careers of black women scientists, it is necessary to examine both educational and personal experiences. Unfortunately, data on the education and employment of scientists are seldom analyzed for both race and sex simultaneously. One must, therefore, often rely on data for either minorities or women, since few data are specifically for minority women.

Precollegiate Education: Critical Preparation for Science Studies

The roots of the dearth of minority women in science reach back as far as elementary school. Minority girls find few examples of minority female role models in their textbooks. A study on sexism in textbooks indicates that in the most widely-used elementary texts in science, math, reading, spelling, and social studies, fewer than a third of the illustrations included girls and even fewer illustrations displayed minority girls engaged in learning activities (Sadker and Sadker, 1979). Even in teacher education textbooks, when the topics of male/female learning differences, sex-role stereotyping and special concerns of minorities are addressed, black women often are described in broad generalizations such as the 'dominant female figure in the black family' (Sadker and Sadker, 1979).

Although conflicting results have been found, desegregation appears to have some effect on black student achievement. For example, Bradley and Bradley's (1977) extensive review of black students in desegregated schools presents conflicting evidence concerning black achievement and adjustment in desegregated schools. They suggest that one of the few positive outcomes of desegregation may be what has been termed the 'lateral transmission of values' (p. 403) from white to black schoolmates. If the values transferred include self-respect and self-confidence, they could, indeed, affect blacks' achievement and attitudes, but the results are not definitive. Another study indicates that, among sixth grade black girls of middle-class socio-economic status, friendship with white classmates is correlated with higher achievement (Lewis and St. John, 1974, in Patchen, 1982). This correlation did not appear when desegregation occurred during the high school years (Patchen, 1982) nor was it found among elementary school boys (Lewis and St. John, 1974, in Patchen, 1982). Although the evidence concerning black achievement is tentative, desegregation does appear to significantly and positively affect black student effort. As Patchen (1982) states,

> Effort among blacks generally was lower when the proportion of blacks in their classes was about half or more than when their classes were predominantly white. This drop in effort with increasing proportions of blacks may reflect lower expectations from teachers and/or a more lax student norm about academic behavior in heavily black classes (p. 264).

During high school, minority females take fewer general or advanced mathematics and science courses than do either white males or females (Marrett, 1981). This may reflect poor counseling: for example, a 1977 study by Erlick and LeBold found that minority females interested in science were more likely than white females to be told by teachers in which courses males and females could expect to be successful (Erlick and LeBold, 1977).

Lower teacher expectations and lower student motivation were two of several factors also cited by successful minority women scientists as detrimental to the education of prospective minority scientists (Hall, 1981). The effect of differential teacher expectations may begin in the primary and secondary grades and continue through graduate school. For example, black teachers in low-income areas described their black students as fun-loving, happy, cooperative, energetic and ambitious; while white teachers perceived the same students as talkative, lazy, fun-loving, highstrung and frivolous (Gottlieb, 1974). Recent research, however, indicates that more positive teacher attitudes and expectations may be found in younger teachers (Karlin, Coffman and Walter,

1969). In 1980 a survey was sent to members of the National Network of Minority Women in Science (MWIS) requesting their suggestions for increasing the number of minority women in science. They offered the following definitive criteria for the improvement of pre-collegiate education for minorities.

1 Attitudes conducive to achievement should be encouraged. Higher self-esteem, success motivation, high academic expectations, self-discipline, willingness to assess and take risks, high regard for the value of education, and realization that educational/career objectives demand hard work and discipline are all requisite for scientific studies. The respondents felt that role models, especially teachers, counselors, parents and science speakers would be excellent sources of encouragement.

2 The quality of the high school curriculum and extracurricular activities should be improved. The respondents stressed the importance of piquing student interest in science at an early point in their education, of relaying the importance of science in the students' world, and of the use of stimulating teaching methods, demonstrations, field trips and microcomputers.

3 Students must have access to adequate counseling and career decision information. Students need to be aware of 'the relationship between high school courses and future career options', the usefulness of science in the student's world, the education requirements for science/mathematics careers, the resulting rewards from those careers, and how to go about choosing an institution suited to the student's particular needs (Hall, 1981).

Counselors especially need to alert minority students to the pitfalls of taking 'easy' courses during high school. Whether due to counseling or to lack of confidence, black students are much more likely to enroll in lower level mathematics courses than are white students (Marrett, 1981). Upon considering a college science major, these students may find themselves lacking over a year's prerequisites for entering a college math sequence. Financially they may not be able to devote the extra time to make up the deficiency. By avoiding 'dead end' courses, counselors can help the minority student keep career options in science and mathematics open. Minority females, especially, need such information. Concerned girls are seeking out counselors, who may be instrumental in expanding their hopes and horizons. For example, nearly 40 per cent of minority girls interested in science reported discussing future education and training with high school counselors three or more times a year. With improved curricula, better counseling, increased achievement, and supportive role models, the number of minority women academically and emotionally prepared for the challenges of a college career should increase significantly.

Collegiate Years: Frustration As the Path to Attrition

In 1978 minorities constituted only 18 per cent of the total undergraduate enrollment (NSF, 1980). However, 57 per cent of all blacks attending a two- or four-year institution were female. Blacks, especially black women, most frequently enroll in the social sciences, education, and psychology. Among the black undergraduate population, only 17 per cent enrolled in biological sciences, 12 per cent in engineering, and 10 per cent in the physical sciences (NSF, 1980). Furthermore, during the course of their college careers, blacks suffer substantial science attrition. For example, blacks earned only 6.6 per cent of all bachelor degrees and only 4.1 per cent of science (including social science and psychology) and engineering baccalaurate degrees in 1978–79 (NSF, 1982a). The loss of minority students from science and engineering is due to withdrawal from college as well as to change in degree programs from science and engineering majors. Among those black students receiving bachelor degrees in 1978–79, twice as many students majored in the social sciences and in psychology as in the life sciences, physical sciences, computer sciences, math, and engineering combined (NSF, 1982a). The lack of black students majoring in science and, within the sciences, the tendency of blacks to avoid the physical sciences represent a substantial loss of potential scientists to the scientific community. Before any recommendations can be made to curb this loss, the underlying reasons must be exposed.

Frustration with the college experience may account for the high attrition rate of minority students from science and engineering programs (Hall, 1981). Frustration with coursework, academic department, or personal aspects of college life may cause students to lose the enthusiasm and dedication required to pass science courses. Minority students frequently are less prepared both personally and academically for the rigors of college studies (Hall, 1981). In addition, they may be less aware of routine information concerning departmental requirements and university graduation policies. They may be naive about the potential personal problems that all incoming freshmen face. This lack of awareness may be attributed to weaker precollegiate education and counseling often received by blacks (Hall, 1981).

On the other hand, according to the American Association of Colleges' (AAC) Project on the Status and Education of Women (1982), colleges themselves may be at fault. Frequently, there is no 'middle of the road' path for black women; that is, they are viewed as either academic incompetents or as academic superstars (AAC, 1982). For example, black women report that they are neglected and overlooked because faculty believe them to be less committed to their studies and frequently ignore and interrupt them. Their interactions with faculty are characterized by excessive physical distance, decreased eye contact, and fewer offers of guidance or criticism. Black women undergraduates, perhaps as a result of these behaviors, frequently attribute their success to luck rather than to ability (AAC, 1982). Female undergraduate students facing such behavior, in addition to the stress of college life, often are frustrated and may wish to quit or change majors. Several solutions for curbing attrition and field-switching among black women are available. First, it is imperative that minority students receive better secondary preparation. Second, minority students need access to support services in order to maintain high academic achievement and personal confidence levels during their college careers. Regular counseling, peer tutors, peer and faculty mentors, and regular monitoring of academic progress have all been suggested as methods to ease the academic and personal pathways for undergraduate minority women (Hall, 1981; NBGE, 1976). As stated by the National Board of Graduate Education (NBGE), ' . . . [This] problem must be addressed during the high school and early undergraduate years to motivate students and ensure adequate academic preparation for advanced work in certain fields such as the natural sciences and engineering' (NBGE, 1976, p. 51).

A solution to the problem of poor faculty relationships may be more difficult to accomplish. Faculty must be cognizant that they have negative attitudes toward both minority and majority women and must be encouraged by their institutions to monitor themselves and their departments for differential behaviors. Table 5.2 offers suggestions for faculty. Minority women students must not be subtly trained to accept such actions as the general attitude of the scientific community. Table 5.3 offers suggestions to women undergraduates on how to avoid becoming the victims of differential behaviors.

Graduate Training: Black Women Face Sexism As Well

According to 1971 data, 57 per cent of black college freshmen compared to 42 per cent of white college freshmen planned to continue to graduate

Table 5.2.   *Behaviors That Can Encourage or Discourage Women Students*

Discouraging Behaviors
— disparaging women's intellectual abilities or professional potential
— using sexist humor in the classroom
— making helpful comments which imply that women are not as competent as men
— discussing women faculty in terms of gender rather than of personal status
— ridiculing specific work because it deals with women's perceptions and feelings
— doubting women students' seriousness and/or academic commitment

Encouraging Behaviors — In the Classroom
— expect both men and women to participate in class discussion; call on women as much as men
— use terminology that includes both men and women
— respond to contributions made by men and women students equally for comparable contributions
— question your reaction to a 'feminine' or 'masculine' response to a question, that is, does 'feminine' delivery imply a poor answer?
— determine if you interrupt women students more than men students; give male and female students equal time to respond to questions
— use parallel terminology when addressing men and women students
— don't reinforce limited views of career choices for men and women
— make eye contact with men and women equally
— watch for non-verbal cues indicating women students' readiness to participate in class
— use the same tone when addressing men and women students
— ensure that women are not 'squeezed out' during the laboratory demonstrations or groups assignments
— pay attention to the questions or comments of women in the class

Encouraging Behaviors — Outside the Classroom
— meet with women students to discuss academic and career goals
— encourage women to pursue 'masculine' jobs or studies when they show interests or abilities
— consider both women and men when choosing classroom or teaching assistants
— consider both women and men for research assistantships in traditionally 'masculine' fields and for nomination for fellowships, awards, and prizes
— ensure that women and men assistants have equal opportunities to pursue their own research
— include women graduate students in the 'informal' interactions of the department and research group; communicate support and acceptance as a colleague
— provide women with both formal and informal feedback concerning quality of their work

Source: Adapted from American Association of Colleges (1982).

studies after finishing their bachelors' degrees (NBGE, 1976). However, 1978 data indicate that minorities comprised only 10 per cent of all graduate students (NSF, 1980). Black students are about half as likely as whites to accomplish the goal of entering graduate school. Among the total black graduate population in 1978, fewer than 3 per cent were studying biology, 4 per cent were enrolled in engineering, and 1.7 per cent matriculated in physical science (NSF, 1980). As a result these three fields, along with mathematics, have the fewest minority professionals (AAAS, 1982). As shown in Table 5.4, 82 per cent of black doctorates, compared to 61 per cent of white doctorates in 1981, were in education, social science, and humanities. On the other hand, fewer

Mildred Collins and Marsha Lakes Matyas

Table 5.3. *Improving the Classroom Climate: Recommendations for Minority Women Students*

— if you feel you're disproportionately interrupted while speaking in class, discuss your problem with other women students to see if they have had the same experience
— give positive feedback to professors who use non-sexist language (nodding, eye contact, or direct communication of approval)
— become familiar with your institution's grievance procedures for sexual harassment; where appropriate, discuss problems of classroom climate with the department chair or dean; if your department is unsupportive, seek out professional organizations for women
— use your student evaluation form to provide positive and/or negative feedback concerning the climate of the classroom
— organize a support group of other minority women majoring in your area; this group can provide a forum for airing problems and developing strategies as well as providing opportunities for supportive collegial relationships
— contact the staff of your minority student center concerning any classroom climate issues.

Source: Adapted from American Association of Colleges (1982).

Table 5.4. *Frequencies and Percentages of Doctoral Degree Recipients by Field and Race, 1982*

Field	Black		White	
	Frequency	Percentage	Frequency	Percentage
Physical Sciences	39	3.5	2807	12.5
Engineering	19	1.7	1092	4.9
Life Sciences	80	7.2	4021	18.0
Social Sciences	223	20.2	4960	22.1
Humanities	93	8.4	2954	13.2
Education	589	53.4	5561	24.8
Professional Fields[a]	59	5.3	984	4.4
Other	2	0.2	21	0.1
Total	1104	99.9[b]	22400	100.0

Source: Data drawn from NRC, 1982.
Notes: a Includes theology, business administration, home economics, journalism, speech and hearing sciences, law, social work, and library science.
b Due to rounding.

than 13 per cent of black, compared to 35 per cent of white, doctorates earned degrees in science and engineering. This may be partially due to field-switching between undergraduate and graduate degrees. Field-switching is frequently done from science to non-science majors, but seldom in the reverse direction.

Many reasons have been suggested for the low number of minority graduate students and, particularly, of minority women graduate students. Financial factors are often cited: 'Although sufficient financial aid does not insure a successful college career, it may be the major inhibiting factor for many minority students' (Kahle, 1982). Nearly 50 per cent of the respondents to the Minority Women in Science survey indicated that financial aid in the form of fellowships, grants, and loans was the most important factor in attracting minority students to graduate studies (Hall, 1981). Graduate schools must compete for minority students against the attractive financial rewards of employment. 'Upon graduation from college, immediate employment opportunities may appear more rewarding than advanced study in view of the prospect of future financial difficulties, the academic risk of graduate study (about half of all doctoral candidates fail to complete the Ph.D. degree), and labor market uncertainties' (NBGE, 1976).

The conspicuous absence of role models, especially black women scientists, also may be a deterrent to black women entering graduate studies in scientific fields. In 1980 black women comprised only 3.1 per cent of the faculty in higher education and only 1.5 per cent of the science faculty in higher education (SMC, 1983). The paucity of minority role models makes it more difficult for minority graduate students to develop mentor relationships with faculty. As the National Board on Graduate Education states. 'The absence of persons with advanced degrees to serve as appropriate role models for the aspiring student weakens the link between wishful thinking and the practical knowledge needed to formulate a meaningful objective and to take the necessary actions to achieve it' (NGBE, 1976, p. 101). Difficulties in establishing faculty relationships must be viewed as a formidable barrier for black women graduate students.

In addition to the difficulties of establishing productive mentor relationships, minority students, especially minority women, have reported problems in establishing mutually supportive collegial relationships with majority graduate students (Hall, 1981). The benefits of a graduate student network include collaboration on research projects, informal teaching of methods and procedures, cooperative generation of hypotheses, and the establishment of professional contacts. They are second in importance only to the major professor/student relationship benefits and cannot be forfeited by minority graduate women aspiring to successful science careers. The potential lack of a cooperative network may lead minority graduate students to enroll in minority graduate schools. However, many minority graduate schools suffer from a lack of funds and equipment necessary for scientific research. Therefore, although their impact on other professions has been substantial, the impact of minority colleges on the production of minority scientists has been minimal (NBGE, 1976). Hopefully, this situation may change; minority graduate schools have cited the acquisition of laboratory space and equipment and the recruitment of qualified science faculty as priority concerns (Kahle, 1982).

Minority students, especially those from small undergraduate schools, may get caught in the 'revolving door' policy, prevalent in some doctorate-granting institutions. According to this policy, students have a specific period of time in which they must complete their qualifying examinations, preliminary examinations, and dissertation. If they delay any step in this process, they may lose financial support. This policy discriminates against any student who enters with an academic deficiency. Since research shows that, on the average, blacks are older than whites when they complete a doctorate and have longer periods between beginning and completing their degrees (NRC, 1982), any policy that decreases flexibility in progress would be detrimental to minorities.

Finally, minority women scientists report that the major difficulties experienced during their graduate studies arise from encounters with sexism (NBGE, 1976). In addition to the difficulties described above, minority women must face the problems encountered by majority women in science. Not only is science viewed as 'non-black', it also is stereotyped as 'masculine'. In choosing a scientific career, therefore, minority women must overcome not one, but two, stereotypes.

Black graduate women may find it necessary to convince both faculty and fellow students of their abilities. They also must accept the teaching assistantships often awarded to women in lieu of research assistantships (NRC, 1982). Married minority women face a potential home/career conflict. Among 1981 doctoral science degree recipients, only 48.4 per cent of females were married, compared to 59.8 per cent of males (NRC, 1982). The female science graduate student may find it difficult to pursue her degree after marriage. Minority women, therefore, bear the compounded burdens of both racism and sexism in their pursuit of a doctorate in science.

Solutions to problems of minority access to graduate studies in science may be found not only in the secondary school changes mentioned earlier but also in changes in undergraduate counseling procedures and graduate science departments. Information provided to undergraduates about graduate schools should include statistics on the numbers of admitted students by race and by sex as well as their respective rates of attrition. In addition, the number of minority faculty as well as information about the general receptiveness of the graduate school toward minority students should be provided (Hall, 1981). Before matriculation, students should receive information specifying the school and departmental expectations and requirements (Hall, 1981). More aggressive recruitment of minority students and more accurate assessment of potential problems also are needed.

After admission, minority students should be quickly integrated into the mainstream of teaching and research activities (NBGE, 1976). Departments should promote minority access to mentor relationships as well as to the informal information networks which are of vital assistance in acquiring job placement references and contacts and in learning grant application procedures (Hall, 1981). Research universities must increase the numbers of minority faculty, both male and female, in order to provide role models for minority graduate and undergraduate students (Hall, 1981; NBGE, 1976). The 'revolving door' policy must be eliminated so that minority students with rectifiable academic deficiencies have the opportunity to complete a doctorate without unusual financial hardship (Hall, 1981). Graduate departments must be responsible for self-evaluation of their overall effectiveness in the aggressive recruitment and maximum development of minority graduate students and scientists (NBGE, 1976).

Minority Women As Working Scientists: The Struggle to Prove Competency

Although data specifically on minority females are sparse at the undergraduate and graduate school levels, they are becoming more available concerning the black female worker in general. Due to their extremely small numbers, however, information concerning minority women scientists is rare. Generalizations concerning minority women scientists, therefore, often must be drawn from the available data on minority scientists and women scientists.

Recent statistics show that the mean annual income for black women working full-time is considerably less than that of white women or black men and is only 52 per cent of the mean annual income of white men (Treiman and Hartmann, 1981). Furthermore, advanced education does not necessarily remove this income disparity. The 1980 census found that the mean salary of black females with five or more years of college was less than that of black males with only one to three years of college and was less than that of white males with only one to three years of high school (Treiman and Hartmann, 1981). In comparing black females with five years or more of college with white or black males of equal training, black women earned only 49.3 per cent of the white male's average salary, and less than 68 per cent of the black male's average salary (Treiman and Hartmann, 1981). Even more alarming are the data analyses which produce occupational segregation indices for all occupations. These analyses show that 'occupational segregation is more pronounced by sex than by race' (Treiman and Hartmann, 1981, p. 28). For example, from 1940 to 1970 occupational segregation indices changed significantly for blacks versus whites, becoming progressively less segregated, but the indices for males versus females remained consistently high (Treiman and Hartmann, 1981). Minority women, therefore, are caught in a 'double bind', and this recent information indicates that their situation has improved little in the last decade.

An analysis of the distribution of black and white female doctorates confirms the importance of sexism in occupational segregation. As Figures 5.2 and 5.3 indicate, black and white female doctorates display similar distributions among their respective fields. For black males (Figure 5.4), the situation is somewhat different: black male doctorates are more evenly distributed among the sciences, with smaller percentages than female doctorates in the life sciences and psychology and larger percentages in the physical sciences, mathematics, and engineering. White male scientists are even more diversified in their fields of study (Figure 5.5).

Data concerning the employment status of women scientists suggest that percentages of both black and white women scientists taking jobs outside science and engineering positions have increased since 1973 (Table 5.5), and that percentages of black and white women doctorates currently holding postdoctoral fellowships are low. It should also be noted that the percentage of white female doctorates holding science and engineering positions was greater in both 1977 and 1979

Table 5.5 *Employment Status of Women Scientists by Race and Year, 1973–79*

| | Percentage of black or white women scientists | | | | | |
| | 1973 | | 1977 | | 1979 | |
	Black	White	Black	White	Black	White
Employed in science/engineering position	84.6	83.6	79.2	81.1	79.0	81.1
Employed in non-science/engineering position[a]	11.5	8.1	13.2	9.1	14.8	10.0
Employed in postdoctoral position	3.8	4.7	5.7	6.5	3.7	6.2
Unemployed, seeking employment	—	3.5	1.9	3.3	2.5	2.7
Total	99.9[b]	99.9[b]	100.0	100.0	100.0	100.0

Source: Data drawn from NSF (1982b)
Notes: a Non-science/engineering positions are those not in the following areas: physical science, environmental science, life science, mathematical science, social science, engineering, psychology, and computer science.
　　　　 b Due to rounding.

Figure 5.2

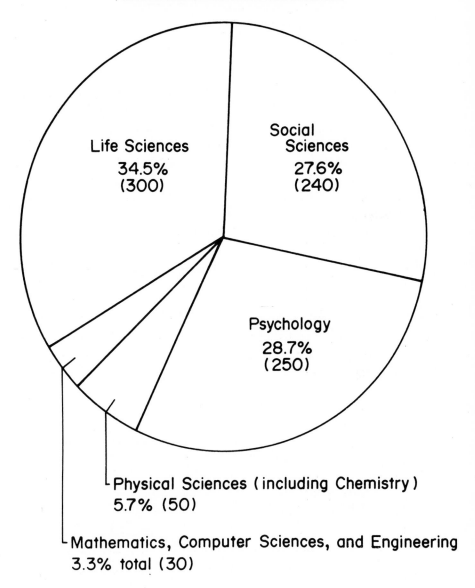

Distribution of Black Women Doctoral Scientists by Field, 1979

Life Sciences
34.5%
(300)

Social Sciences
27.6%
(240)

Psychology
28.7%
(250)

Physical Sciences (including Chemistry)
5.7% (50)

Mathematics, Computer Sciences, and Engineering
3.3% total (30)

Note: Numbers in parentheses indicate actual frequencies

Source: Data from NSF (1982b).

Figure 5.3

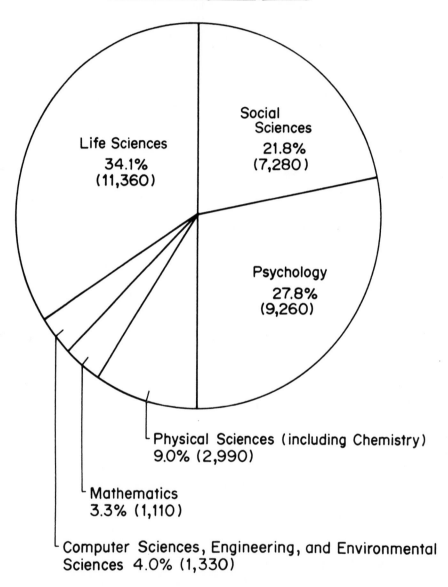

Distribution of White Women Doctoral Scientists by Field, 1979

Social Sciences
21.8%
(7,280)

Life Sciences
34.1%
(11,360)

Psychology
27.8%
(9,260)

Physical Sciences (including Chemistry)
9.0% (2,990)

Mathematics
3.3% (1,110)

Computer Sciences, Engineering, and Environmental Sciences 4.0% (1,330)

Note: Numbers in parentheses indicate actual frequencies

Source: Data from NSF (1982b).

Figure 5.4

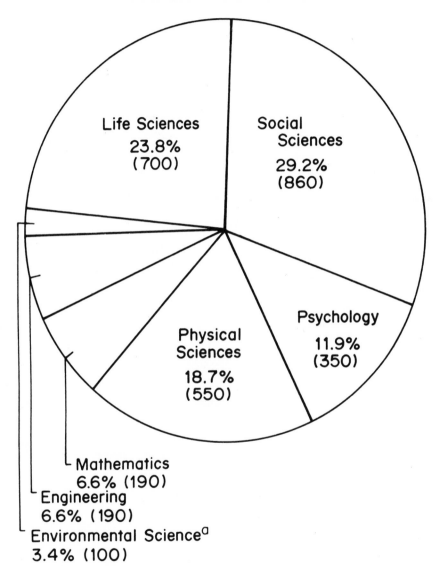

Distribution of Black Male Doctoral Scientists by Field, 1979

Life Sciences
23.8%
(700)

Social Sciences
29.2%
(860)

Psychology
11.9%
(350)

Physical Sciences
18.7%
(550)

Mathematics
6.6% (190)

Engineering
6.6% (190)

Environmental Science[a]
3.4% (100)

Note: Numbers in parentheses indicate actual frequencies
[a]No subjects were classified as computer scientists.

Source: Data from NSF (1982b)

117

Figure 5.5 **Distribution of White Male Doctoral Scientists by Field, 1979**

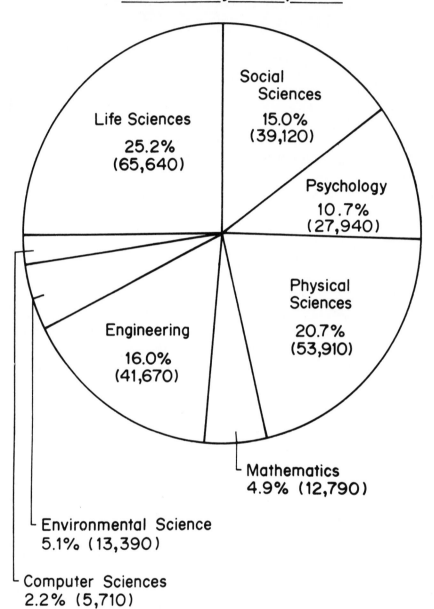

Note: Numbers in parentheses indicate actual frequencies

Source: Data from NSF (1982b).

than that of black women scientists, and that a smaller percentage of white, compared with black, women doctorates was employed in non-science and non-engineering positions in all three surveys.

Although 79 per cent of black female doctoral scientists are employed in science and engineering fields (Table 5.5), the status of black female scientists within the realm of science and engineering is, for the most part, unknown. Some information may be drawn, however, from the status of women scientists in general. In academe, entering women doctorates earn lower salaries than males at every age and status level. The gap between male and female scientists' salaries widens as their years of experience increase. This salary differential is due largely to the lag in promotions and in granting of tenure to women. Salary and promotion differences do not appear to be related to marital status, family, or choice of field (Vetter, 1981). As stated in Chapter 4, however, they may be due to the small but significant difference in publication productivity found between male and female doctorates with the same number of years of experience. Causes for this difference have been explored in Chapter 4.

Recently, reasons for inequities reported by minority women were suggested by respondents to the Minority Women in Science survey. First, they indicated that society's view of the minority woman scientist was negative, suggesting disapproval and resentment. Second, they frequently have encountered those who believe 'that minority women enjoy special privileges and advantages due to affirmative action' (Hall, 1981, p. 15). Results of a 1982 survey of the National Association of Biology Teachers indicated, however, that few biology teachers at either the secondary or tertiary level found that affirmative action had made any changes in the proportions of women and/or minorities in their departments (Douglass, Matyas and Kahle, in press). Therefore, the belief that affirmative action has afforded special privileges to minority women may be unfounded. Third, minority women scientists face all the obstacles described previously that women scientists face. In addition, minority women may be inaccurately prejudged as 'non-performers' (Hall, 1981).

For example, black women scientists also have been viewed as non-performers by employers, whose attitudes are even more critical to the woman scientist's career. MWIS survey respondents stated that there is a significant failure to recognize the potential and accomplishments of minority women scientists (Hall, 1981). They have endured lower pay, slower advancement, less utilization of their talents, fewer rewards, less recognition, and less job security (Hall, 1981). In addition, they are frequently overloaded with committee work during which they are called upon to offer 'the black woman's point of view' but seldom their own personal opinions (Hall, 1981).

Perhaps the most frustrating situation black women face is the negative attitudes of co-workers and colleagues. Science is a social discipline and profits from collaboration and cooperation among scientists (Reskin, 1978). Minority women scientists, viewed as a threat to co-workers, encounter resentment and prejudice, and they may be ignored when colleagues choose collaborators, when training or job opportunities open, or when social functions are planned (Hall, 1981). These inequities result in a professionally crippling isolation in which minority women suffer a general lack of recognition as a legitimate and valuable part of the peer group' (Hall, 1981, p. 17), and the benefits which accompany that membership.

Personal Considerations: Stereotypes and Battle Scars

Minority women scientists have encountered negative attitudes from high school counselors and teachers, college faculty, departmental administrations, and professional colleagues. As a result, many feel a 'perpetual drive to prove one's competency, to remove all doubt that others may have about one's fitness, capability and performance. This often results in the minority woman's pushing herself to do more and be better than her colleagues, and, where other personal responsibilities compete, to approach them with a similar desire to excel' (Hall, 1981, p. 17).

Despite their hard work, minority women scientists still may fail to receive the personal recognition they deserve. Even after years of successful schooling and training, a lack of positive reinforcement may lower one's self-esteem and lessen one's personal satisfaction in work. When minority women scientists do receive reinforcement or are asked to collaborate, the opportunity may have little to do with their own work or success. Black women frequently are seen only as representative of 'women' or 'blacks' and not as individuals: '. . . they have been singled out, not as individuals, but as representatives of their particular ethnic group — as when a minority woman is called upon to give the "black woman's view" of an issue rather than her own view' (AAC, 1982, p. 12).

In addition, minority women, even more than white women, are socialized to serve in non-leadership positions (Jones and Welch, 1979). This socialization process appears to affect achievement attribution. For example, black females often perceive themselves as less successful than white males or females and they tend to externalize their source of failure by stating that a task is difficult (Erkut, 1979). Furthermore, Erkut found that any slight decrease in success may dramatically decrease a black female's expectancy for future progress.

One of the most effective methods for combating many of the isolation and personal worth problems encountered by minority women in science is the development of a support network. A good example is the National Network of Minority Women in Science (Hall, 1981). Another approach to the establishment of minority women scientist networks has been taken by the National Institute of Education. The NIE supported a project to promote research and publication skills among minority women science faculty at southern minority institutions. In addition to the development of a support network, the participants also gained experience in educational research techniques, grant proposal application, publication production, and research presentation at scientific meetings (Kahle, 1982). Active participation in such activities, and especially in the formation of local support networks, may provide minority women with critical support and encouragement.

Summary

Minority women who choose science careers face all the social stigmas and personal constraints encountered by white women. In addition, they must cope with the obstacle of racism. Inadequate counseling, lack of emphasis on academic achievement, and few role models during high school may leave black girls poorly prepared to study science in college. The frustation of continued low academic achievement or of remedial work may result in attrition from school or from science majors. The continued lack of role models and a poor psychological support structure on the college campus does little to alleviate such frustration.

At the graduate level, black women may encounter additional financial hardships and difficulties in establishing collegial relationships. They find that encounters with sexism are increasing and that mentor relationships are difficult to cultivate. After graduation, they must work not only as scientists but also as public relations personnel, trying to dispel unfounded myths about their own abilities. Black women scientists must strive to maintain high self-esteem and high expectancies for success while they struggle to ignore criticisms by employers and colleagues. If the scientific endeavor is to maintain its high standards of excellence, it must not waste the resources of minority women. Diversifying the backgrounds of scientists in no way threatens the objectivity of science, nor does it eliminate opportunities for males or females of other ethnic groups. As Hall (1981) states,

> We have a responsibility to understand the significance of the personal values, experiences, and interests of the scientist in the conduct of science. These factors influence every aspect of scientific activity including the selection of research questions, the formulation of hypotheses, the analysis of data, and the setting of program and funding priorities. It is possible that the closest we shall ever come to objectivity in science will be when we achieve a totally diverse population of scientists. Improving the access of minority women to the training and professional opportunities in science is a step toward strengthening the health of the scientific enterprise (p. 26).

References

AMERICAN ASSOCIATION FOR THE ADVANCEMENT OF SCIENCE (AAAS) (1982) 'Data briefs and research reports', *Meshwork News*, 1, pp. 7–8.

AMERICAN ASSOCIATION OF COLLEGES (AAC) (1982) 'The classroom climate: A chilly one for women?' *Project on the Status and Education of Women*, February, pp. 1–22.

BRADLEY, L.A. and BRADLEY, G.W. (1977) 'The academic achievement of black students in desegregated schools: A critical review', *Review of Educational Research*, 47, 3, pp. 399–449.

DOUGLASS, C.B. MATYAS, M.L. and KAHLE, J.B. (in press) 'Professional equality as reported by biology educators', *Journal of Research in Science Teaching*.

ERKUT, S. (1979) Sex and Race Effects in the Attribution of Achievement and Expectancy for Success (Center for Research on Women, Working Paper No. 30), Unpublished Manuscript, Wellesley College, Wellesley, MA.

ERLICK, A.C. and LeBOLD, W.K. (1977) *Factors Influencing the Science Career Plans of Women and Minorities*, West Lafayette, IN, Purdue Research Foundation.

FORD FOUNDATION'S COMMITTEE ON THE HIGHER EDUCATION OF MINORITIES (1982) Text of the recommendations of the Ford Foundation's panel, *Chronicle of Higher Education*, 23, 3 February, pp. 10–14.

GOTTLIEB, D. (1974) 'Teaching and students: The views of negro and white teachers', *Sociology of Education*, pp. 345–53.

HALL, P.Q. (1981) *Problems and Solutions in the Education, Employment and Personal Choices of Minority Women in Science*, Washington, DC, American Association for the Advancement of Science.

HART, D. (1977) 'Enlarging the American dream', *American Education*, 13, 4, pp. 10–17.

JONES, J. and WELCH, O. (1979) 'The black professional woman: Psychological consequences of social and educational inequities upon the achievement of high-status careers in leadership positions', *Journal of the NAWDAC*, Winter, pp. 29–33.

KAHLE, J.B. (1982) *Double Dilemma: Minorities and Women in Science Education*, West Lafayette, IN, Purdue Research Foundation.

KARLIN, M., COFFMAN, T.L. and WALTER, G. (1969) 'On the fading social stereotypes: Studies in three generations of college students', *Journal of Personality and Social Psychology*, 13, pp. 1–16.

MARRETT, C.B. (1981) *Minority Females in High School Mathematics and Science* (NIE report on the Program on Student Diversity and School Processes), Madison, WI, Wisconsin Center for Education Research.

NATIONAL BOARD ON GRADUATE EDUCATION (NBGE) (1976) *Minority Group Participation in Graduate Education*, Washington, DC, National Board on Graduate Education.

NATIONAL RESEARCH COUNCIL (NRC) (1982) *Summary Report 1981 Doctorate Recipients from United States Universities*, Washington, DC, National Academy Press.

NATIONAL SCIENCE FOUNDATION (NSF) (1980) *Science Education Databook* (SE–80–3), Washington, DC, National Science Foundation.

NATIONAL SCIENCE FOUNDATION (NSF) (1982a) *Science and Engineering Education: Data and Information* (NSF 82–30), Washington, DC, National Science Foundation.

NATIONAL SCIENCE FOUNDATION (NSF) (1982b) *Women and Minorities in Science and Engineering* (NSF 82–302), Washington, DC, National Science Foundation.

PATCHEN, M. (1982) *Black-White Contact in Schools: Its Social and Academic Effects*, West Lafayette, IN, Purdue University Press.

RESKIN, B.F. (1978) 'Sex differentiation and the social organization of science', *Sociological Inquiry*, 48, pp. 6–37.

SADKER, M.P. and SADKER, D.M. (1979) *Beyond Pictures and Pronouns: Sexism in Teacher Education Textbooks*, Washington, DC, Women's Educational Equity Act Program of US Department of Health, Education, and Welfare.

SCIENTIFIC MANPOWER COMMISSION (SMC) (1983) 'Women and minorities in the sciences', *Manpower Comments*, 20, pp. 16–22.

TREIMAN, D.J., and HARTMANN, H.I. (Eds.) (1981) *Women, Work and Wages: Equal Pay for Jobs of Equal Value*, Washington, DC, National Academy Press.

US DEPARTMENT OF LABOR (1980) *Twenty Facts on Women Workers*, Pamphlet published by Women's Bureau, US Department of Labor, December.

VETTER, B.M. (1981) 'Women scientists and engineers: Trends in participation', *Science*, 214, pp. 1313–21.

6 Women's Role in Professional Scientific Organizations: Participation and Recognition

Frances S. Vandervoort
Kenwood Academy, Chicago, Illinois

Although the past decade has seen a notable increase in the number of women entering scientific professions, women still lag far behind men both in absolute numbers and in proportion. Among the scientific elite women are rare indeed. Only five of the 345 scientists who have received the Nobel Prize have been women. Only thirty-four, or 2.6 per cent, of the 1361 members of the National Academy of Sciences have been women (Cole, 1981). For every woman who has achieved distinction in the scientific community, untold numbers have failed, either due to discouragement from seeking advanced training in their field or by consignment to second-class status within their profession.

Before 1900 the scientific community was populated almost exclusively by men. Indeed, to speak of 'scientists' was almost invariably to speak of 'men of science'. Women were considered emotionally, physically, and intellectually unfit for the rigors of scientific work (Rossiter, 1982). In view of the widespread disregard for women with scientific interest, it is astonishing that there were any women scientists at all. The rare individuals who succeeded often had scientist husbands or other male relatives willing to support them or collaborate with them. Astronomer Caroline Herschel, for example, probably would have had little claim to fame had not her brother, Sir William Herschel (discoverer of the planet Uranus in 1781), been an astronomer too. The joint research on radioactivity by Marie Curie and her husband, Pierre, earned for them the Nobel Prize for Physics in 1903. In 1947 Gerty and Carl Cory were granted the Nobel Prize in Physiology and Medicine for investigating the role of enzymes in carbohydrate metabolism.

The first decades of the twentieth century saw little change. Few women studied for advanced degrees, and fewer still attained recognition once they received the degree. Women who succeeded had extraordinary motivation, thick skins, exceptional ability, and courage (Rossiter, 1982; Gornick, 1983; Keller, 1983). It was necessary for them to overcome the triple penalty facing women choosing to work in a traditionally male field. The triple penalty has been defined by Cole (1981) in the following way,

1 Science was culturally defined as an inappropriate career for women; few women were recruited into science, and few sought it out.
2 Women who surmounted the first barrier continued to be hampered by the belief that women were less competent at science than men. Whatever the validity of this belief, it contributed to women's ambivalence toward work and reduced motivation and commitment to scientific careers.
3 Women encountered significant discrimination within the scientific community.

Cole describes women who managed to attain the PhD during the first half of the century as 'survivors' who, throughout their lives, faced discrimination, frustration, and a sense of isolation. ¯

By the mid-1960s women had begun to take a new look at their talents, attributes, and goals. They were motivated by the greater emphasis given to secondary school science following the 1957 launching of the first Russian satellite, Sputnik, an increased awareness of the wide range of career opportunities in the sciences, and recognition of their potential as scientists. Also, many women of all ages were profoundly affected by the writings of Betty Friedan, Kate Millet, Gloria Steinem, and other feminist authors of the 1960s. They were eager to take on the challenging frontiers of science.

Although women are coming closer than ever to a full partnership with men in the scientific community, they are still a long way from genuine acceptance based solely on scientific merit. Until they are accepted, society will continue to be deprived of the talent and commitment of an important segment of the population.

Women's Roles in Science and in Scientific Societies

The following section analyzes opportunities, problems, and rewards in a variety of scientific fields. Although this survey is not comprehensive,

Frances S. Vandervoort

it provides an overview of what might be expected by women considering a career in the sciences or engineering.

The Biological Sciences

Biology. Women choose careers in biology more than in other scientific fields. The percentage of life science doctorates awarded to women
has increased steadily from 10.4 in 1965 to 34.6 in 1980 (Vetter, 1981).
Furthermore, women are earning biological science doctorates in a wide
variety of areas (Table 6.1). By 1978, 36,200 female life scientists (57.3
per cent) were employed in science or engineering positions, 42.6 per
cent were employed, but not in science or engineering positions; and
1.9 per cent of the total were unemployed and seeking employment

Table 6.1.   Percentages of Women Receiving Doctorates in Biological Sciences by Area of
Specialization

Area of specialization	Percentage of female biological sciences degrees
Biochemistry	19.2
Biophysics	1.0
Biostatistics	1.2
Anatomy	4.9
Cytology	1.4
Embryology	1.0
Immunology	6.1
Botany	4.2
Ecology	5.3
Microbiology/Bacteriology	10.4
Physiology (Plant and Animal)	9.2
Zoology	4.8
Genetics	6.3
Entomology	1.3
Molecular Biology	6.9
Nutrition (Dietetics)	6.0
General Biological Sciences	6.1
Other Biological Sciences	4.7

Source: From NRC (1982).

(NSF, 1982). According to the Office of Scientific Manpower, among
women life scientists employed in science positions, the large majority
were employed by educational institutions (73.5 per cent); others found
positions in government (9.1 per cent), business and industry (7.9 per
cent), or hospitals and clinics (4.0 per cent). Historically, male biologists
have been more evenly distributed among employment categories than
have female biologists. In 1979 the percentage of male life scientists
working in industry was nearly twice the percentage of females, and the

percentage of male life scientists in governmental positions was 1.4 times the percentage of females in similar situations. Sex differences in job distributions exist among life scientists employed at educational institutions. In 1979, 75.8 per cent of females (compared to 83.6 per cent of males) were faculty members, 11.0 per cent of women (6.6 per cent of males) were non-faculty research staff, and 8.4 per cent of women (4.8 per cent of males) held postdoctoral appointments (Vetter, 1981).

Gender disparities also exist in salaries and unemployment rates of life scientists. The salaries of female life scientists have consistently been lower than those of their male counterparts. In 1973 the average salaries for female doctoral life scientists were only 76.6 per cent of those for male doctoral life scientists. This improved in 1975 and 1977 to 83.6 per cent and 83.7 per cent respectively, but by 1979 had again dropped to 79.6 per cent. In that respect, employment in the life sciences is one of the worst areas for women. In comparison, women's 1979 salaries (as a percentage of men's) ranged from 84.3 in social studies to 80.0 in the physical sciences. Furthermore, the 1979 unemployment rate for all female doctoral scientists was 3.5 per cent, more than three times that of their male counterparts. With the current economic constraints found in most universities, those salary and unemployment disparities are unlikely to change in the near future.

As Table 6.1 indicates, more than 10 per cent of female biological scientists earning PhDs in 1981 specialized in microbiology/bacteriology. In a survey of the members of the American Society for Microbiology, Kashket, Robbins, Leive and Huang (1974) found that, as a result of unequal opportunity throughout their training and careers, the status of female microbiologists was lower than that of male microbiologists. In 1974 the salary of women microbiologists averaged $11,400 compared to $16,000 for men. The salaries for women are less at every level, and median additional income (from consulting, for example) averages $1200 for women and $1900 for men. Women doctorates earn less than men at every period after graduation, and the difference in salary increases with seniority.

An interesting finding of this survey was that although the employment status of women doctorates was lower than it was for men, there was no significant difference in the status of women microbiologists without doctorates. In fact, men with only a bachelor's degree in microbiology were found to have an unemployment rate nearly twice that of women at the same level. At the master's degree level, the unemployment rates for men and women in microbiology were equal. But at the PhD or ScD level, the unemployment rate for women was ten times higher than that for men. These data suggest that women are employed in technical positions requiring an MS degree. However, securing high level positions after the doctoral degree has been more difficult for women.

In academe, most women in microbiology had positions as associate professors or research associates. Women were three times as likely to be appointed as research associates as men, but only one-third as likely to be full professors. In 1974 there were no women microbiologists who were department heads or academic administrators. Women attained the rank of full professor an average of twenty years after the PhD, whereas men attained the same rank from ten to nineteen years after their doctorates.

In summary, although women microbiologists appear to work as hard as men, remain at their jobs as long as men, publish as frequently as their male counterparts, and have basically the same motivations as men for working outside their homes, women are not afforded equal treatment by employers or the scientific establishment. They feel handicapped by lack of proper encouragement and role models. Women students in microbiology generally receive little advice regarding their professional futures and seldom are pushed to take the most demanding positions. If that pattern is to change, the change must begin during a student's undergraduate years. As suggested in Chapter 4, institutions must be willing to recognize and encourage the talents of an important segment of the nation's future biologists.

Pharmacy. Pharmacy is a promising field for women interested in a career that combines biology, chemistry, and health care. Pharmacists are always needed; in 1980 Americans visited pharmacies more than five billion times for prescription needs, over-the-counter-drugs, health supplies, and advice (Brody, 1982). The United States is one of the few Western countries where male pharmacists outnumber female pharmacists. In Germany, for example, nearly 98 per cent of all pharmacists are women. Pharmacy is an attractive career to many women because of the flexible hours common in the profession. Part-time or evening employment is often available to women raising families. Once children reach school age, it is easy for women to assume full-time positions. Of the 143,000 pharmacists currently registered in the United States, approximately 17 per cent are women, an increase of 10 per cent since 1970 (Brody, 1982). The United States Department of Health and Human Services predicts that that proportion will grow to 33 per cent by 1990 (Sabatini, 1982). In 1982 women accounted for more than 53 per cent of the first year enrollment in pharmacy; 47 per cent of the 1982 pharmacy graduates were women (Scientific Manpower Commission, 1983).

Approximately 40 per cent of women pharmacists work in hospitals, 30 per cent in independent community pharmacies, and 10 per cent in industry, colleges, and universities (Sabatini, 1982). Government service offers security and variety. Opportunities exist in the US Public Health Service, the Veterans Administration, the Food and Drug Administration, and the Drug Enforcement Administration, agencies that have historically provided positions for women. Specialized areas of pharmacy include work with drug wholesale firms, pharmaceutical trade organizations, and teaching at colleges and universities. Nuclear pharmacy is a rapidly developing field that primarily involves compounding and dispensing radioactive isotopes used for diagnostic purposes. Its growth may provide additional jobs for women pharmacists.

In January 1981 the American Pharmaceutical Association (APhA) appointed a task force to address the needs of women in pharmacy and to assess the impact of the increasing number of women pharmacists on the public and in the profession (Sabatini, 1982). The task force recommended that the APhA form an office of women's affairs to launch new programs and activities designed to provide information, communication services, and assistance in professional development to women pharmacists. Since, historically, the feminization of any profession (botany, teaching and nursing, for example) has resulted in both lower salaries and lower status, the concerns of the APhA are warranted. If the gradual feminization of pharmacy does not have these negative effects, perhaps, for the first time a profession which employs primarily women will maintain its status and high salaries. Some experts still wonder, however, whether APhA is addressing the issue to protect women pharmacists or to limit the number of women entering pharmacy.

Biology teaching. Although biology teaching has long been a predominantly masculine endeavor, increasing numbers of women are teaching biology at both the secondary and tertiary levels; in 1977, 24 per cent of all high school science teachers were female. Many of those teachers belong to the National Association of Biology Teachers (NABT), a national association dedicated to improving biology education at all academic levels. In 1982 NABT charged its committee on the Role and Status of Women in Science with the task of surveying its membership in order to describe the roles, salaries, assignments, professional activities, and evidences of discrimination within its ranks. The results of the survey, discussed in Chapter 7, indicated that proportionately more males than females teach advanced high school biology and are employed in larger institutions. Furthermore, males receive higher salaries, attend more national professional meetings, and are involved in more research activities than are their female counterparts. Finally, 19 per cent of female respondents compared to 7 per cent of male respondents felt they had experienced sex discrimination in their professional lives (Douglass and Kahle, 1983).

Those responses suggest that women biology teachers still encounter difficulties as females working in a masculine field. Although women biology teachers appear to have a firm foothold in teaching in high schools, middle schools, and colleges, additional effort from professional organizations such as NABT will be required to delineate and find solutions to the problems of equity for women in biology teaching.

These associations of microbiologists, pharmacists, and biology teachers are not unique in their concern for the status of women life scientists. The American Association of Immunologists, the American Society for Cell Biology, the American Society of Biological Chemists, and the Biophysical Society have each established committees to investigate opportunities for advancement among women members. Furthermore, several associations have been created specifically to advance the cause of all women scientists, including life scientists. These include the Association for Women in Science, the National Network of Minority Women in Science, and Sigma Delta Epsilon Graduate Women in Science. As a communications network among women life scientists grows, women will continue to derive benefits such as opportunities to collaborate, support networks, and financial and honorary sources of encouragement. It is possible that strong networks of communication and action will enable more women life scientists to attain status equal to that of male life scientists. Unfortunately, many associations have not established sections or committees to assist women in attaining full professional status or recognition.

The Physical Sciences

Astronomy. Women have been making significant inroads in the physical sciences. Astronomy, one of the oldest sciences, was among the first to appeal to women. I have already spoken of the contributions of Caroline Herschel. Some women astronomers currently hold important positions in several of the nation's observatories and research institutions. In 1980 the Committee on the Status of Women of the American

Astronomical Society (AAS) reported that of the approximately 3600 society members 8.2 per cent were women (Liller, Cowley, Hodge, Keer and Morrison, 1980). That is a slight increase over the 7.9 per cent identified in a similar study in 1973. It is, however, far below the maximum percentage of women, about 17 in the early 1940s. Eighty-nine per cent of the women astronomers held the doctorate as their highest degree, 8 per cent the master's degree, and 3 per cent the bachelor's degree. The report cites a survey showing that, although the percentage of women with the rank of associate professor had increased since 1973, the percentage of women holding full professorships was below that for men. However, the 1973 and 1979 surveys showed approximately equal percentages of men and women at the level of assistant professor. Unfortunately, more women held the less prestigious position of instructor in 1979 than in 1973. The 1979 survey included sixty-six departments with 769 individuals, 571 of whom held professorial rank (assistant, associate, or full professors). The survey showed that although 5.5 per cent of the astronomers were women, only 3.9 per cent of the professional positions were held by women.

An interesting sidelight of the 1980 study is the high percentage of married women in astronomy whose husbands also work in astronomy or a closely related field. In the last six years that percentage has increased from 48 to 68. A comparison of the salaries and job titles of those astronomical couples shows that, although job titles for the female partners do not differ greatly from those of women astronomers in general, single women earn significantly better salaries than women members of those couples. In fact, in astronomy single women earn slightly more than single men.

An examination of the relationship between job satisfaction and type of employer shows that the satisfaction for both men and women is at or above average in research institutions, observatories, government, and private industries. Women at universities are noticeably less happy with their jobs than are men. The most common complaint from women concerns employers' nepotistic practices, which cause women to take left-over jobs and to be treated as second-class citizens. Several respondents reported encountering overt hostility toward women in academe (Liller *et al.*, 1980).

Although women contributed much to early astronomical studies, their contributions were frequently unacknowledged (Rossiter, 1982). Today their status has improved. For example, when compared to men in astronomy, women astronomers show essentially no differences in the publication rate of scientific papers. An increasing number of women are being asked to review papers for journals, serve on advisory boards, and present invited papers. The most critical problem presently facing women astronomers faces men also: that is, shortage of permanent jobs. Unfortunately, that situation is unlikely to improve in the foreseeable future. If women can maintain the status quo during a period of low job availability, their future acceptance and activity is assured.

Chemistry. Chemistry has long attracted women with an interest in the sciences, and some of the most notable discoveries in the field have been made by women. However, discrepancies between women and men in salary and employment status are greater in chemistry than in almost any other field. The number of women chemists who are unemployed and seeking employment is twice as large as that of men at the bachelor's level and four times as high at the doctoral level (see Table 6.2). Salaries of women with PhDs are lower than those of men at every level of experience except the entry level. The differences in salary increase with years of experience at every degree level.

Table 6.2. Women Chemists' Salaries As a Percentage of Men's by Highest Degree and Years of Experience, 1974–79

Survey year	Years of experience							
	0 to 1	2 to 4	5 to 9	10 to 14	15 to 19	20 to 24	25 to 29	30 to 34
				BS or BA				
1974		93.0	85.7	84.8	83.3	78.5	76.5	74.7
1977	104.3	94.3	89.8	94.6	74.3	79.2	88.5	88.7
1979	107.1	103.2	90.2	70.6	93.5	74.8	83.3	88.3
				MS or MA				
1974		88.3	83.3	80.5	77.9	79.1	67.1	71.7
1977	71.4	84.4	94.4	79.2	81.5	77.0	74.1	66.7
1979	87.0	93.3	90.0	83.3	90.6	74.1	78.6	88.6
				Ph.D.				
1974		87.9	76.0	84.9	82.1	81.7	79.5	68.0
1977	76.2	84.0	86.4	74.8	70.9	72.6	77.3	72.7
1979	103.6	87.0	80.0	73.7	73.4	68.0	62.2	71.1

Source: Adapted from Vetter, B.M. (1981) 'Women scientists and engineers: Trends in participation, *Science*, 214, pp. 1313–21.

When women chemists are employed, they secure positions in government, industry, and academe. Their relative proportion in these areas differs by specialized field and by level of academic attainment. Women are likely to specialize in biochemistry and to be employed in biochemistry or pharmaceutical chemistry. Women who work for non-academic employers are less likely than men to be in manufacturing, coatings, and metal-related industries. A significant percentage of women chemists is associated with the pharmaceutical industry, the government, or non-profit organizations. Doctoral women chemists, compared with men, are more likely to be employed in academic institutions (49 per cent compared to 34 per cent respectively), although they may not hold faculty tenure track position.

Women chemists are underemployed and underrepresented in chemistry departments across our nation, and their fate in academe is related to both their academic degree and to their gender. Since 1940, 3740 women have earned PhDs in chemistry, 7.5 per cent of the total awarded. Those women are as likely as men to have matriculated at a top-rated department (Vetter, 1981). Since 1945, 9500 master's degrees and 58,000 bachelor's degrees in chemistry have been awarded to women (Vetter, 1981). However, when we examine the employment records of these women, we find that 30 per cent of women, compared to 8 per cent of men, are in non-professional positions in universities that grant a doctorate in chemistry. In addition, only 15.6 per cent of women, compared to 18 per cent of men, chemists who are employed full-time are able to find employment of any kind in doctoral granting institutions. Of all PhD chemists employed full-time in colleges or universities, 39 per cent of women, but only 31 per cent of men, are assistant professors (NAS, 1979). Chemistry departments in the nation's top universities have been, and continue to be, almost exclusively male. That situation has continued despite the substantial number of women obtaining doctorates in chemistry. In 1978, 1.5 per cent of full-time faculty members at the 180 doctorate-granting chemistry departments were women. By 1980 the proportion had increased to 3.1 per cent. Half of the chemistry departments of doctoral institutions employ no women faculty today, and only fourteen employ two or more women above the rank of instructor (Vetter, 1981).

In 1927 women chemists established the Women Chemists' Committee of the American Chemical Society (ACS). Goals of the committee include encouraging women to take an active interest in ACS activities, serving as a forum for the problems of women in chemistry, providing means of increasing and improving participation of women in the ACS, and increasing membership of women chemists in the society. The importance of chemistry to a technological society cannot be overestimated. It offers great opportunity for specialization in a variety of fields. Women have a right to be involved in the advancement of this vital field.

Geoscience. Geoscience, historically considered one of the most 'masculine' of sciences (Rossiter, 1982), is currently experiencing an unprecedented influx of women. In 1974 women constituted only 4 per cent of approximately 35,000 geoscientists in the United States, but they made up 17 per cent of all students pursuing degrees in that field (Schwartzer, 1977). In 1973 women received 4 per cent of all PhDs granted in geoscience, and in 1977, 11 per cent of all PhD candidates were women. The reason for the sudden surge of interest in geoscience is not entirely clear, but it is apparent that underrepresentation of women in this demanding field may soon be ending.

Traditionally, women geoscientists have pursued careers as teachers, librarians, or cartographers. Today women with degrees in geoscience are working alongside men in physically demanding and sometimes hazardous conditions. Most, however, are employed in academe — 52 per cent as compared with 20 per cent of men in the profession. In 1977 colleges and universities employed 28 per cent of the approximately 1500 women geoscientists. Women geoscientists are rarely found in some fields, including geological engineering, geophysics, and exploration geology. They are also conspicuously absent from management and consulting positions.

In addition to being underrepresented in geoscience, women typically have been underpaid (Henderson, 1975). In 1974 there was a differential of more than $10,000 between men and women with bachelor's or master's degrees in the petroleum industry and at the bachelor's degree level in the mining industry. For a woman doctorate, salary discrepancies were small (ranging from $800 to $3800), but still significant. A possible reason for the lower salaries of women geoscientists may be the number of years of work experience. It is not known, for example, whether women geoscientists have interrupted their careers to raise families. This point is important because, in 1970, 58 per cent of women geoscientists responding to a nation-wide survey were under 40. That is a large percentage generally and professionally. In 1977 census data showed 44.4 per cent of all women in the United States to be under 40, and the median age for women faculty members at four-year colleges was 36; at junior colleges, 45; and at secondary schools, 40.

In academe women geoscientists have made progress at each employment level, although problems still exist. From 1968 to 1969 the percentage of women at the full professor level dropped from 2 to 1. During the same period the percentage of women at the associate professor level climbed from 1 to 3. Four per cent of assistant professors in 1976 were women, 7 per cent in 1977, and 6 per cent in 1979 (Schwartzer, 1977). However, substantial salary differences exist between men and women with comparable work experience, and the discrepancies increase with experience. In 1974 a survey by the National Research Council showed that of all science and engineering PhDs in the country, the salaries of women, compared with men, were lowest in chemistry and earth sciences (Vetter, 1981). By 1977 median salaries for newly hired women (bachelor's degree with less than one year of experience and master's degree with two to four years of experience) were slightly higher than for men with similar qualifications. Those gains are generally attributed to the enforcement of equal opportunity legislation, rather than to changes in attitudes toward or status of women geoscientists. Provisions of such legislation are more enforceable at entry levels where there is greater flexibility in setting salary levels (Schwartzer, 1977). Women with bachelor's or master's degrees in geoscience have commonly become teachers in secondary schools (27 per cent of women compared to 5 per cent of men). However, salary discrepancies are also found at this level. In her 1975 study Henderson found that the lowest salary paid to a secondary school earth science teacher ($5000) was earned by a woman with a master's degree. The lowest salary for a man ($6000) was earned by a male teacher with a bachelor's degree.

As in the other scientific fields, industry and government also employ women geoscientists. After educational institutions (including high schools), local, state, and federal agencies provide the largest sources of jobs for women geoscientists. Approximately 24 per cent of all women geologists are employed by governmental agencies, including 13 per cent by the United States Geological Survey.

In 1977, although 68 per cent of all geoscientists were employed by industry, only 18 per cent of women geoscientists worked for industry (272 women compared to 25,000 men). The median age of women in industry was less than 30, reflecting the recent hiring of new graduates. In 1978 male geoscientists averaged approximately fifteen years more experience than women.

In 1973 the Women Geoscientists Committee of the American Geological Institute was founded to encourage women to enter fields of geoscience and to increase professional recognition of women employed in that area. Although the undergraduate and graduate enrollments of women in geoscience are expected to stabilize or decrease slightly in the early 1980s, the employment field holds much promise.

Meteorology. Meteorology is one of the most promising scientific fields for women. Perhaps due to the small number, women with doctorates in meteorology earn salaries comparable to males (LeMone and Waukau, n.d.). This favorable state of affairs is aided by the employment of a significant proportion of women by governmental agencies, large corporations, or universities where there are strong affirmative action programs and above average salaries. Furthermore, the small size of the meteorological community enhances women's prospects for employment; their individual abilities may be more quickly recognized and used as bases for judgment by potential employers. Also, their relative youth gives them an advantage; for they are too young to have encountered the severe discrimination of the past. The number of women entering the field of meteorology is growing. In mid-1978 only 2.4 per cent of the 6500 professional members of the American Meteorological Society (AMS) were women. However, among 1100 student members of the society, more than 10 per cent were women. AMS estimates indicate that women represent 10 per cent of all recipients of bachelor's and master's degrees in meterology each year. Women earn between 4 per cent and 5 per cent of all PhDs granted in meteorology.

The four major employment categories in meteorology are: (1) government operations, which include forecasting and air pollution monitoring and control for state, local, or federal agencies; (2) federal governmental research; (3) military forecasting; and (4) military research. Opportunities, in private industry include television weathercasting, consulting, forecasting, and research.

Most meteorologists with bachelor's degrees are involved in operational work for government and private industry and are primarily forecasters. More recipients of master's degrees work at colleges and universities where they are often engaged in research. Women doctorates in meteorology are strongly concentrated in academe, reflecting the general tendency for women with advanced degrees in sciences to join university or college faculties in greater numbers than men. LeMone and Waukau also found that of women faculty members surveyed, five were assistant professors, five were associate professors, and one was a full professor. Promotion was directly correlated with age; all the assistant professors were between 30 and 35, and all the associate professors were between 35 and 45.

LeMone and Waukau offer several explanations for women's success in meteorology. First, small colleges, which traditionally pay women lower salaries than men, seldom have meteorology departments. Second, many women are employed in the federal government or by large private firms where salary discrepancies between males and females are closely controlled. Third, because the meteorological community is small, recognition of ability quickly replaces prejudice (LeMone and Waukau, n.d.). Thus, discrimination on the basis of sex has rarely been a problem at the doctoral level. At the master's and bachelor's degree levels, however, some instances of discrimination and lower salaries have been reported.

Women are beginning to make inroads into management level positions in meteorology. Some have assumed positions in state and federal agencies, including the National Aeronautics and Space Agency (NASA), and some have been promoted to middle level management in private industry. Also, women are receiving recognition by the American Meterological Society for their accomplishments.

Physics. Physics is often regarded as the most difficult of the sciences. Physics is concerned with properties of matter, atomic particles, electricity, magnetism, and the laws that govern their behavior. Physicists' interests range from the smallest quantities of matter and energy to the universe itself. There is plenty of room for women in so wide a field.

To most people physics is a man's field. Despite the world-wide acclaim accorded Marie Curie, Lise Meitner, and Maria Mayer, relatively few women become physicists. Today only about 3 per cent of physics doctorates and 4 per cent of the members of the American Physical Society are women (Simmons, 1982). Even more striking is the paucity of women faculty members at the associate professor or full professor rank in American colleges and universities that grant PhDs in physics. In a recent study Baranger and Eisenstein (1981) found that among 171 physics departments there are 4176 faculty members who are assistant professors or above; only seventy-nine (1.9 per cent) are women. Women comprise 1.5 per cent of all associate and full professors in the nation's physics departments. Furthermore, 125 physics departments, with 2304 senior faculty members, have no women at all. The American Physical Society formed its Committee on the Status of Women in Physics a decade ago in an effort to address this problem (Windham, 1980). The goals of the committee are: to stimulate the interest of young women in college physics, to develop support networks for women college graduates and postdoctoral fellows, and to assist junior and senior high school counselors and teachers in advising and encouraging young women to enter science careers. By working with counselors and teachers, committee members hope to decrease unconscious sex-role stereotyping and to increase sensitivity to the problems of women students in the sciences and mathematics. Although this committee recognizes that parity for women in physics is some years away, the members are convinced that they have made positive steps toward that goal.

In 1980 the newly formed Committee on Women in Physics of the American Association of Physics Teachers began complementary efforts to reduce barriers to the entry of women into the physical sciences and mathematics (Windham, 1980). Although more women have been finding entry-level jobs in physics and technology than ever before, the increase in the proportion of women in academic physics has been insignificant. The American Physical Society has addressed that problem by forming a panel on faculty positions for women physicists (Simmons, 1982). The panel is seeking to identify women physicists who possess the necessary talent and experience in teaching and research, but who are not currently in academe. For example, women who have developed notable careers in industry or government laboratories are considered prime candidates for the committee's efforts. The American Physical Society's panel members believe that increasing the number of women in university physics departments will demonstrate to junior women that progress in careers in physics need not be blocked by gender.

Other Scientific Fields

There are other scientific fields where women are gaining recognition. Two will be considered in this section, immunology and anthropology. Immunology is the study of the ability of living systems to resist foreign organisms or their products. Organ transplants, immunization programs, and certain kinds of cancer research have prompted widespread public interest in this vital area. Experts in immunology are needed in greater numbers than ever before. The American Association of Immunologists reports that at present there are 3400 active members of the society, 10 per cent of whom are women. Primary places of employment are hospitals, government and private research facilities, and pharmaceutical companies.

The history of women in anthropology has been punctuated by outstanding discoveries and acrimonious debate over status. Mary Leakey's accomplishments equal or surpass those of any other living physical anthropologist. With her late husband, Louis Leakey, she spent many years in Africa unearthing and analyzing some of the oldest fossils of human ancestors ever discovered. Although her husband died in 1972, Mary Leakey has carried on the family tradition of persistence, creativity, and incisive interpretation in tracing the earliest history of human development.

Yet, aside from a few obvious exceptions, women anthropologists have not been accorded the recognition given men. That is especially true among college and university faculty. In 1972 the American Anthropological Association passed and ratified a resolution calling on departments of anthropology to adopt fair hiring practices for women. However, anthropology departments are shrinking in response to deteriorating economic conditions, and the situation for women is unlikely to improve, despite the resolution.

Women's Roles in Engineering and Engineering Societies

The field of engineering offers tremendous promise to a young woman with an independent spirit, self-discipline, and a consummate curiosity about the way things work. Women have responded to the nation's growing need for trained engineers by enrolling in college engineering programs in record numbers, a trend expected to continue for several years. In 1980, 49,000 women were enrolled in full-time engineering programs, up from fewer than 4000 in 1970. That number represents an increase in the percentage of women from 1.5 to 13.4 of all engineering undergraduates. In 1980, 9.7 per cent of the total number of bachelor's degrees in engineering were awarded to women.

In 1979, 63 per cent of women in engineering programs were concentrated in six fields (Table 6.3). Chemical engineering was chosen most commonly, followed by electrical and civil engineering. Enrollment of women is increasing in newer fields, including nuclear, environmental, and petroleum engineering. In 1978, 21,700 (1.6 per cent) of all engineers were women. This represents a dramatic change from 1974, when women made up only 0.5 per cent of the engineering population. Of those 21,700 women engineers, 1200 (3.4 per cent) were unemployed in 1978, leaving the total number of working women engineers at 19,800. The greatest percentage of employed women

Table 6.3   Enrollment of Full-time Engineering Students by Field and Sex, 1979

	Number of students		
	Women	Men	Total
Chemical	6,477	24,926	31,403
Civil	5,048	39,269	44,317
Computer	2,094	8,814	10,908
Electrical	5,341	64,782	70,123
General	8,991	50,972	59,963
Industrial	2,571	9,600	12,171
Mechanical	4,821	54,557	59,378
Other	6,684	45,541	52,225
Total	42,027	298,461	340,488

Source: From Engineering Manpower Commission of the American Association of Engineering Societies (1981).

engineers work in mechanical engineering, followed by chemical and electrical engineering. The greatest concentration of women is in mechanical engineering (Table 6.4).

Table 6.4. *Distribution of Experienced Women Engineers by Engineering Discipline, 1978*

Discipline	Number	Percentage
Aeronautical	1,200	6.1
Chemical	2,600	13.1
Civil	1,600	8.1
Electrical	1,900	9.6
Mechanical	3,300	16.7
Other	9,200	46.4
Total	19,800	100.0

Source: From Engineering Manpower Commission of the American Association of Engineering Societies (1981).

Sixty-three per cent of the practicing women engineers are employed at the bachelor's degree level. Twenty-eight per cent have master's degrees, and only 6 per cent of women engineers have doctorates (Society of Women Engineers, 1980). The salaries paid women engineers at the entry level are higher than those paid women entering any other field (Table 6.5). Those salaries also exceed entry

Table 6.5. *Starting Salary Offers to Women Bachelor Degree Recipients by Field, 1980*

Field	Dollars per month
Engineering	1,725
Computer Science	1,508
Chemistry	1,434
Mathematics	1,427
Accounting	1,292
Business, General	1,142
Marketing and Distribution	1,131
Health Professions	1,130
Biological Sciences	1,084
Humanities	1,042
Social Sciences	1,013

Source: From Engineering Manpower Commission of the American Association of Engineering Societies (1981).

level salaries offered to male engineers. On the other hand, women engineers who have worked fifteen years have salaries only 84.9 per cent of men. The average age of male engineers is 39, while the average female engineer is approximately 27 years of age (Society of Women Engineers, 1980). More than half the women engineers entered the labor market fewer than five years ago. On the average, women engineers have eleven fewer years' work experience than male engineers. Despite gains in the number of women entering the field, in reality the number of women — fewer than 2 per cent of the total number of engineers — is spread very thinly throughout industry, government, and education.

In 1977 a study of engineering students at the University of Cincinnati compared women students with their male counterparts (Durchholz, 1977). Researchers investigated differences and similarities between male and female students in terms of academic qualifications, parental attitudes, socio-economic status, and non-academic variables including sports, extracurricular activities, time in life when students chose to enter an engineering program, and non-engineering electives taken in college. Questionnaire data from both male and female freshmen showed that:

1   Women in the population scored twenty-four points higher on average on the SAT (Scholastic Aptitude Test) composition test than did men. The ACT (American College Test) did not show a great difference between men and women freshmen engineering students.

2   Women scored slightly but insignificantly lower than men in math, but were almost thirty points ahead in verbal skills. On ACT English and ACT math scores women performed as well as men.

3   The average incoming freshman engineering student, male or female, had taken four high school science courses. Approximately 13 per cent more men than women had taken more than four science courses in high school. More men than women took second year chemistry, general science, earth science, and electronics, but significantly more women than ´men had taken biology.

4   More women (89.3 per cent) than men (78 per cent) received awards, including sports awards, in high school. Twenty per cent of the women and 14 per cent of the men had received five or more awards.

5   A comparison of fathers' and mothers' attitudes toward the students' choice of engineering in college showed that both males and females received strong support from their fathers. Mothers favored their sons' choice of an engineering career only slightly more than their daughters' choice of engineering. Significantly, mothers' support of their daughters is equal to the fathers' support of either daughters or sons.

6   When asked to pick three people who most influenced their choice of engineering as a career, male students ranked their fathers significantly higher than did females. Females ranked their fathers fairly highly, but the strongest influence for women was math or science teachers and recruiters from engineering schools. When students were asked whether they had ever known any engineers before they had entered college, 73 per cent of both males and females answered affirmatively. Students had either a neighbor or relative who was an engineer, had worked with an engineer, or had friends whose fathers were engineers. Sixty-two per cent of women and 37 per cent of men had had personal encounters with engineers.

7   A study of the socio-economic status of the respondents showed that the fathers of female students have more education than the fathers of male students. More than 54 per cent of the female students' fathers had a bachelor's degree or higher, were professionals in engineering or science, or were skilled workers. Fewer than 40 per cent of the male students' fathers had obtained bachelor's degrees. The men and women students seemed to have mothers with approximately equal levels of education. The families of female students were more affluent; 44 per cent of the women compared to 31 per cent of the men came from families with incomes exceeding $23,000.

8   The survey showed that both female and male students ranked math, chemistry, and physics in that order as being the subject they enjoyed most in school, although women mentioned math more often than did men.

9   In general, factors analyzed show remarkable similarities between male and female engineering freshmen: aspirations for graduate degrees, type of work, study habits, and goals for life were astonishingly similar for both groups. Even the birth order of individuals in the groups was similar — approximately 3 per cent of both men and women were only children, and 30 per cent were the oldest child.

10 The only two areas where differences were noted between males and females were the age when students first considered engineering as a career, and whether or not the student had joined or attended meetings of a professional society at the University of Cincinnati. In the first instance, 80 per cent of the women replied that they had first considered engineering as a career in their junior or senior year of high school. Close to

40 per cent of the males had considered engineering before the junior year in high school. In the second case, 40 per cent of the females but only 9 per cent of the males answered affirmatively.

In summary, the University of Cincinnati study indicates that if more women are to become engineers, recruitment must begin in high school. Teachers and guidance counselors must be sensitive to girls showing traits similar to those of boys entering engineering programs, and they must be cognizant of the special support girls will need in selecting an engineering program appropriate to their interests.

In 1950 the Society of Women Engineers was established as an educational, non-profit organization representing all disciplines of engineering. The organization's objective is to inform young women, their parents, their counselors, and the public of qualifications, achievements, and opportunities for women in engineering. The society also provides a network of support for women professionals and students in the field. As the number of women undertaking careers in this challenging field increases, the number of obstacles to success will decrease. It is reassuring to know that so many women seek to overcome obstacles that still exist.

Summary

Since 1970 women desiring careers in the sciences have made remarkable progress. More women than ever are enrolling in science and engineering programs in college, and more are obtaining advanced degrees. Those trends are expected to continue.

Enthusiasm about those gains must be tempered by the recognition that women are still a long way from becoming full citizens of the scientific community. Their salaries are lower than those of men with equal background and experience. Their working conditions are less attractive, they have fewer opportunities for promotion, and they are frequently burdened with heavy teaching loads or administrative tasks that drastically reduce time available for research. Because so many women received their academic appointments within the past decade, women in colleges and universities have had little time to establish the seniority needed for job security. Thus, they are particularly susceptible to reductions in staff caused by the nation's current economic situation. Affirmative action programs, equal pay legislation, and Title IX of the Education Amendments of 1972, which forbid discrimination by sex in all federally assisted programs, are all threatened by the wave of conservatism prevalent in America.

We need a national commitment to overcome barriers to the full participation of women in the sciences. We need to persuade bright, energetic young women that a career in the sciences is both appropriate and desirable. That is no easy task; recent studies show that from early childhood girls are treated differently from boys both at home and in school. Teachers too often discourage girls from developing skills necessary for science by praising boys for independent thought and creativity, while complimenting girls for docile feminine submission (Rossi, 1965). At home, girls learn that their fathers, who spend much of the day away from home, are doing something important. The contributions of mothers, at least those who stay home, are undervalued, and children learn that women's activities are so unimportant that they may be interrupted casually.

What differences are there between female and male attitudes toward themselves and their work? Yalow (1982) attributes the tendency of women to choose professions in the biological and social sciences to lower scores on the mathematical components of pre-collegiate aptitude tests. Recent studies by Gilligan (1982) show that most women orient their lives toward relationships, interdependence, and subordination of personal achievement to caring for others. Thus, women are more often found teaching science than doing it. Women college teachers prefer appointments with 'good students' and 'desirable colleagues'; whereas male college teachers stress 'opportunity to do research', and 'freedom and independence' (Rossi, 1965). Both traits — choice of professions in biology or social science, and attitudes based on relationships — appear to be related to the degree of training in independence a child receives at home and in schools. Much more needs to be understood about the values and goals of young people. We need to know, for example, why girls who are only children or have all female siblings become scientists or engineers more often than girls with siblings of both sexes. We need ways to overcome persistent attitudes in both males and females that marriage and a career are not compatible for women. We need methods of counseling adolescent girls that enhance the development of individual goals and responsibilities. There must be greater acceptance of women scientists and engineers by males in the field. Traditionally, men in the sciences have been able to benefit from an informal collegiality that exists among members of their profession and allows them to hold informal discussions and debates in formal (offices and laboratories) or informal (coffee shops and cocktail parties) settings. Such informal contact enhances the dissemination of information about research developments, job opportunities, and a host of other issues vital to progress in the sciences. Too often, women in science and engineering are considered to be deviates from the norm, and are thereby excluded from activities that could help them attain full membership in the scientific and engineering communities. Men need to overcome the double standard that allows them to attribute mistakes of a woman scientist to the fact that she is a woman, while holding a man responsible for his errors on the basis of his professional attributes.

The lack of role models for girls with interest in science and engineering has hindered recruitment in the past, but the situation is changing as the number of women in scientific professions increases. We need to know much more about the social and psychological processes that influence selection of a career. Our nation can no longer afford to deprive young women of rewarding, productive careers critical to the survival of a modern technological society.

Fortunately, today — in contrast with the past — scientific and engineering societies are taking positive steps to ensure the entrance and retention of women in scientific fields. Professional associations have been the primary influence in increasing the number of women in both physics and engineering. Both groups have developed and distributed excellent brochures and instructional materials that encourage high school girls to continue in science. The National Association of Biology Teachers, supported by the National Science Foundation, has attempted to study and identify professional and personal attributes of science teachers who successfully encourage girls to pursue technological careers. In addition, the pharmaceutical association is attempting to prevent any negative attitudes associated with the feminization of pharmacy by active, positive public relation campaigns. Immediately, these positive steps will help ameliorate the perception of girls that science and engineering are men's work. In the long run, they may lead to actual equal pay and promotion for women in scientific and technological positions.

References

AMERICAN ANTHROPOLOGICAL ASSOCIATION (n.d.) *Unfinished Business*, Unpublished report.

AMERICAN CHEMICAL SOCIETY (1981) *Women Chemists 1980*, Washington, DC, American Chemical Society.

AMERICAN CHEMICAL SOCIETY (1974–81) *Report of Chemists' Salaries and Employment Status, 1974–1978: Report of Chemists' Salaries, 1979, 1980 and 1981*, Washington, DC, American Chemical Society.

Frances S. Vandervoort

AMERICAN PHARMACEUTICAL SOCIETY (1981) *APHA Task Force on Women in Pharmacy*, Washington, DC, American Pharmaceutical Society.

BARANGER, L. and EISENSTEIN, E. (1981) *Survey Completed for the Committee on the Status of Women in Physics*, New York, American Institute of Physics.

BRODY, R. (1982) 'Pharmacy', *The Working Woman*, April, pp. 138–40.

COLE, J.R. (1981) 'Women in science', *American Scientist*, 69, pp. 385–92.

DOUGLAS, C.B. and KAHLE, J.B. (1983) 'A profile of NABT: The results of the 1982 national survey of the National Association of Biology Teachers', *American Biology Teacher*, 45, pp. 418, 414, 423.

DURCHHOLZ, P. (1977) 'Women in a man's world: The female engineer', *Engineering Education*, 67, pp. 292–9.

ENGINEERING MANPOWER COMMISSION OF THE AMERICAN ASSOCIATION OF ENGINEERING SOCIETIES (1981) 'Women in engineering', *Engineering Manpower Bulletin*, April, p. 52.

GILLIGAN, C. (1982) *In a Difference Voice*, Cambridge, MA, Harvard University Press.

GORNICK, V. (1983) *Women in Science: Portraits from a World in Transition*, New York, Simon and Schuster.

HAHN, O. (1966) *Otto Hahn: A Scientific Autobiography*, New York, Scribner.

HENDERSON, B.C. (1975) 'As you might guess men are paid more', *Geotimes*, 20, 3, pp. 30–1.

KASHKET, E.R., ROBBINS, M.L., LEIVE, L. and HUANG, A.S. (1974) 'Status of women microbiologists', *Science*, 183, pp. 488–94.

KELLER, E.F. (1983) *A Feeling for the Organism: The Life and Work of Barbara McClintock*, San Francisco, CA, Freeman.

LEMONE, M.A. and WAUKAU, P.L. (n.d.) *Women in Meteorology*, Boulder, CO, National Center for Atmospheric Research.

LILLER, M.H., COWLEY, A.P., HODGE, P.W., KERR, F.J. and MORRISON, N.D. (1980) 'Report of the committee on the status of women', *Bulletin American Astronomical Society*, 12, 2, pp. 624–35.

LYONS, D.M. (1982) 'Salzman, Freda (Obituary)', *Physics Today*, 35, 2, pp. 89–90.

NATIONAL ACADEMY OF SCIENCES (NAS) (1979) *Climbing the Academic Ladder: Doctoral Women Scientists in Academe*, Washington, DC, National Academy of Sciences.

NATIONAL RESEARCH COUNCIL (NRC) (1982) *Summary Report 1981 Doctorate Recipients from United States Universities*, Washington, DC, National Academy Press.

NATIONAL SCIENCE FOUNDATION (NSF) (1982) *Women and Minorities in Science and Engineering* (NSF 82–302), Washington, DC, National Science Foundation.

ROSSI, A. (1965) 'Women in science: Why so few?' *Science*, 148, pp. 1196–202.

ROSSITER, M.W. (1982) *Women Scientists in America: Struggles and Strategies to 1940*, Baltimore, MD, Johns Hopkins University Press.

SABATINI, G.R. (1982) *Opportunities for Women in Pharmacy*, Paper presented at the Hygea Banquet, Lambda Kappa Sigma School of Pharmacy, West Virginia University, Morgantown, WV, 18 March.

SACHS, R. (1982) 'Maria Goepart Mayer — two-fold pioneer', *Physics Today*, 35, 2, pp. 46–51.

SAYRE, A. (1975) *Rosalind Franklin and DNA*, New York, W.W. Norton.

SCHWARTZER, T.F. (1977) 'Women in geoscience', *Geotimes*, 22, 4, pp. 20–4.

SCIENTIFIC MANPOWER COMMISSION (1983) *Manpower Comments*, 20, 4, p. 16.

SIMMONS, R.O. (1982) 'More senior women in physics', *Physics Today*, 35, 3, p. 120.

SOCIETY OF WOMEN ENGINEERS (SWE) (1980) *A Profile of the Women Engineer*, New York, Society of Women Engineers.

VETTER, B.M. (1981) 'Women scientists and engineers: Trends in participation', *Science*, 214, pp. 1313–21.

WATSON, J. (1968) *The Double Helix*, New York, Athenaeum.

WINDHAM, B. (1980) *American Association of Physics Teachers Committee on Women in Physics*, Unpublished report, Palatine, IL.

YALOW, R.S. (1982) 'Men and women are not the same,' *The New York Times*, 31 January, p. E21.

7 Discrepancies Between Men and Women in Science: Results of a National Survey of Science Educators

Claudia B. Douglass
Central Michigan University

The previous chapter discussed the role and status of women in professional organizations in the United States. Its brief historical introduction revealed that few women have held positions of prominence in science or in scientific associations. Unfortunately, that bleak situation continues today. This chapter focuses on a specific national organization, the National Association of Biology Teachers (NABT), which recently formed a committee to investigate and report on the role and status of women in biology. In addition, this group warrants close examination because women earn approximately half of all baccalaureate degrees in the biological sciences. Therefore, they have entered biology teaching in large numbers and their resulting roles and status merit examination.

The Committee on the Role and Status of Women in Biology, formed in 1981 by the NABT, surveyed the membership of the National Association of Biology Teachers in order to determine the general professional characteristics, roles, salaries, assignments, professional activities, and equity of its members. The survey focused on identifying any discrepancies between the role and status of female and male biologists who were primarily concerned with teaching. Although the study described the characteristics of all biology educators, this chapter focuses on the female component of the sample only.

A National Survey

Many questionnaires of professional characteristics and attitudes were previewed before including the following areas in the national survey:

general demographics, guidance into the profession, institutional and instructional characteristics, earning characteristics, professional memberships and activities, and perception of professional self-concept and discrimination.

The survey included sixty-three items; the first seventeen were Likert-type and the remaining were multiple choice items. If the choices provided were not applicable, the respondents were able to write additional information on the questionnaires; these written comments were included in the analyses of the results. Since limited time and funds prohibited surveying the entire membership of over 5000 biology educators, every fifth member was sent a questionnaire. Five hundred and nine members completed and returned the questionnaire for a response rate of 48 per cent. This sampling method approached a simple random sample (Douglass and Kahle, 1983).

Answers to the survey supplied interesting and intriguing data which were difficult to synthesize. Therefore, responses were grouped into four categories. First, items which described the general demographics of the sample were analyzed. Next, items that assessed professional guidance and financial support received during college were analyzed. Then, characteristics of the respondents' positions, including teaching assignments, institutional characteristics, professional experience, and income sources were studied. Last, items regarding self-concept and professional equity were evaluated.

Demographics

As noted in the previous chapter, most of the members of any professional, scientific organization are men; only 37 per cent of NABT members are women. However, of those returning the questionnaire, 44 per cent were women and 56 per cent were men. Proportionately more women than men took time to respond to the survey and, therefore, to contribute to our findings.

The distribution of married and single respondents is shown in Figure 7.1. Sixty-five per cent of the female respondents were married in contrast to 77 per cent of the male respondents. As Figure 7.1 shows, proportionately more married men and single women taught at the college level; the reverse was true in middle schools. High school faculties, on the other hand, showed the most even distribution between single and married respondents. Although nearly three-quarters of those returning the questionnaire were married, 50 per cent reported having no dependent children at home. In addition, a signi-

Figure 7.1

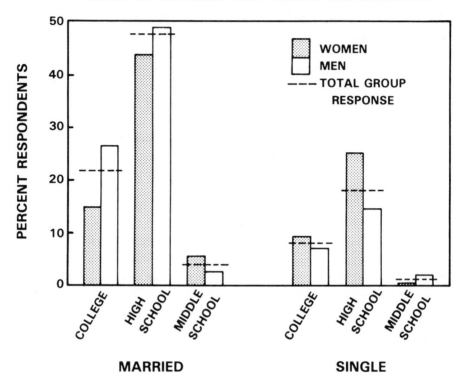

DISTRIBUTION BY SEX AND TEACHING
LEVEL OF MARRIED AND SINGLE RESPONDENTS

ficant relationship between gender and the number of dependent children was found. For example, 54 per cent of the women and 46 per cent of the men reported having no dependent children. More than 70 per cent of those who reported having two or more dependent children were men. These responses followed the pattern previously found among women scientists; that is, although many women professionals marry, they leave the work force after having three or more children (Cole, 1979).

The age distribution of the respondents, shown in Figure 7.2, followed that of other national science teaching samples; for example, 75 per cent of all respondents were between 30 and 55 years old, while 53 per cent were in the range of 35 to 50 years. However, it was interesting to note that 61 per cent of the respondents under 30 years of age were women. In addition, past age 60, more of the respondents were women. These data suggest that the gender distribution of biology teachers has

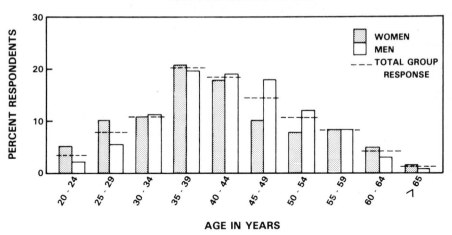

Figure 7.2

AGE DISTRIBUTION BY SEX

changed with more women continuing in the profession longer than men have. For the sample as a whole, the age stratification might be explained in terms of current economic and population statistics. Declining enrollments have forced many young teachers out of the classroom. Often only teachers with more than twelve years of experience are retained. The age stratification has obvious relationships to both years of experience and salary level, which will be discussed later.

Guidance into the Profession

When asked to react to the statement, 'I was encouraged to pursue science in high school', men and women responded similarly. Overall, 59 per cent of the respondents indicated that they were encouraged to pursue science in high school. However, 39 per cent of the respondents, discouraged from pursuing science in high school, went on to become biology teachers. Possibly they received encouragement elsewhere; for example, parents, family physicians, and adult acquaintances working in science were mentioned in the written responses. Research investigating factors influencing a student's decision to pursue science reveals that most decisions are made during childhood. The single most important group of factors are school-related. They include both the support of teachers and successful academic experience (Douglass, Richardson and McBurney, 1985). Thus, early encouragement to pursue science may have significant, lasting effects in the life of the student.

151

When asked about encouragement to continue scientific studies during college, differences between men and women were found, as shown in Figure 7.3. Eighty per cent of all respondents were encouraged in college, probably because they entered a specific program. However, 18 per cent of the respondents reported that they still did not receive positive reinforcement to pursue scientific careers while in college.

Figure 7.3

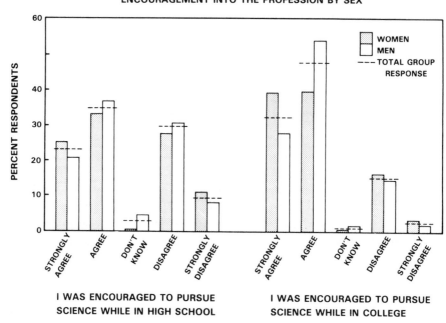

ENCOURAGEMENT INTO THE PROFESSION BY SEX

Incentives, such as opportunities for financial aid, often serve as sources of encouragement at the college or university level. Sources of graduate support were similar for men and women students; they consisted of teaching assistantships, research assistantships, scholarships, and fellowships. However, fewer than 60 per cent of all respondents received financial assistance as graduate students. Scholarships or fellowships formed the largest category of aid. Considering the age distribution of the respondents and the federally-sponsored master's degree programs of the 1960s, this finding was not surprising. Thirty-four per cent of those returning the survey had benefited from such programs. Thirty-three per cent received teaching assistantships, while 18 per cent held research assistantships. The remaining 40 per cent of the respondents did not receive financial support during their graduate careers. Those students might have been part-time, summer, or evening students who were ineligible for such aid. Also, students enrolled in non-degree courses are often ineligible for financial aid. Nearly 10 per cent of those returning the survey reported that they did not have a faculty sponsor, advisor, or mentor during graduate school. Although they enrolled in courses and completed programs, those teachers/students did not benefit from the personal interest and guidance and of an advisor. However, proportionately more men than women reported having adequate support by a faculty sponsor.

Teaching Assignment and Institutional Characteristics

Teaching assignments varied between men and women, as shown in Figure 7.4. As noted in previous chapters and as reported by Cole (1979), academic positions at prestigious institutions are more often filled by men.[1] Among college biology teachers, two-thirds of those teaching courses for biology majors were men, while only slightly more than half of those teaching courses for non-majors were men. The vast majority of the respondents taught in high schools where general biology courses were equally distributed between men and women teachers. However, a larger percentage of men than women taught a second course, usually advanced or honors biology. Although few respondents were involved in teaching life science at the middle school level, the percentages of men and women teaching at that level were nearly equal.

Forty-two per cent of the respondents taught in schools with enrollments ranging from 1000 to 3000 students. Twenty-three per cent taught in schools with 500 to 1000 students, while 17 per cent were employed in schools with fewer than 500 students. A significantly greater percentage of men taught at the larger schools, while more women were found in very small schools (500 students or fewer). Thus, men might hold positions in institutions with greater resources and with greater opportunities for advancement and recognition.

Teachers at all levels were asked how they divided their class time into the following activities: lecture, discussion, laboratory, and field work. The great variety in their responses probably reflected differences in their available facilities. However, at all levels, the most classroom time was spent in lecture and discussion, and the least amount of time was spent in field experiences. The common belief that female, compared to male, science teachers spend less time in laboratory and field activities was disproved by the results of the survey; women conducted laboratory experiences and field excursions as often as men did.

Figure 7.4

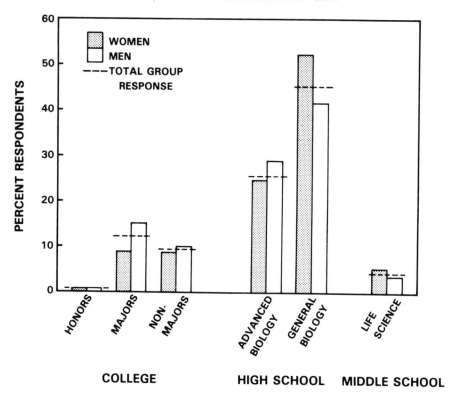

TEACHING ASSIGNMENT BY SEX

Experience and Income Characteristics

The respondents were experienced biology teachers as suggested by their age distribution. Forty-two per cent of all the responding teachers had eleven to twenty years of teaching experience, 18 per cent had six to ten years of experience, while only 24 per cent had five or fewer years of experience with their present employer. Years of experience varied significantly with sex, as shown in Figure 7.5. A higher percentage of women than men had ten or fewer years of experience, while equal percentages of men and women had eleven to fifteen years' experience. Although the percentage of men greatly exceeded that of women in every other category, twice the percentage of women as men reported having thirty or more years' experience, undoubtedly reflecting the age distribution reported earlier.

Figure 7.5

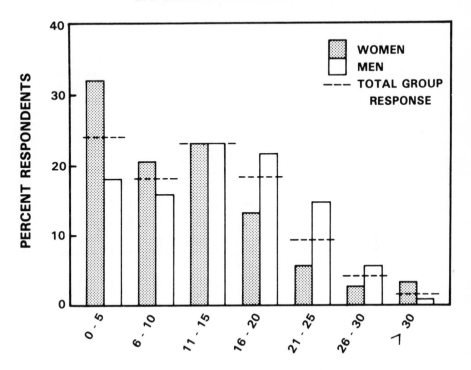

EXPERIENCE DISTRIBUTION BY SEX

YEARS OF EXPERIENCE WITH PRESENT EMPLOYER

Seventy-five per cent of those who completed the survey earned between $15,000 and $20,000 for an academic year. The salary range approximated a normal distribution, and 89 per cent of the respondents earned between $10,000 and $30,000 annually. Salaries also significantly differed by gender (Figure 7.6). Overall, higher percentages of women, compared with men, were found at every salary level below $20,000, while larger percentages of men were found at all higher salary levels. The difference was influenced by differences in teaching assignments, in types of institutions, and in years of experience.

Forty-three per cent of those returning the questionnaire reported little or no supplemental income. Many responded that they were too tired to work at night and that they filled their summer months with course work. Higher percentages of women than men reported no supplemental income. Thirty-six per cent of the respondents with supplemental incomes claimed earnings between 10–19 per cent of their base salaries; 14 per cent reported additional earnings between

Figure 7.6

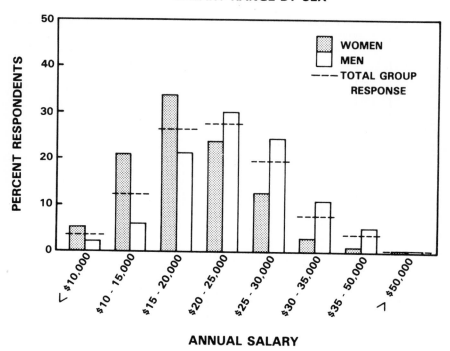

SALARY RANGE BY SEX

20–29 per cent of their base salaries. Income sources were typically summer teaching, other summer employment, coaching, curriculum writing, consulting or, for a few, an after-school job. High school teachers reported receiving the greatest percentage of supplemental income. A few earned more than 50 per cent of their base pay in another position.

Professional and Research Activity

Both the men and women who responded to the survey were professionally active and influential. More than 90 per cent of the respondents reported that they were active in the professional matters of their scholastic departments and that they influenced departmental policies. The percentage dropped to between 80–85 per cent when asked about their professional activities and influential powers at the institutional level. There were no significant differences in influence or activity found at any of the three teaching levels (college, high school, middle/junior high school), or between men and women. Many institutions based promotions, in part, on the professional activities of teachers. Contrary to the belief that women have less time commitment to professional activities, the women in this survey were as professionally active as the men. Therefore, they met this prerequisite for recognition and reward.

Responses to the statement, 'I am included in the informal social gatherings of my department', varied by gender. Proportionately, more men than women gave a positive response (strongly agree or agree), while more women than men responded negatively (disagree or strongly disagree). Since policy decisions might be reached at such gatherings, those not involved might not have opportunities to be influential; many women respondents wrote comments that suggested that they did not have informal, or social, contacts with their colleagues.

An important way to increase one's professional activities is to attend state and national meetings of professional or learned societies. Over 40 per cent of all respondents reported attending professional meetings less than once a year, while 22 per cent reported attending only once a year. Twenty-five per cent of all respondents had never attended a meeting, while only 10 per cent reported attending more than one meeting a year. Attendance at professional meetings varied by gender, with men attending more frequently than women. For example, as Figure 7.7 shows, 52 per cent of those who stated that they never attended a meeting were women, while only 28 per cent of those who attended frequently were women.

The record of professional activity can be explained partially by other responses in which nearly one-half of the biology educators surveyed reported they covered their own expenses for professional meetings. According to Figure 7.7, only 30 per cent of the responding teachers received institutional support for professional activities. Of those who attended professional meetings, more men (66 per cent) than women (34 per cent) received funds from their institutions, while more women (55 per cent) than men (45 per cent) used other sources, often personal or family resources, of funding.

Another important aspect of professional life is research, which may be stimulated by reading professional journals. Half of all respondents reported reading two or three journals regularly. The only significant difference in reading habits of respondents by gender was found at the college level where men reported more time to read professional journals than women did. This difference was due primarily to the fact that 21 per cent of the college level teachers reported regularly reading

Claudia B. Douglass

Figure 7.7

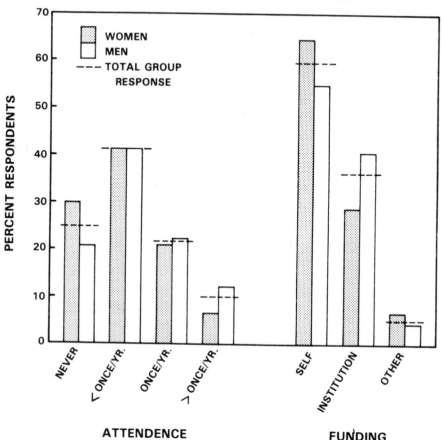

ATTENDENCE AT AND FUNDING FOR TRAVEL TO
PROFESSIONAL MEETINGS BY SEX

more than seven professional journals. Most respondents read between
one and five journals regularly.

Research activities may be judged, in part, by one's publication
record. Fewer than 20 per cent of the respondents reported publishing
more than one paper in the last five years. In addition, there was a
significant difference in the numbers of published papers reported by
men and women. Twenty-two per cent of all male respondents had
published two or more papers in the last five years, while only 10 per
cent of the female respondents had published as many. The difference
was even greater at colleges and universities where 43 per cent of the

158

men, compared to 17 per cent of the women, reported publishing two or more papers.

Assistance for research activities may be in the form of personnel, funds, or both. Respondents at all three academic levels surveyed reported research activities. However, 67% of all respondents did not have research assistants. High school students assisted with the research of 24 per cent of the high school teachers.

Funds for research were secured by biologists and biology teachers at all academic levels. Many institutions and departments funded research. In addition, 15 per cent of the college respondents reported that they had received federal funds, while 5 per cent of the high school personnel had received federal support. More teachers at the high school than the college level received state, local, foundation, or industrial support for their research efforts. There was no significant difference in the distribution of research monies to men and women teachers.

Professional Self-Concept

The following types of items, concerning self-concept, were included in the survey: (1) respondents' perceptions of their success, (2) respondents' judgments of their sphere of influence, and (3) respondents' perceptions of their contentment with their current position. Over 90 per cent of all respondents reported that professional success was important to them. In addition, when compared with men or women of similar age and qualifications, respondents of both sexes stated that they were successful. These results were similar for men and women at all academic levels. Likewise, 93 per cent of all respondents indicated they have had opportunities to influence the policies of their academic departments. However, the percentage of positive responses dwindled to 80 per cent when teachers were asked about influencing the policies of their institutions. Neither set of responses showed a significant difference by gender or by teaching level.

Some of the most interesting responses concerned happiness, or contentment, with one's current position. For example, the item, 'If I were to begin my career again, I would seek a position similar to that which I now hold', received mixed responses. Fifty-two per cent indicated discontent with a present position, while 58 per cent indicated a general satisfaction with it. However, 89 per cent reported that they frequently think of leaving their present job; this response is consistent across all teaching levels and for both sexes.

Perceived Professional Equality

Participation of both men and women in the administrative affairs of their institution was surveyed. The respondents reported that 73 per cent of their department chairpersons were men. Although there were no statistically significant differences among academic levels, higher percentages of women were found as science department chairpeople at the middle school level. Forty-one per cent of the middle school, 29 per cent of the high school, and 21 per cent of the college and university respondents reported that a woman served as the department chair.

As shown in Figure 7.8, 44 per cent of all respondents reported that fewer than 10 per cent of their administrators were women. Another 13 per cent reported that fewer than 20 per cent of their administrators were women, and 10 per cent of the respondents reported that fewer than 30 per cent of their administrators were women. Altogether, 85 per cent of all respondents reported that women held fewer than 50 per cent of their institution's administrative positions. The percentage of women in administration varied significantly with academic level. As can be seen in Figure 7.8, there were relatively fewer women in college and university administrative positions than in high school positions. Written comments suggested that women held secondary roles, such as curriculum consultant or guidance counselor. Usually these positions have less prestige and, ultimately, less influence.

The dearth of women in administration might be due to the few women found in biology faculties. Over one-third of the respondents reported that women comprised less than 20 per cent of their department. The proportion of female faculty members varied significantly by academic level, as seen in Figure 7.9. As expected, proportionately more women were found in science departments at the middle and secondary schools than were found in science departments in colleges and universities.

Surprisingly, most male (60 per cent) and female (56 per cent) respondents at all academic levels disagreed with the statement, 'Affirmative action has produced a more balanced number of women and minorities in my department.' The same trend was observed when teachers were asked about the effects of affirmative action on hiring at the institutional level. In this case, differences in the responses of faculty at the various academic levels emerged; at the college and university level, proportionately more men disagreed with the statement, while more women agreed with it. Since there are many more male than female biologists at the college level, an increase of a few women may double or triple the number of women in a department.

Figure 7.8

FEMALE REPRESENTATION ON THE ADMINISTRATION

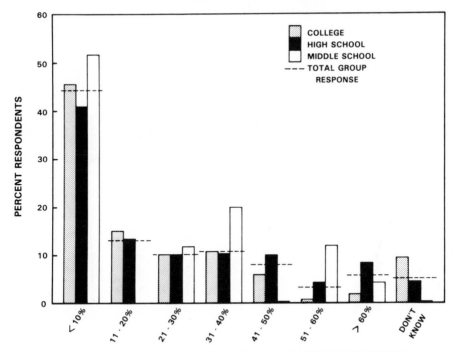

PERCENT FEMALE ADMINISTRATORS IN RESPONDENT'S INSTITUTION

Women faculty in colleges and universities, therefore, may be more aware of these changes.

Middle school teachers were offered more jobs and received more serious inquiries about jobs than all other teachers, while colleges and university faculty received the fewest offers and/or inquiries. Proportionately more men than women received serious inquiries about jobs, but proportionately more women than men reported receiving actual job offers.

Perceptions of equality in promotion, tenure, and salary decisions were included in the survey. There was a significant difference in the responses of men and women to the statement, 'At my school, males are generally treated in a manner that is preferential to that received by females where matters of professional advancement are concerned.' Thirty-four per cent of women respondents strongly agreed or agreed with that statement, while 56 per cent disagreed or strongly disagreed. However, only 13 per cent of the men responded positively, while 76 per cent responded negatively. When the reverse was stated, 'At my

Figure 7.9

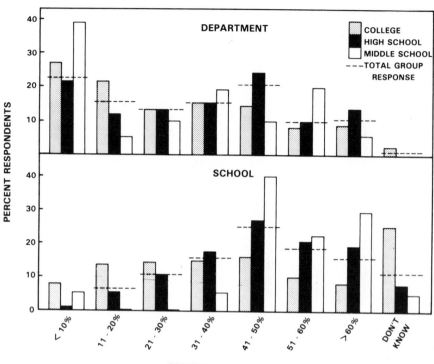

FEMALE REPRESENTATION ON THE FACULTY

PERCENT FEMALE FACULTY

school, females are generally treated in a manner that is preferential . . .',
5 per cent of the women strongly agreed or agreed, and 84 per cent
disagreed or strongly disagreed. Eleven per cent of the males responded positively, and 78 per cent responded negatively (Figure 7.10).
There is little difference in the reaction to either statement by those at
various academic levels. Again, there was a significant difference in the
responses of men and women biologists to the statement, 'At my school,
promotions are awarded equitably to males and females.' Figure 7.11
graphically represents this difference. Overall, 67 per cent of all
respondents strongly agreed or agreed with that statement. Proportionately more men than women responded positively, while proportionately more women than men responded negatively. Therefore,
men appeared to be satisfied with promotion procedures, while a
significant percentage of women felt that promotion policies were not
equitable. There was no significant difference in the response of men
and women to the statement. 'At my school, professionals of equal rank

Figure 7.10

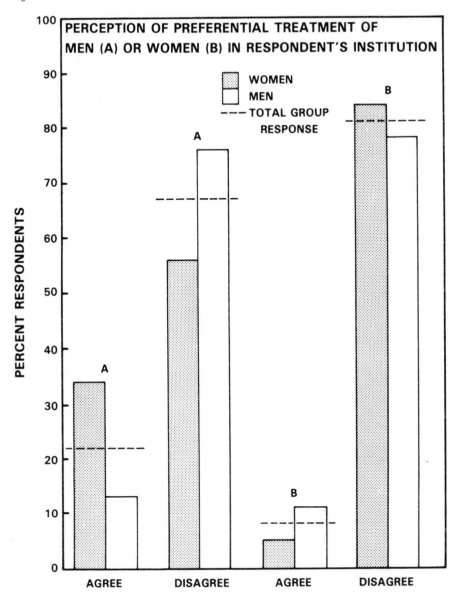

RESULTS OF THE 1982 NABT MEMBERSHIP SURVEY

Figure 7.11

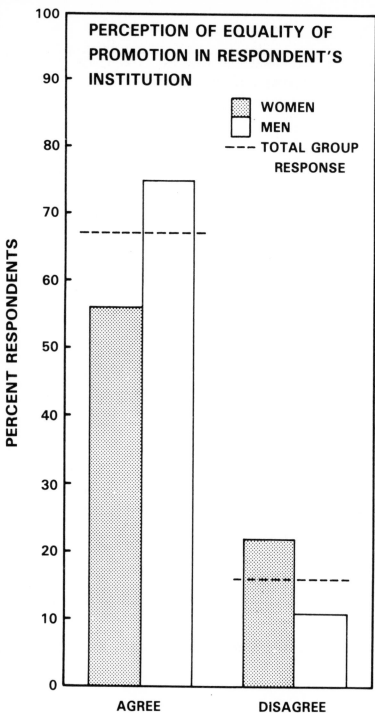

PERCEPTION OF EQUALITY OF PROMOTION IN RESPONDENT'S INSTITUTION

WOMEN
MEN
--- TOTAL GROUP RESPONSE

PERCENT RESPONDENTS

AGREE   DISAGREE

RESULTS OF THE 1982 NABT MEMBERSHIP SURVEY

and tenure are paid equally for the same work, regardless of sex.' This finding undoubtedly reflected the effectiveness of the collective bargaining procedures common among teachers' unions and associations.

However, the statement, 'I have experienced some form of sex discrimination as a professional', brought significantly different responses from men and women. As shown in Figure 7.12, three times the percentage of women as men agreed with that statement. Similarly, proportionately more men than women disagreed with it. The pattern of responses was the same when the item concerned sex discrimination against others. There were no significant differences in the responses of those teaching at the various academic levels to either statement. These results suggested that women experienced more professional discrimination at all levels and that they were more sensitive to the discrimination experienced by others.

Summary

The information in this chapter is based largely upon responses to a questionnaire sent to members of the National Association of Biology Teachers in the spring of 1982. The purpose of the survey was to characterize biology educators with regard to roles, salaries, assignments, professional activities and professional equity.

Members of the NABT, who are usually biology educators at colleges, universities, high schools, and middle schools, responded to the survey. The majority were male and white. Racial and ethnic minorities composed a small part (5 per cent) of the respondents. Most of the respondents were married. However, noticeably fewer women than men were married, and women reported having fewer dependent children than had men. It appeared that professional women might forfeit or delay traditional family roles for careers. Since both teaching and childrearing demand time and energy, women may choose only one role.

The respondents generally were encouraged to pursue careers in science in high school and college. During college and graduate school, many respondents were assisted financially by fellowships, assistantships, and grants-in-aid. On the other hand, many teachers struggled through degree programs as part-time, evening, and/or summer students without financial assistance. Many respondents lacked the advantages of an academic advisor.

The teaching assignments of the respondents were highly desirable. Most (65 per cent) of the respondents taught general or advanced

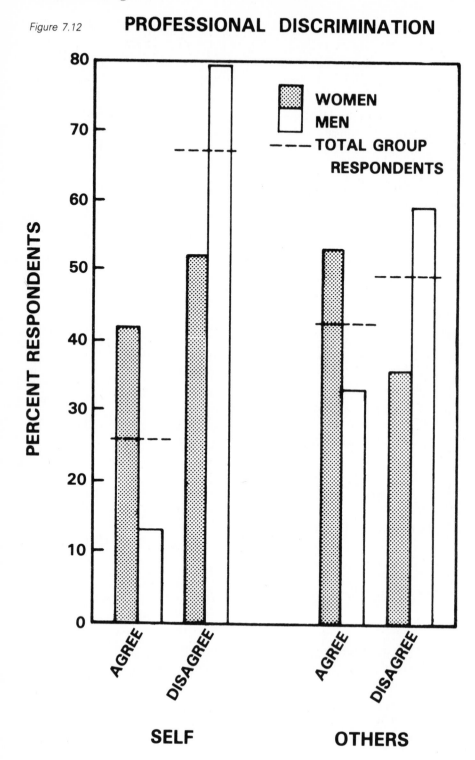

Figure 7.12 **PROFESSIONAL DISCRIMINATION**

biology in the high schools. Thirty per cent of the respondents instructed college biology majors or non-majors. The smallest group of respondents (5 per cent) taught middle school life science courses. At all educational levels, proportionately more men than women taught advanced classes. Women either chose to teach introductory classes, or they received less desirable courses. Higher percentages of men were found at large institutions, while smaller institutions had higher percentages of women on their staffs. Men were found in the universities, colleges, junior colleges and large high schools, while women taught in smaller schools. Since women teachers may be in the position of having fewer students, their potential as positive role models for girls interested in science is limited.

The respondents as a whole had considerable experience teaching. Higher percentages of women were found both among young teachers and among those with the most experience. Although women work longer than men, they do not draw the highest salaries.[2] Proportionately more women than men had incomes less than $20,000, and men outnumber women at all higher salary levels. Three times the percentage of women compared with men earned no supplemental income. Those women who were able to secure additional income taught in the summer, while men more often found employment in other fields. Until recently, the higher paying, labor-intensive, summer jobs such as painting, construction, etc. have been open only to men.

One way to aid one's professional advancement is to be more visible. According to our survey, men attended more professional meetings than did women. They also were more successful at securing travel funds than women were. College and university faculty attended more meetings than did professionals at the other academic levels. Attendance at these meetings was a significant source of professional visibility and of potential research contacts. Compared with women, proportionately more men engaged in research. Since this may be one criterion for promotion, women may be hampered by their limited exposure to and contacts in research. Women must become more visible in the professional world by attending meetings, presenting papers, and publishing in research journals if they are to advance to the higher paying positions or to become eligible to fill administrative openings.

Few women among those who returned the survey held administrative positions. Men held over 90 per cent of the administrative positions and composed the majority of the science faculties. When women were found as administrators, they were in middle schools, rather than in high schools, or colleges and universities. Most repondents did not think that affirmative action programs had balanced the number of minorities and women in their departments and/or institutions. In general, the respondents did not feel that either sex was treated preferentially with regard to professional advancement. If these feelings regarding professional equity are true, then women must become more professionally active to fulfill qualifications for administrative or research positions.

At present, women are in the minority as administrators and do not have financial support to attend professional meetings and/or to conduct research studies. However, the data indicate that many younger teachers at all academic levels are women. It will be interesting to note the differences in the responses to future questionnaires when women become among the most qualified in their departments for positions of leadership. Will they receive the higher salaries, research and travel support, more desirable teaching assignments, and administrative appointments? Will they really desire those challenges? A subsequent survey may indicate the changing status of women biology educators.

Notes

1 In most cases, and in this one, prestigious institution refers to one of the top ten of the nation's universities in amount of research money received.
2 These data are confounded by the fact that more women than men respondents were members of religious orders. Therefore, the salary data are biased.

References

COLE, J.R. (1979) *Fair Science: Women in the Scientific Community*, New York, The Free Press.
DOUGLASS, C., RICHARDSON, R. and McBURNEY, W. (in press) 'Factors motivating students to science', *School Science and Mathematics*.
DOUGLASS, C. and KAHLE, J. (1983) 'A profile of NABT: The results of the 1982 national survey', *The American Biology Teacher*, 45, pp. 418, 414, 423.

8   International Perspectives on the Status and Role of Women in Science

Ann E. Haley-Oliphant
University of Cincinnati

> I wonder whether the tiny atoms and nuclei or the mathematical symbols or the DNA molecules have any preference for either masculine or feminine treatment (Wu, 1965).

It is doubtful that the inanimate objects described above have a preference for being studied by females or males. Yet an examination of the disparity of women in the scientific community indicates that a selection process must be discouraging women from pursuing scientific careers. Whether or not that selection process is unique to a specific country or culture is the subject of this chapter.

Researchers have cited a combination of biological, cultural, attitudinal, educational, and economic forces that discourage women from entering the sciences in representative numbers (Kelly, 1976; Tosi, 1975). Although separate philosophies have developed among Eastern European, Western European, North American, Australian, and developing countries in Africa and Asia regarding women in scientific and technological careers, there is an underlying, recurrent problem of the prevalence of women in positions of lower status in scientific occupations in all countries surveyed. This issue will be examined by analyzing representative research on the status of women scientists internationally and by examining various efforts to improve the access of women to science in several areas of the world.

A brief overview of the percentage of women doctors and engineers in ten countries will form the foundation of our comparison. According to Table 8.1, Eastern European countries have been far more successful than Western European nations and the United States in educating women for medical and engineering careers. Yet numbers alone do not fully describe the situation for women scientists as the following analysis of individual countries will show. Many countries are not discussed in

Table 8.1.   Percentages of Women Physicians and Engineers in Ten Countries.

	Physicians	Engineers
Western countries		
Britain	17	0.5
Canada[a]	33	8.2
France	15	2.0
USA	10	1.0
West Germany	30.6	7.8
Eastern countries		
East Germany	53	10
Hungary	42	—[b]
Poland	44	11
Russia	75	44
Developing countries		
Burma	50	15
Mexico	34.7	6.7

Note: Adapted from data from Kelly, 1976; Lapidus, 1978; Tosi, 1975; Turi, 1980; Shaffer,
1981; Thein, 1980; Scott, 1981; Srinivasan, 1982.
a Enrolled in professional schools.
b Data unavailable.

this chapter, due to the lack of information regarding the current status of women in science in those countries. Our observations and conclusions, therefore, cannot be generalized to all countries. In addition, limitations of space and time have allowed us to present an overview only, not a detailed analysis of women in science internationally.

Women in Science in England and Australia

England

As Table 8.2 indicates, from the Ordinary (O level) examinations onward, boys outnumber girls in science studies by ratios ranging up to 17 to 1. Nearly four times as many British men as women receive doctorates in biology and nearly ten times as many men as women in the United Kingdom earn doctorate degrees in mathematics and physics (Kelly and Weinreich-Haste, 1979). However, girls' rates of attrition from science, compared to girls' attrition from other academic areas, are fairly constant after the O level examinations (Kelly and Weinreich-Haste, 1979). It appears, then, that the factors affecting female attrition from science studies in England and Wales take effect before age fourteen.

Although many theories have been proposed to explain early attrition, one that has been well supported is the view of science as a

Table 8.2   Ratios of Numbers of English Males to Females Studying Science at Various Levels of Educational Attainment, 1975/76

Level of education	Biology	Mathematics	Subject Chemistry	Physics	All subjects
Attempt O-level exams	0.6	1.5	2.1	3.8	1.0
Attempt A-Level exams	1.1	3.8	2.4	4.9	1.4
Obtain first degree	1.3	2.6	4.7	7.2	2.0
Do postgraduate research	2.6	8.0	7.0	9.6	4.1
Obtain PhD	3.8	9.7	9.7	17.1	6.3

Source: Adapted from Kelly and Weinreich-Haste (1979).

masculine endeavor. A 1979 study has indicated that English school children perceive physics, chemistry, and mathematics as masculine subjects. However, this same study showed that boys think that biology is a masculine subject, while girls view it as a neutral subject (Wein-reich-Haste, 1981). When asked to describe 'a scientist', both boys and girls in English schools described a person with clearly masculine characteristics, and over 33 per cent of them specifically referred to a scientist as male (Weinreich-Haste, 1981). In a recent British study on sex-role stereotyping and attitudes toward science among eleven-year-old school children, Kelly and Smail found that children who accepted sex stereotypes, when compared to those who did not, showed less interest in the branches of science traditionally associated with the opposite sex.[1] This finding suggests that children may be closing vocational doors before they take subjects such as chemistry and physics in school. As Kelly (1975) points out, the curriculum available to girls in some English schools is limited due to informal barriers. This limitation may restrict their future opportunities to study science and to pursue scientific careers.

Once women earn scientific or technological degrees, they still face considerable obstacles in attaining high status and/or high salaries positions. Currently in England, 10 per cent of the scientists and technologists are women, yet they account for fewer than 2 per cent of the practicing research scientists, technologists, and managers (Curran, 1980). The other 8 per cent occupy low-paying, less prestigious positions categorized as technician, teacher, or laboratory assistant (Curran, 1980; Dauber and Cain, 1981). The women scientists who do attain research positions frequently are not recognized for their achievements. As Table 8.3 indicates, only 4 per cent of British women scientists are full or corresponding members of the Fellows of the Royal Society.

The situation for English women scientists, therefore, appears

Table 8.3.   Percentages of Women Scientists Holding Memberships in Academies of Science.

	Full Members	Corresponding Members
Western countries		
Belgium	0	7.4
Britain	3	1
Finland	4.2	0
The Netherlands	3	1.3
New Zealand	6	—[a]
Sweden	0	—[a]
USA	1.5	—[a]
Eastern countries		
Czechoslovakia	0	2.2
East Germany	2.9	0
Hungary	0.47	5
Russia	1.2	2
Yugoslavia	0.96	3.2

Note: Adapted from data from Kelly, 1976; Lapidus, 1978; "Distribution by Sex of Principle Scientific Awards and Memberships in Academics of Science," 1975.
a No data available.

analogous to that of women scientists in the United States, which has been reported in other chapters. Science is viewed as a predominantly masculine career and academic subject, and the number of women participating reflects this view. In addition, those women who do participate in science are frequently in the lower ranks of their profession and, therefore, have less status and receive lower salaries than do their male counterparts. As stated by Kelly and Weinreich-Haste (1979):

> Girls who cannot or will not learn science are cut off at an early age from a wide range of careers and interests. By conforming to a feminine stereotype which excludes science, they are moving towards traditional women's occupations, and the low pay and low status which frequently accompanies such occupations (p. 280).

Australia

The pattern of employment and the status of Australian women scientists are similar to those of American and English women scientists. In Australia, there are no federal regulations concerning sex discrimination; there are, however, some state regulations. Jones and Lovejoy (1980) reported that, although females comprise 50 per cent of the

Australian population, they earn only 34 per cent of all bachelor degrees granted and 14.6 per cent of all higher degrees conferred. Women comprise approximately 12 per cent of full-time, Australian University faculty. Like their English and American sisters, female Australian scientists are concentrated at the lower ranks and at lower salary levels in academia. In 1976, only 3 per cent of Australian university women in research and teaching positions held the rank of professor or associate professor. Therefore, only one of every seven professors or associate professors was female, an increase of only 0.4 per cent since 1972. As Table 8.4 indicates, Australian women academics are concentrated in the lower ranks, with 37 per cent holding Senior Lecturer/Lecturer positions and 60 per cent holding Junior Staff positions (Jones and Lovejoy, 1980). In Australia, as in other Western countries, women are found primarily in teaching, not research, positions within universities.

Table 8.4. Percentages of University Research and Teaching Staff in Various Status Categories, 1976

Status	Males	Females
Professor	11.1	0.9
Associate Professor	11.3	2.1
Senior Lecturer/Lecturer	57.8	37.0
Junior Staff	19.8	60.0
Totals	100.0	100.0

Source: From Jones and Lovejoy (1980).

Jones and Lovejoy (1980) also reported that when academic faculties were asked about unfavorable treatment, males complained about 'teaching duties, administrative tasks, secretarial assistance, technical assistance, and equipment/resources/space'. In addition to those complaints, women academicians in the same study complained of unequal appointments and promotions. Women also indicated that they were discriminated against due to their gender, their academic and marital status, and their age. On the other hand, men described nationality, political beliefs, and racial origin as major reasons for their personal discrimination. According to Table 8.5, Australian women academicians think that covert sex discrimination is far more frequent than overt sex discrimination.

In conclusion, although Australia has been described as one of the most highly urbanized societies in the world with 86 per cent of its population living in modern urban centers, one finds sex-stereotyped career patterns similar to those found in other English-speaking countries. Factors similar to those found in the US and Great Britain may be affecting women scientists in Australia.

Table 8.5. Percentages of Australian Academics Believing There Is Overt and Covert
Discrimination against Women Academics in Australia, by Sex, 1976

		'Do you believe there is overt discrimination?' (Percentage responding)			
Sex	Total	Yes	No	Don't know	No response
Female	100.1[a]	24.4	29.0	20.4	26.3
Male	100.0	12.8	50.4	27.9	8.9
		'Do you believe there is covert discrimination?' (Percentage responding)			
Female	100.0	59.0	10.7	20.9	9.4
Male	99.9[a]	27.9	27.1	39.1	5.8

Source: From Jones and Lovejoy (1980).
Note: a Due to rounding.

Programs Designed to Encourage Girls in Science in Western Europe

In recent years, Western countries have been especially active in developing programs designed to encourage girls to pursue scientific or technological careers. Some of those programs are described in Figure 8.1. Some programs have risen to fill a void of opportunities in schools and industries in the United States, Canada, Great Britain, Norway, the Netherlands, and numerous other countries. Those programs are designed to encourage girls to understand the potential value of scientific careers both to themselves and for their society.

Figure 8.1 includes some British efforts to alter girls' images of

Figure 8.1. Selected International Programs to Encourage Females Toward Scientific and Technological Careers

Country	Title of Program	Focus of the Program
Canada	'Science and Education Committee' of the Science Council of Canada	Assess current status of Canadian science education to determine the status of girls in science courses.
Egypt	'Al-Ahram Science Club' — International Coordinating Committee for the Presentation of Science & the Development of Out-of-School Scientific Activites	Set up small labs for after school hours to enhance girls' and boys' understanding of international happenings in science.

Figure 8.1. Continued

FDR West Germany	'Modellversuche' Federal Government, Employers and Other Organizations	Encourage girls to enter into technical and craft apprenticeships in industry.
Netherlands	'HANDROVER' Project	Examine textbooks for sex bias. Perform case studies on different subjects to determine the problems posed to girls due to sex-stereotypes.
	'MENT' Project	Encourage boys and girls to choose science by providing successful experiences with science activities.
Norway	'Girls & Physics' Group at the Centre for School Science at Oslo University	Provide a link between schools and the University; aid teachers through inservice workshops and curriculum development.
Portugal	'Changing Attitudes' Project	Produce written, visual, and audio-visual materials as well as intervention activities to promote non-stereotyped attitudes among students
Sweden	'Sex Equity Department' of the Government	Develop special programs to encourage girls into technology.
United Kingdom	'Engineering Industry Training Board' (EITB)	Work with employees and with universities to encourage girls to become student professional engineers or engineering technicians.
	'Manpower Services Commission' (MSC)	Fund programs to assist re-entry of women engineers and scientists to careers in technological fields. Also, begin starter courses for older women to enter technological careers for the first time.
	'Loughborough University Women in Engineering Project and School Link Programme' 'INSIGHT'	Encourage girls toward engineering careers. Link secondary schools with the university in a career counseling capacity.
	'Girls into Science & Technology' (GIST); 'VISTA'	Improve girls' attitudes to physical sciences and craft subjects. Sponsor visits from women scientists and engineers to schools to discuss their careers.
	Equal Opportunities Commission and Engineering Council	Declare 1984 to be "Women in Science and Engineering (WISE) Year."

Note: Adapted from Chivers, 1984; Romao, 1981; Raat, 1981; Sjøberg and Lie, 1981; Chivers, 1981; Mottier, 1981; Ferguson, 1981; Galai, 1970.

scientists and to expand their knowledge of possible scientific careers. A project entitled *Girls into Science and Technology* (GIST) has been conducted recently in ten schools in Greater Manchester (UK). The project's sponsors, the Manchester Polytechnic Commission and the Social Science Research Council, hope to encourage more girls to enroll in a variety of science options in secondary school (Smail, Whyte and Kelly, 1981; Ferry, 1982). The three major goals of the initial stages of the GIST program were to:

1 raise teachers' awareness of girls' under-achievement and help them realize that they can do something about it;
2 test children's entering attitudes and knowledge in science and technology for comparison with their later performance and choice;
3 arrange a series of visits to schools by women working in scientific and technological jobs who could act as role models for girls.

(Smail, Whyte and Kelly, 1981, p. 241).

During the final two years of GIST, the program focused on craft curriculum and careers.

Another British program, sponsored by the Engineering Industries Training Board (EITB), annually provides 400 girls with opportunities to attend a university for a week to explore engineering careers. EITB also provides funding to universities for women who are earning their first engineering degree, and it offers grants to industries employing women as trainee technicians (Ferry, 1982).

Mutschellers (1969) provides another explanation for the lack of women in scientific and technological careers in Western Europe; that is, the lack of career guidance. According to Mutschellers, 'Of course we do not have enough boys and girls going in for a scientific career or a vocational and technological career. Why not? Because they don't know enough about the facts and about the circumstances of their future professions' (p. 226). Many of the programs described in Figure 8.1 are designed to provide students with contacts with actual scientists and engineers. Chivers (1981) claims that the United Kingdom has the lowest proportion of women professional engineers in the developed world and he attributes this to a misunderstanding of the role of engineers in society. The Loughborough University Women in Engineering Project was devised to counteract the false image of engineers in young women's eyes. The project provides girls with opportunities to learn the roles, aspirations, and ideas of young women scientists, technologists, and engineers who are established in successful careers. Chivers (1981) reports on a British study of 345 women engineers; only 2 per cent felt that their schools had influenced them in the selection of their careers. Projects such as the one at Loughborough University may help to alleviate the current lack of career guidance. ·

In other Western European countries, projects have also been initiated. Because only 16 per cent of all university students studying mathematics and natural sciences in the Netherlands are women and because women students comprise only 4 per cent of all engineering students in that country (de Raaff, 1981), the 'HANDROVER' project was undertaken. One of its early objectives was to reduce sex bias in textbooks. In addition, Eindhoven University of Technology developed a program which provided girls with actual experiences with mechanical equipment; with guidance concerning technology's impact on people and society; and with meeting practicing women engineers. Another Dutch project, the MENT-project was developed to provide positive science experiences for twelve to fifteen-year-old girls.

The project 'Girls and Physics', founded by the Centre for School Science, Oslo University, was designed to link schools with the university in hopes of attaining the following two goals:

1 Changes in course and career decisions made by girls.
2 Changes in subject and classroom practices.
   (Sjøberg and Lie, 1981, p. 228).

As was done during the Portuguese 'Changing Attitudes' project and the Dutch 'HANDROVER' project, an analysis of Norwegian textbooks was performed for sex-bias and unnecessary use of sex-role stereotypes. A preliminary analysis found only 10–20 per cent of science texts' illustrations pictured females. Furthermore, when girls and women were illustrated, 'the message is often of a sexist character: They are shown in a narrow and traditional range of occupations, and often in passive roles' (Sjøberg and Lie, 1981, p. 234).

Science education in West Germany is limited since only 26 per cent of all students continue their education beyond primary school (Mutschellers, 1969). When the percentage of young women attending secondary schools is examined, only 10 per cent of the physics students are found to be female (Hoffman, 1981). Hoffman claims that in West Germany there are currently no curriculum projects designed to encourage girls to pursue scientific or technological careers. In addition, she hypothesizes that girls may stop their physics studies because of a lack of stress on the importance of physics in daily life.

Currently there are numerous attempts to increase the involvement of girls in science studies and scientific careers in Western Europe. Most of the programs focus on adolescent or older girls and involve role modeling, career guidance, positive science experiences, reduction of sex-bias in textbooks, and an increase in teacher awareness of the underachievement of girls in science. Since sex-role stereotypes are learned at early ages, programs designed for pre-school and primary school girls may provide girls with experiences which will foster scientific abilities and interests in girls. One future direction, then, is the development and implementation of such early intervention programs.

Women in Science in Some Eastern European Countries

Soviet Union

The country with the greatest success in training women physicians and engineers is the Soviet Union. Research indicates that this is primarily due to three critical factors: academic study, work experience, and propaganda (Kelly, 1976). Kelly also reports that 50 per cent of the scientists and 33 per cent of the technologists in Russia are women. As seen in Table 8.1, 75 per cent of Soviet physicians and dentists are female. In addition, Lapidus (1978) cites mechanical engineering and metallurgy as predominantly female careers in the Soviet Union. Indeed, 44 per cent of Russia's engineers and technicians are women. The Russian pattern has influenced engineering education in satellite countries as well. Goodyear (1977) found that in Eastern Europe, the number of young women enrolled in engineering majors approaches that of young men. On the other hand, in most Western societies engineering is regarded as a masculine profession to which women may have difficulty adjusting. In fact, Souter and Winslade (in Kelly, 1976) found that in Russia women were so accepted as engineers that Russians had difficulty understanding the lack of women engineers in other countries.

Although reports indicate that women have gained equality in science and engineering in the USSR, their situation is not ideal. Although the number of women in science is impressive, more women than men are found in the lower levels of the scientific professions, a situation common throughout the world (Pfafflin, 1982). Only 10 per cent of the academicians, corresponding members, and professors in

Russia are women (Lapidus, 1978). As Table 8.3 shows, only a small percentage of Russian women scientists are members of scientific organizations such as the USSR Academy of Science. In Russia and other Eastern European countries, proportionately more women are found in the lower ranks in scientific and technological positions.

Hungary

Turi (1980) described the situation for women in science in Hungary. Before World War II, a fairly large number of girls entered universities to study math, chemistry, pharmacy, and medicine. However, after receiving a degree in mathematics, a woman usually had only two career options: teacher or insurance mathematician. Options for women graduating in science were equally limited. After World War II women were admitted to technical universities in much larger numbers, yet Hungary's women, then and now, are not readily accepted into positions in experimental research or in industrial technology. For example, only 28.2 per cent of the research scientists in Hungary are female (Turi, 1980; Tosi, 1975). In an attempt to remedy this situation, one-third of Hungary's women graduate students are granted scholarships to further their education (Turi, 1980).

Hungarians have, however, placed greater emphasis on their children's science education than have citizens of many other nationalities. Comber and Keeves (1973) report on the IEA (International Association for the Evaluation of Educational Achievement) which surveyed science education in nineteen countries during the 1970s. The IEA data indicate that, within each country, males outscore females in biology, chemistry, and physics. However, girls in some countries score higher than do boys in other countries. For example, Hungarian girls score higher in biology than boys of every country except Hungary (Comber and Keeves, 1973; Kelly, 1981). Kelly (1981) has analyzed the IEA data pertaining to students' attitudes toward science to detect reasons for gender differences in science achievement. In examining the attitudinal data, Kelly (1981) has found that, of all countries surveyed, Hungarian children have the most positive attitudes toward science. Hungarian boys and girls also have been reported to be actively involved in science hobbies and activities. According to Simpson's (1977) work in seventeen countries, student attitudes correlate more highly with achievement in science than with achievement in other subject areas. Hungarian girls' science achievement supports Simpson's findings, since they have the most positive attitudes. Nevertheless,

Hungarian boys still out-perform Hungarian girls on all of the science achievement tests. Hopefully, Hungarian educators will investigate ways to translate the positive attitudes towards science, espoused by Hungarian girls, into improved achievement levels in science by girls.

Poland

Compared with the four other countries tabulated in Table 8.6, a higher percentage of Poland's undergraduate students in science are women. Prior to World War II, women accounted for less than 5 per cent of Polish technology students. By 1981, women comprised 45 per cent of all students in two year programs and 30 per cent of students in four year programs at the Institute of Technology (Chivers, 1984). Lewicka (1975) accounts for the higher percentage of women in the Polish work force by referring to Poland's history after World War II.

> Losses were particularly heavy among the intellectual leaders, who were deliberately exterminated ... Consequently, at the beginning of the post-war period, education at all levels was staffed mainly by elderly teachers or young people who were inadequately trained. Women played a considerable part in the efforts made to rectify this situation (p. 155).

Table 8.6.   *Percentages of Women Enrolled in Undergraduate Science Programs in Five Countries*

	Biology	Chemistry	Physics
Eastern countries			
Poland (1971–72)	83	66	43
East Germany (1974)	41.8	45.2	—[a]
Western countries			
Canada (1976)	40	29	15
Britain (1978)	44	21	10
Developing countries			
Burma (1975–76)	61	46	50

Note: Adapted from Shaffer, 1981; Thein, 1980; Ferry, 1982.
a No data available.

Role and Status of Women in Science in Various Developing Nations

In examining the role of women in science and technology in developing countries, one must consider several factors: educational programs and policies; economic structure, labor market, and working conditions; cultural, socioeconomic, and religious ideologies; and the role that science plays within the boundaries of each country. Although there are notable exceptions, women are often found in low-paying, less prestigious, relatively unskilled occupations in the formal labor market of most developing countries due to a complex array of economic, historic, social, and cultural institutions (Tadesse, 1982). Industrialization comprises only a small proportion of the total sector of the economies of those countries. Women often occupy the 'nonsupervisory "feminine" occupations such as nursing and elementary school teaching' (Tadesse, 1982, p. 24) as well as food and textile positions and as public employment. Smith (1978) reports that many women in the developing countries live as American women did in the 16th and 17th centuries, which implies primarily an agricultural/domestic existence. We shall assess their more traditional role in agriculture-based science and their newer roles in developing scientific industries.

Women's Role in Agriculture

Although women traditionally have been involved in agriculture in developing countries, the influx of agricultural technology into those countries has not necessarily improved women's status or working conditions. One report describes the situation in the following way.

> New techniques based primarily on know-how such as application of fertilizer or the use of improved seed varieties, obviously do not carry an inherent sex designation for utilization. But to a certain degree, the acceptance and use of improved agricultural methods depends on education. And unequal education for the sexes with primarily boys sent to school or boys remaining in school longer than girls, creates an ever widening gap between the sexes (Deere, 1977, in Tadesse, 1982, p. 87).

Tadesse (1982) emphasizes the importance of women in agriculture in Africa, Latin America, and Asia. While men in Africa migrate to industrial opportunities in the cities, mines, or ports, labor by women accounts for 60 per cent to 80 per cent of the cultivation of foodstuffs. Likewise, 75 per cent to 85 per cent of Asian women, living in rural areas, spend an inordinate amount of time involved in agricultural activities. In Latin America, men migrate seasonally to plantations, mines, or other industries to seek additional income. This seasonal migration leaves women to tend to the family's agricultural activities. Finally, Tadesse reports a direct relationship between women's participation in agriculture and regional development. If new technology has not been incorporated into an area, then more women are found as permanent agricultural labors. For example, in Swaziland, a recent need for scientific and technological labor has opened up science education opportunities for women. However, it is too soon to determine the impact of such programs (Makubu, 1984). Historically, women were found in:

agriculture
food processing
family care
education
health services (Makubu, 1984).

Since women are the primary agriculturalists in many developing regions, one might expect little discrimination with regard to extension services and education. Unfortunately, this is not the case. Women from developing countries have unequal access to new information and techniques. Srinivasan (1982) points out the importance of agriculture and related activities in Mexico as well as the role played by women in farming, yet only 5 per cent of Mexican agricultural scientists and technicians are women. Clearly, women's role in agriculture in developing countries has not provided them with increased opportunities.

Women's Role in Science and Technology

The current status of women in science in Mexico reflects the trends found in the rest of the developing world. Srinivasan (1982) reports that only three persons in 100,000 in research and development branches of science are women. Overall, women account for only 20 per cent of Mexican scientists and technologists. In specific disciplines, 34.7 per cent of physicians, 21.6 per cent of natural scientists, 8.6 per cent of physicists, and 6.7 per cent of engineers are women. According to one source, 'Primary and secondary school teaching, medicine, nutrition, and social sciences tend to attract women, and women find that they have better chances of finding employment in these areas rather than in hard-core science and technology' (Srinivasan, 1982, p. 122). This situation reflects the fact that there are no specific programs aimed at increasing or encouraging female participation in vocational, technical, and professional courses and careers in Mexico (Srinivasan, 1982).

India and Burma have been able to produce a number of women who have excelled in the sciences (Ghosh, 1975; Thein, 1980). In Burma, 50 per cent of the surgeons and physicians are women. In addition, at one of Burma's universities, women comprise 42 per cent of the teaching staff (Thein, 1980). This situation may be the result of favorable timing. As explained by Thein, 'Whereas the Western scientific establishment has existed and been dominated by men for centuries, science in Burma came into being only in the years after World War II. Men have not yet had the time to entrench themselves' (p. 15). Historical development, therefore, may be a factor which has allowed fairly equal access to science careers for men and women in Burma.

A second factor may be the structure of the Burmese society itself. Unlike many Western societies, the Burmese society has a matriarchal foundation in which women retain their individuality after marriage. For example, women retain their own surnames and property (Thein, 1980). This tradition may have resulted in more equal treatment in the Burmese scientific enterprise as well. Despite favorable conditions, there are still scientific fields in which Burmese women are inadequately represented. They include forestry, geology, dentistry, and veterinary medicine (Thein, 1980). Girls hoping to enter those fields must have school grades superior to those of their male peers.

Educational opportunities in many countries are related to an individual's socio-economic status. Although the number of girls enrolled in Indian schools has increased, many girls still leave school at the elementary level (Tadesse, 1982; Razafy, 1969). In India, a girl's education may place an added financial strain upon her family which must provide a larger dowry so that an educated daughter may marry a man of equal or higher educational level (Jones, 1980). However, among urban, middle, and upper class families, a girl's education is respected for the prestige it carries (Jones, 1980; Gonzalez, 1984).

In the Philippines, one researcher has related the high proportion of educated and professional women to cultural and social differences between the Philippines and other nations (Useem, 1984). She reports that at the college level more women than men pursue degrees and that more than half of university faculty (including administrators and scientists) are female. In addition, a study of Filipino research scientists who have published indicated that 40 per cent are women. In addition, 68 per cent of all Filipino chemists are women. She attributes these high proportions to the extended family support network as well as to social structure provided by individual barrio priests. However, she notes that the high proportion of women scientists in academia reflects the lack of opportunities for them in industry and the military. Positions in more lucrative positions are filled by men (Useem, 1984).

One problem in educating girls to be scientists in developing countries may be the curriculum. Courses 'suitable for women' such a sewing, childcare, and embroidery are based on the view that many girls will leave school for domestic duties. 'Thus, the educational system, both formal and informal, preselects women away from scientific and technological subjects and continues to reproduce the sexual division of labour and resultant subordination of women' (Tadesse, 1982, p. 103). However, Egypt, Lebanon, Chile, and some Arab countries are encouraging girls to seek technical careers by providing training and encouraging employment (Tadesse, 1982; Adibe, 1981; Galai, 1970). For example, some Egyptian schools offer an Al-Ahram science club for students interested in developing scientific knowledge and talent through out-of-school activities. Small laboratories are set up for use by the students after school hours to enhance their understanding of science and to acquaint them with seminars and conferences held in Egypt and abroad. The Al-Ahram science clubs are formed in conjunction with the International Coordinating Committee for the Presentation of Science and the Development of Out-of-School Scientific Activities (ICC). ICC is a UNESCO sponsored program which offers scientific opportunities for children in fifteen developing countries (Galai, 1970).

A national project in Thailand is attempting to develop scientific expertise among its most exceptional high school students. For three years, commencing in 1983, thirty upper secondary school students will be selected for special training and advanced study in science. Selected on the basis of science aptitude, knowledge, and attitudes, these students will enroll in special after school science activities, attend summer science camps, and receive free undergraduate and graduate educations. Among the first twenty-nine participants are seven girls. Although limited in number, some Thai girls are receiving the best science education their country can offer (Kahle, 1984).

Educational opportunities for women are increasing throughout the world. For example, in 1970, women constituted 46 per cent of the student body at the University of Chile. In Japan, Western Europe, Latin America, and some Arab counties, women now comprise 33 per cent of all university students (Gonzalez, 1984; Dorozynski, 1976). In the Philippines and India, 55 per cent and 22 per cent, respectively, of university students are women (Gonzalez, 1984). Unfortunately, many well educated women may be employed in clerical and other low-paying jobs. Gonzalez (1984) claims that in Egypt, China, and India women who are trained in medicine, law, and agriculture cannot locate jobs outside of government clerical offices.

Different Careers, Same Status

Although women in Eastern European countries, the Soviet Union, and some developing nations seem to have easier access to scientific and technical training, many experience difficulties on entering and progressing in scientific careers. Generally, women throughout the world are relegated to positions of lower status in science-related careers. Research suggests that once women enter a profession in considerable numbers, society's image of that profession changes. The profession is characterized as one that is less deserving, less creative, and less prestigious (Tosi, 1975; Janson-Smith, 1980). For example, a medical doctor in the United States is highly respected; only one out of ten physicians in the US is a woman. In the Soviet Union, seven out of ten doctors are women, and a medical doctor in the USSR has lower status than does his/her American counterpart. Curran (1980) summarizes this situation in the following way, 'If a job has high status, in terms of money, power, and prestige, you can be sure it will be a job done predominantly by men' (p. 23). Deckard (1975) further illustrates this situation by examining the medical profession in the United States. The data in Table 8.7 illustrate that as the pay and prestige of a medical speciality increase, fewer women are found in that speciality.

Table 8.7. Percentages of Women in/and Corresponding Rank of Various Medical Specialties, 1969

Specialty	Rank of specialty (out of 10) in pay and prestige	Percentage of women in field
Surgery	1st	1
Psychiatry	7th	11
Pediatrics	9th	19

Source: From Epstein in Deckard (1975).

In addition, McCabe (1965) suggests that women are more apt to be accepted in a career field when there is a shortage of people to fill the available openings. Recently this phenomenon can be noted in the computer industry. McCabe's assertion is reinforced by the observation that the Eastern European countries may have more women in science primarily due to the loss of labor experienced during recent wars (Tosi, 1975). With a decrease in the number of men, women's contributions have been essential to rebuilding some societies. Although women in Eastern European societies often pursue science in greater numbers than do their Western sisters, they also have failed to gain access to the upper ranks of management in industry or in academia. The same situation is analogous in some Asian countries such as Burma and the Philippines.

Shaffer (1981) cites an interesting contrast between the attitudes prevalent in Eastern and Western Europe by examining the attitudes toward women in science found among East and West Germans. In 1960, faculty members at West German institutions of higher education were surveyed regarding their attitude toward female students. Sixty-four per cent were opposed to women studying at higher institutions of learning and maintained that 'female students, in spite of greater diligence, have less ability' than do male students (p. 129). In addition, they saw women as being unable to think critically, and as lacking in creative-productive abilities, initiative, and self-confidence.

Stereotypically, then, women of West Germany are considered less capable than men, even though a recent survey found that faculty in West German universities viewed women students as being more diligent than men, more eager to learn, more receptive, and equipped with a better memory. However, the faculty opinion suggests that those attributes are less important in the scientific professions than are the attributes of logic, intelligence, and critical thinking. Although negative attitudes persist, West German women have entered medical school in impressive numbers. They comprised over thirty per cent of the medical students in the 1978–79 school year (Shaffer, 1981).

The faculty of East Germany's universities do not share the attitudes of West German faculty. Efforts are being made to encourage women students to obtain higher educations (Shaffer, 1981). In East Germany, more and more women can be found in the 'masculine' disciplines, although there is still a high proportion of women in typical 'female' careers such as in nursing, teaching, and social work.

Women from developing and developed countries may respond differently to society's resistance to their entrance into primarily 'masculine' fields. Ghosh (1975), for example, states that women in developed countries often face discrimination in scientific research, engineering, medicine, and business management with 'a certain restlessness, a discontent with their subordinate role in the working world, and a willingness to organize themselves and protest against sexual discrimination' (p. 102). Women in developing countries may face societal resistance to their entry into scientific and technological careers with more tolerance and accommodation than do women from the West. Sex discrimination is far from absent in developing countries, but women may accommodate to it more easily than they do in developed ones.

Summary

Throughout the world, women have less access to education than men, and when they do have access to education beyond the primary level, they are likely to be channeled into traditional women's fields, such as domestic science or education, not into the more technologically oriented training programs (Pfafflin, 1982, p. 180).

Throughout developing and developed countries, certain similarities exist for women. First, women are still predominantly employed in 'feminine' professions. This is true for the most technologically advanced countries as well as for developing nations. Second, the Eastern European countries have more women in science; but, as in Western European countries as well as in the US and Australia there are few women found in the upper ranks of management and research. Third, throughout the reports, there is an underlying theme that women's domestic responsibilities hamper their chances for significant contributions to science. For example, Professor Trina Rabokobolskaya, head of the Cosmic Rays and Space Physics Department at Moscow University, has said that 'When a scientist is a woman it is still difficult, though possible, to combine serious research with the woman's traditional role of wife, mother and homemaker' (in Ferry, 1982, p. 13). Pfafflin (1982) explains further that limited resources allocated for domestic consumption require Soviet women to spend an inordinate amount of time and energy in maintaining a household. Along the same line, Saraga and Griffiths (1981) state, 'In education and employment women can never be equal to men as long as the sexual division within the family, and the family itself, remains unchallenged' (p. 91). They suggest that some challenges have resulted in changes in Russia, but not in other Eastern European countries. They add that Britain's leaders still stress the importance of the family.

Bunting (1965) suggests that before society can plan a woman's education and her employment in the sciences, society must first provide an optimum environment for women in the work force, observe the results, and finally proceed to make accommodations and changes. In other words, until we reduce the anxiety women feel regarding their 'split' careers (home and work), a judgment cannot be made as to whether women scientists can be as productive, creative, and responsible as male scientists are. Alison Kelly emphasizes the importance of women's contributions to society, stating: 'Science changes society — without women in scientific roles many technical and cultural changes will be decided by men. Women need to have an equal opportunity to debate the controversial issues as well as men' (Kelly, 1981, p. 13). It is hoped, therefore, that women scientists around the world will work to gain equal access to the higher, decision-making ranks of scientific professionals.

Finally, every nation must face the issues raised concerning their own cultural, social, and economical values. The following six steps are appropriate for instigating change:

1　Greater access to education for all young people.
2　Increased teacher awareness regarding the loss society suffers by the underachievement of girls in science.
3　Increased funding for scientific and technical education for women.
4　Legislation which eliminates practices discriminatory to women scientists.
5　Provision of more opportunities for girls to meet young women scientists, engineers, and technologists as well as the elimination of sex-biased materials from textbooks.
6　Increased numbers of women involved in policy making, government panels, and international delegations as well as scientific organizations.

Without the changes suggested above, the number of girls in science courses and the status of women in science careers will remain lower than those of their male counterparts. The pool of young women, as yet untrained in science, is an international resource which must be tapped to help nations, both developed and developing, reach their full technological potential.

Note

1 SMAIL, B., and KELLY, A. (1984) *Sex Stereotypes and Attitudes to Science Among Eleven-year-old School Children*. Unpublished manuscript, Manchester Polytechnic, Manchester, England.

References

ADIBE, N. (1981) 'Arab women in science and technology', *Arab Perspective*, pp. 39–42.

BUNTING, M.I. (1965) 'The commitment required of a woman entering a scientific profession,' in MATTFELD, J.A. and VAN AKEN, C.G. (Eds.), *Women and the Scientific Profession*, Cambridge, MA, MIT Press.

CHIVERS, G. (1984) 'A comparative international study of intervention strategies to reduce girls' disadvantages in science and technology education and vocational training.' Paper given at Interests in Science and Technology Education, IPA Symposium, Kiel, Germany, April 12–16.

CHIVERS, G. (1981) 'Loughborough University Women in Engineering Project,' in RAAT, J.H., HARDING, J., and MOTTIER, I. (Eds.), *Contributions GASAT Conference 1981*, Eindhoven, the Netherlands, Eindhoven University of Technology.

COMBER, L.C., and KEEVES, J.P. (1973) *IEA Report Science Education in Nineteen Countries*, New York, Wiley.

CURRAN, L. (1980) 'Science education: Did she drop out or was she pushed?' in Brighton Women & Science Group (Eds.), *Alice Through the Microscope*. London, Virago.

DAUBER, R., and CAIN, M. (1981) 'Women, technology, and the development process,' in DAUBER, R. and CAIN, M. (Eds.), *Women and Technological Changes in the Developing Countries* (AAAS Selected Symposium, No. 53), Boulder, CO, Westview Press.

DECKARD, B.S. (1975) *The Women's Movement: Political, Socioeconomic, and Psychological Issues*, New York, Harper & Row.

DE RAAF, I. (1981) 'Special activities for women entering engineering at Eindhoven University,' in RAAT, J.H., HARDING, J., and MOTER, I. (Eds.), *Contributions GASAT Conference 1981*, Eindhoven, the Netherlands, Eindhoven University of Technology.

Distribution by sex of principle scientific awards and membership in academies of science (Table) (1975) *Impact of Science on Society*, 25, 2, p. 154.

DOROZYNSKI, A. (1976) 'Science, technology and education in the Arabian peninsula', *Impact of Science on Society*, 26, pp. 193–8.

FERGUSON, J. (1981) 'The science education of girls in Canada: A strategy for change,' in RAAT, J.H., HARDING, J., and MOTTIER, I. (Eds.), *Contributions GASAT Conference 1981*, Eindhoven, the Netherlands, Eindhoven University of Technology.

FERRY, G. (1982) 'How women figure in science,' *New Scientist*, 95, pp. 10–13.

GALAI, S. (1970) 'Current trends of scientific activity in Arab and Islamic countries,' *Impact of Science on Society*, 20, pp. 173–4.

GHOSH, D. (1975) Comment, *Impact of Science on Society*, 25, pp. 99–104.

GONZALEZ, N.L. (1984) 'Professional women in developing nations: The United States and the Third World compared,' in HASS, V.B., and PERRUCCI, C.C. (Eds.), *Women in Scientific and Engineering Professions*, Ann Arbor,

University of Michigan Press.

GOODYEAR, A.S. (1977) 'Engineering education today, comment,' *Impact of Science on Society*, 27, p. 348.

HOFFMAN, L. (1981) 'Consequences for science education based on the results of girls' learning interest,' in RAAT, J.H., HARDING, J., and MOTTIER, I. (Eds.) *Contributions GASAT Conference 1981*, Eindhoven, the Netherlands, Eindhoven University of Technology.

JANSON-SMITH, D. (1980) 'Sociobiology: So what?' in Brighton Women & Science Group (Eds.), *Alice Through the Microscope* London, Virago.

JONES, C. (1980) 'Observation on the current status of women in India,' *Internatonal Journal of Women's Studies*, 3, pp. 1–18.

JONES, J.M., and LOVEJOY, F.H. (1980) 'Discrimination against women academics in Australian universities,' *Signs: Journal of Women in Culture and Society*, 5, pp. 518–26.

KAHLE, J.B. (1984) 'US/Thai cooperative project: Team leader report.' Final Report. Washington, DC, National Science Foundation, International Section.

KELLY, A. (1975) 'Why do girls study biology?' *School Science Review*, 56, pp. 628–32.

KELLY, A. (1976) 'Women in science: A bibliographic review,' *Durham Research Review*, 36, pp. 1092–1108.

KELLY, A. (Ed.) (1981) *The Missing Half*, Manchester, England, Manchester University Press.

KELLY, A., and WEINREICH-HASTE, H. (1979) 'Science is for girls?' *Women's Studies International Quarterly*, 2, pp. 275–93.

LAPIDUS, G.W. (1978) *Women in Soviet Society*, Berkeley, CA, University of California Press.

LEWICKA, H. (1975) 'The professional woman in modern Poland (an interview),' *Impact of Science on Society*, 25, pp. 155–8.

McCABE, R. (1965) 'The commitment required of a woman entering a scientific profession (panel discussion),' in MATTFELD, J.A. and VAN AKEN, C.G. (Eds.) *Women and the Scientific Profession*, Cambridge, MA, MIT Press.

MAKUBU, L. (1984) 'Impact of women on international development,' *Abstracts of Papers, AAAS Annual Meeting*, New York, May 24–29. Washington, DC, American Association for the Advancement of Science.

MOTTIER, I. (1981) 'Girls and physics textbooks in the HANDROVER-project,' in RAAT, J.H., HARDING, J. and MOTTIER, I. (Eds.) *Contributions GASAT Conference 1981*, Edinhoven, the Netherlands, Eindhoven University of Technology.

MUTSCHELLERS, F.K. (1969) 'Science education in West Germany,' in GILLON, P., and GILLON, H. (Eds.) *Science and Education in Developing States*. New York, Prager Publishers.

PFAFFLIN, S.M. (1982) 'Some reflections on women in science and technology after UNCSTD,' in D'ONOFRIO-FLORES, P.M. and PFAFFLIN, S.M. (Eds.) *Scientific-technological Change and the Role of Women in Development*,

Boulder, CO, Westview Press.

RAAT, J.H. (1981) 'Intervention strategies in favour of girls' achievement in science (physics) and technology in the MENT-project,' in RAAT, J.H., HARDING, J., and MOTTIER, I. (Eds.), *Contributions GASAT Conference 1981*, Eindhoven, the Netherlands, Eindhoven University of Technology.

RAZAFY, E. (1969) 'Integration of science and education in Africa,' in GILLON, P., and GILLON, H. (Eds.) *Science and Education in Developing States*, New York, Praeger Publishers.

ROMAO, I. (1981) 'The changing attitudes project,' in RAAT, J.H., HARDING, J., and MOTTIER, I. (Eds.), *Contributions GASAT Conference 1981*, Eindhoven, the Netherlands, Eindhoven University of Technology.

SARAGA, E., and GRIFFITHS, D. (1981) 'Biological inevitabilities or political choices? The future for girls in science,' in KELLY, A. (Ed.) *The Missing Half*, Manchester, England, Manchester University Press.

SCOTT, J.P. (1981) 'Science subject choice and achievement of females in Canadian high schools,' *International Journal of Women's Studies*, 4, pp. 348–61.

SHAFFER, H.G. (1981) *Women in the Two Germanies: A Comparative Study of a Socialist and a Non-socialist Society*, New York, Pergamon Press.

SIMPSON, R.D. (1977) 'Relating student feelings to achievement in science,' in ROWE, M.B. (Ed.) *What Research Says to the Science Teacher*, (Vol. 1). Washington, DC, National Science Teachers Association.

SJØBERG, S., and LIE, S. (1981) 'Girls and physics,' in RAAT, J.H., HARDING, J., and MOTTIER, I. (Eds.) *Contributions GASAT Conference 1981*, Eindhoven, the Netherlands, Eindhoven University of Technology.

SMAIL, B., WHYTE, J., and KELLY, A. (1981) 'Girls into science and technology: The first two years,' in RAAT, J.H., HARDING, J., and MOTTIER, I. (Eds.) *Contributions GASAT Conference 1981*, Eindhoven, the Netherlands, Eindhoven University of Technology.

SMITH, D.R. (1978, Summer) 'Women still denied access: Can you help?' *Journal of the National Association of Women Deans and Counselors* (NAWDAC), pp. 162–164.

SRINIVASAN, M. (1982) 'The impact of science and technology and the role of women in science in Mexico,' in D'ONOFRIO-FLORES, P.M., and PFAFFLIN, S.M. (Eds.) *Scientific-technological Change and the Role of Women in Development*, Boulder, CO, Westview Press.

TADESSE, Z. (1982) Women and technology in peripheral countries: An overview, in D'ONOFRIO-FLORES, P.M., and PFAFFLIN, S.M. (Eds.), *Scientific-technological Change and the Role of Women in Development*, Boulder, CO, Westview Press.

THEIN, M.M. (1980) Women scientists and engineers in Burma, *Impact of Science on Society*, 30, pp. 15–22.

TOSI, L. (1975) 'Woman's scientific creativity,' *Impact of Science on Society*, 25, pp. 105–14.

TURI, Z.F. and colleagues. (1980) 'Women technical graduates in Hungary,'

Impact of Science on Society, 30, pp. 23–32.

USEEM, R.H. (1984) 'The anomoly of a scientific community without gender inequality: An empirical study of Philippines women scientists,' *Abstract of Papers, AAAS Annual Meeting*, New York, May 24–29, Washington, DC, American Association for the Advancement of Science.

WEINREICH-HASTE, H. (1981) 'The image of science,' in KELLY A. (Ed.) *The Missing Half*, Manchester, England, Manchester University Press.

WU, CHIEN-SHIUNG. (1965) 'The commitment required of a woman entering a scientific profession (panel discussion),' in MATTFELD J.A. and VAN AKEN, C.G. (Eds.) *Women and the Scientific Profession*, Cambridge, MA, MIT Press.

9   *A View and A Vision: Women in Science Today and Tomorrow*

Jane Butler Kahle
Professor of Biological Sciences and Education
Purdue University

> Our children and our students are participants in a complex process that equips one sex with math, science, and technical skills indispensable to functioning in the adult world, while it fails to encourage the same development in the other sex. Although the lives of individual women are the most negatively and directly affected, the loss to both sexes is immense. (Skolnick, Langbort, and Day, 1982, p. 2.)

Factors contributing to the under-representation and under-utilization of women in science have been analyzed in research studies in both the United States and Western Europe. We have attempted to synthesize the findings in order to present a view of women scientists and would-be scientists. Explanations, presented in the preceding chapters, for gender differences in the development and productivity of scientists have ranged from differences in elementary science classroom activities to inequalities in graduate school research groups to differential memberships in professional associations. Although the lack of women in advanced science courses and in scientific and technological careers is accepted, the causes of this situation are argued. We have seen that some maintain that society itself is responsible; others argue that biological differences are the reason; and still others suggest that Western culture is at fault. The pervasiveness of the problem and the complexity of its underlying causes defy simply solutions. Although other writers have examined historical, sociological, and cultural factors contributing to the under-representation of women in science, we have presented a more narrow view, focusing on education, professional, and employment factors in the hope that changes may be made in those areas which will increase the number of women in science as well as improve their role and status.

A View of Today

In this final chapter, we will review our findings and observations in order to present a view of women in science today. We will also suggest changes which may lead to an enhanced and expanded vision of women in science tomorrow. New or additional information will be provided as we examine educational, professional, and employment obstacles facing women in science courses and careers.

Educational

The obstacles which girls and women must overcome to receive comparable scientific educations are many. In Chapter 2 Matyas discussed some of the results of the third National Assessment of Educational Progress survey of science (NAEP, 1978b). She contrasted and compared the responses of boys and girls in order to assess any gender differences. She described gender differences both in achievement levels in science and in attitudes toward science and scientists.

In 1981–82 a limited national survey of science was conducted by researchers at the University of Minnesota. This survey, supported by the National Science Foundation, followed the procedures developed by and used the items constructed by the National Assessment of Educational Progress. It tested a national random sample of 18,000 9-, 13-, and 17-year olds and its findings may be compared to those of earlier national science assessments (Hueftle, Rakow and Welch, 1983). Using the results of those two surveys, the achievement levels of girls fell from between 1.6 to 2.5 points below the national mean for each cognitive item in 1977 to 1.7 to 6.7 points below the national mean for cognitive items in 1982 (NAEP, 1978b; Hueftle, Rakow, and Welch, 1983). In addition, preliminary results of the Second International Science Study showed that boys outperformed girls at both the fifth- and ninth-grade levels (*Report on Education Research*, 1984).

In addition to assessing science achievement, both the 1977 and 1982 national assessments also included items concerning attitudes toward, opportunities in, and beliefs about science. Analyses of these items help to explain the lower science enrollment levels of girls. For example, in 1977, girls' responses to National Assessment items concerning opinions of science classes and feelings toward science as a career were consistently negative. As presented in Chapter 2, in 1977 female responses to attitudinal items overwhelmingly documented poorer attitudes toward science, less understanding of science, and less interest in scientific careers. Unfortunately, the situation had not improved in 1982. Hueftle *et al.* (1983) stated that females showed significant declines in their attitudes toward science and in their beliefs that science could solve world problems. In addition, Willson's (1983) meta-analysis of studies concerning science attitudes and achievement revealed that poor attitudes were directly related to lower achievement levels, especially among high school students. Observations, discussed in Chapter 3, indicated that attitudes were closely related to enrollment in elective science and mathematics courses.

The status of advanced courses in science and mathematics as elective courses in high school curricula coupled with negative female attitudes toward both subjects may explain differential enrollment data. Although Benbow and Stanley (1980, 1983) argue that quantitative ability, not differential enrollments, accounts for boys achieving higher than girls do on the quantitative portion of the Scholastic Aptitude Test, other researchers refute that claim. For example, Pallas and Alexander (1983) document the existence of different enrollment patterns, and Fox (1980) suggests that comparisons of mathematical ability between 17-year-old boys and girls are truly comparisons between students with three to four years of mathematics and those with 1-2 years of math. In a typical school district girls may outnumber boys in advanced eighth grade math classes, but by twelfth grade twice as many boys as girls are enrolled in calculus (Skolnick *et al.*, 1982).

The persistent barrier of mathematics to the access and success of women in science is taking on a new ramification. According to a recent *Report on Education Research* (1983), Stanford University researchers have turned up evidence of a 'growing gender gap' in computer literacy. More elementary school boys, compared with girls, report having home computers, and they are three times as likely as girls to attend computer camps. Linn (1984) reports that girls become more scarcely represented as the cost of the computer camp goes up. Furthermore, computer software is slanted toward typical male interests. Out of seventy-five titles, appropriate for middle-school children, more than a third have been rated as being exclusively for males. Only four titles, 5 per cent, have been identified as being of primary interest to girls. The titles of the feminine programs are: 'Typing Tutors', 'Consumer Buying', 'Typing Fractions', and 'Counting Calories'. As boys and girls progress through elementary school to high school the 'computer gender gap' widens. Among eighth grade algebra students, half the boys, but less than a fifth of the girls, report having home computers (*Report on Education Research*, 1983).

In the past ten years, considerable research has been done on factors affecting the achievement and enrollment levels of girls in mathematics, and those of us concerned about science can learn from those studies. Much of the work has been summarized by Fox (1980), who identifies the following factors as those which may influence girls and boys to study, or not to study, mathematics in high school: counselors, teachers, parents, peers, self-confidence, perception of usefulness, perception of math as masculine, and tracking or grouping. She suggests general directions for change, including observational studies, remediation, intervention, and prevention of negative attitudes. Stage and her colleagues at the Lawrence Hall of Science have found that two factors, math achievement and perception of its future usefulness, are the best predictors of continued math enrollment (Davis and Humphreys, 1983). Stage (1982) proposes a systems approach for intervention programs which, in order to be successful, must be:

1 sought out by interested teachers,
2 supported by the entire community, and
3 based upon collaborative efforts between schools and universities.

Fortunately, recent intervention programs have been successful. The percentage of women who expect to take four years of high school math in the US has risen from 37 per cent to 57 per cent in the last decade, and the two point rise in the 1982 Scholastic Aptitude Test's quantitative scores may be attributed to gains made by women.

However, lack of training in mathematics may explain the findings that although females comprise over one-third of all students in higher education in England, they account for less than one of every seven undergraduates in physics and for fewer than one in six in chemistry (Head, 1979). In the United States, differences in number of mathematics courses may explain why twice as many college-bound senior boys as girls have had three years of physical science. Typically, a girl who wishes to pursue advanced science courses finds her fear that girls don't become scientists reinforced clearly by the ratio of boys and girls in the classroom (Skolnick *et al.*, 1982). As they explain, 'While for boys math and science successes can heighten masculine self-esteem, girls must walk a tight rope between pride in their achievement on the one hand and a threat to their feminine self-image and social support on the other' (Skolnick *et al.*, 1982, p. 42). Recent studies in England have concluded that girls lose interest in science as they progress in school. Likewise, they do not view science as a worthwhile subject to study (Wilce, 1983).

The National Assessment data, the research concerning women in mathematics, and the study discussed in Chapter 3 all suggest that different science teaching strategies must be adopted from kindergarten through graduate school. For example, laboratory and demonstration activities which provide spatial experiences may enhance the spatial abilities of females. As Treagust (1980) points out. 'A student with poorly developed spatial abilities should not be taught primarily by verbal means' (p. 95). Skolnick *et al.* (1982) suggest a variety of science activities which range from recognizing similar shapes from different perspectives to converting two-dimensional patterns to three-dimensional objects and vice versa. Recently Linn and Petersen (1984) have reported few differences between boys' and girls' spatial abilities. This finding, discussed in Chapter 2, suggest that research bias, rather than inherent differences, may account for some of the reported discrepancies. In other words, some obstacles to women in science may be artifacts of our society and culture rather than intellectual barriers. Girls, therefore, must be encouraged to enroll in mechanical drawing, industrial education, and other courses which have activities designed to develop spatial abilities.

As the successful teachers described in Chapter 3, demonstrated, laboratory groups must be carefully structured so that girls actually work with science apparati. Laboratory activities, career information, and non-sexist teaching behaviors and learning materials ameliorated the masculine image of science and led to higher enrollments in elective courses. In addition, Chapter 3 suggested that science teachers as well as school counselors and administrators must guard against unconscious bias in their presentation of science courses and careers and in their scheduling of elective courses. For example, physics should not conflict with honors English, advanced French, or other courses traditionally selected by girls. The written and verbal use of non-sexist language in the classroom as well as in texts and other instructional materials was identified as important. The textbook analysis in Chapter 3 and the historical perspective in Chapter 1 indicated that the contributions of women must be portrayed seriously in narrative as well as illustrative materials. The inclusion of women photographed in lab coats was inadequate; their real contributions must be discussed. Our studies suggested that if the repeated message from teacher and text was that scientists were males, adolescent girls, unsure of their femininity, would shy away from science or, if enrolled, would perform poorly.

However, changes had occurred in the last decade among students whose teachers have consciously or unconsciously used specific teaching behaviors or techniques. Briefly, Chapter 3 concluded that teachers who successfully encourage girls in science:

* maintained well-equipped, organized, and perceptually stimulating classrooms;
* were supported in their teaching activities by the parents of their students and were respected by current and former students;
* used non-sexist language and examples and included information on women scientists;
* used laboratories, discussions, and weekly quizzes as their primary modes of instruction and supplemented those activities with field trips and guest speakers;
* stressed creativity and basic skills;
* recommended the need for further courses in science and mathematics;
* provided information about science-related career opportunities and the prerequisites for them;
* avoided sex-stereotyped views of science and scientists which are fostered by texts, media, and many adults;
* developed spatial-visual skills through activities and exercises.

Although these strategies were effective in encouraging all students to continue in science, they were disproportionately effective for girls. As Table 9.1 shows, the percentage of girls in case study classes who responded positively to selected items assessing attitudes toward science

Table 9.1.   Percentages of Females Responding Positively to Selected Items in 1977 NAEP Survey and 1983 NABT Survey

	1977	1983
How often have science classes made you feel . . .		
curious	48.1	86.1
stupid	52.3	49.7
confident	16.4	60.2
successful	24.1	63.5
How often do you like to go to science classes?		
often	31.9	67.2
Would you like to work in a science-related job?		
yes	28.6	47.2
Would you like to know more about jobs in a science-engineering field?		
yes	41.5	54.3

Source: Kahle, J.B. (1983) *Girls in School: Women in Science* (Final Report: #83–3D–0798), Washington, DC, National Science Board, National Science Foundation, October.

classes and careers was double the national percentage. However, for each item, higher percentages of boys in case study classrooms responded positively. The common theme throughout the classroom observations, reported in Chapter 3, was that good teachers made a difference. Each teacher, successful in encouraging girls as well as boys to continue in science courses and careers, was also an exceptional teacher. For example, they were active professionally, were involved in science activities in their communities, were skilled in a variety of instructional techniques, and were informed about science careers and their educational requirements.

Recently, our findings and analyses have been substantiated by a national report by Berryman (1983). She points out that in 1980 a randomly selected male in an appropriate age group was three times as likely as a randomly selected female in the same age group to receive a quantitative PhD. Furthermore, she states that the recent increase in women in quantitative areas has been due to an increase in the total number of doctorates awarded to women rather than to changes in female field choices. Although women earned increasing percentages of quantitative degrees at the bachelor's, master's, and doctoral levels during the 1970s, their rate of increase in quantitative degrees has been slower than their rate of increase in other degrees.

In her discussion of potential scientists and engineers she analyzes how people enter the technological and scientific pool and why they exit from it. She refers to this process as 'the pipeline' to scientific and technological careers. Furthermore, she suggests major policy implications, based on her findings, which are directed toward increasing access to the pipeline and, eventually, to the pool. According to Berryman, *The pool appears to reach its maximum size prior to senior high school, subsequently declining in size through graduate school . . .* [N]umerous studies show that *after high school migration is almost entirely out of, not into, the pool* (p. 67; author's italics). In contrast with all non-Asian minorities, women leave the pipeline at its end. As she states, 'For females the losses are concentrated at the end of the pipeline: at the PhD level' (p. 5). Relative to men, women have had stable and lower losses at the high school level in the most recent decade (1970–80). However, for both women and all non-Asian minorities[1] entrance to the pool basically occurs during the high school years. As Berryman states, 'Female science BA graduates tended to select science as their major field of interest somewhat later than their male counterparts, but by grade 12 even 90 per cent of the women had chosen science as their major field' (p. 66). Berryman states that high math achievement at grade 9 results in increased interest in quantitative careers during high school. As both Tables 9.2 and 9.3 illustrate, girls consistently choose fewer courses in mathematics during high school. According to Table 9.2, approximately equal percentages of girls and boys enroll in required academic math courses; however, boys select elective, advanced courses far more often than girls do. The percentage

Table 9.2. Percentage of Mathematics and Science Courses of High School Seniors by Sex and Course Title, 1980

Course	Male	Female
Algebra	79	79
Geometry	58	55
Algebra II	51	47
Trigonometry	30	22
Calculus	10	6
Chemistry	39	35
Physics	26	14

Source: National Center for Education Statistics (1981) *High School and Beyond: A National Longitudinal Study for the 1980's,* Washington, DC, p. 5. Adapted from *Women and Minorities in Science and Engineering* (NSF 84–300) (1984) National Science Foundation, January, p. 154.

of boys, compared with girls, is also higher in general and vocational mathematics courses, as shown in Table 9.3 Berryman suggests, therefore, that 'the key for women is pre-high school interests ... [which] trigger an educational sequence that ultimately results in underrepresentation among quantitative doctorates' (p. 84). She ponders the affect of attitudes toward science on enrollments, and our studies, reported in Chapter 3, indicate that positive attitudes are related to enrollments. Berryman attributes the decline in students' positive attitudes toward science between grade 3 (50 per cent) and grade 8 (20 per cent) to the

Table 9.3. Percentage of High School Seniors Taking Three or More Years of Mathematics and Science by Sex

Curriculum	Total	Male	Female
Mathematics			
Academic	55	63	47
General	22	26	18
Vocational	18	22	15
Science			
Academic	41	48	35
General	13	15	10
Vocational	9	11	7

Source: National Center for Education Statistics (1981) *High School and Beyond: A National Longitudinal Study for the 1980's,* Washington, DC, p. 5 and unpublished data. Adapted from *Women and Minorities in Science and Engineering* (NSF 84–300) (1984) National Science Foundation, p. 153.

fact that the overwhelming majority of elementary teachers are women who are less apt to like science or to feel competent in it.[2] In addition, Berryman maintains that the high school tradition of offering advanced math courses as electives interacts with girls' lesser interest in math to close doors to technological and scientific careers. According to the data presented in Table 9.4, less than half as many women as men indicate that they intend to select a quantitative college major either as high school seniors or as college freshmen. Furthermore, this disparity in numbers has been stable over almost a decade. As Berryman succinctly states. 'Removing choice during high school would preserve it after high school' (p. 84). The culminative effect of both negative attitudes and lower enrollments results in fewer girls entering the pool and more women exiting the pipeline, in comparison with their male counter-

Table 9.4.   Percentage of High School Senior SAT Test-Takers and of College Freshmen[a] Who Plan a Quantitative Major[b] by Sex and Year (1973–81)

Year	SAT test-takers[c]		College freshmen[d]	
	Men	Women	Men	Women
1973	36.0	15.0	26.3	9.1
1975	31.5	11.8	26.2	9.2
1977	29.6	9.8	27.5	9.2
1979	31.7	10.8	29.5	9.6
1981	35.7	13.2	32.6	11.6

Source: From Berryman, Sue E. (1983) *Who Will Do Science?* New York, The Rockefeller Foundation, November, p. 87.
Note: a College freshmen are defined as full-time, first-time freshmen.
        b Quantitative majors include biological sciences, computer sciences, engineering, mathematics, and physical sciences.
        c Source: College Entrance Examination Board (1973, 1977, 1981) *National College-Bound Seniors.*
        d Cooperative Institutional Research Program at the University of California at Los Angeles, *The American Freshman: National Norms* series for 1973, 1975, 1977, 1979, and 1981.

parts.
   Using data from the *National Longitudinal Study of the High School Class of 1982*, Dunteman *et al.* (1979) analyzed factors affecting the choice of a college science major.[3] Although they introduced several reasonable factors, for example, family and community orientations, they could not eliminate the negative effect of being a woman on the selection of a college science major. They found that even when men and women were statistically equated, women were 10 per cent less likely than men to choose a science major. From this and other studies Berryman concludes that:

Information on the dynamics of the scientific/mathematical pool and on the causes of women's underrepresentation identify early college tracking and an early orientation toward quantitative careers and training as important precursors of college entry and choice of a quantitative college major (p. 89).

Berryman suggests that the policy implications of the findings are two-fold. First, if interests drive skills and those in turn lead to access and retention in scientific training and careers, then interventions must include early career exposure. Second, if skills drive interests, then interventions must stress math skills. The study discussed in Chapter 3 indicates that high school teachers, successful in retaining women in Berryman's hypothetical pipeline, stressed basic skills (graphing, metrics, conversion formulas, etc.) and provided scientific and technological career information to their students.

As one moves up the educational ladder, the discrepancies between boys and girls in high school mathematics and advanced science courses result in differences in educational opportunities and rewards. Although half of all undergraduate enrollments and degree recipients are women, in 1981 women earned only 35 per cent of all (including advanced) science and engineering degrees (NSF, 1984). As Table 9.5 shows, in 1979 women received over 40 per cent of bachelor degrees awarded in the biological sciences, mathematics, psychology, and social sciences. Yet their percentages fell dramatically in each area between the BS and PhD degree. Between 1970 and 1981 women increased their proportion of all master's degrees by more than half and their proportion of doctoral degrees by almost a third. However, in the same time period women increased their percentage of all science and engineering master's degrees by 10 per cent (from 17 per cent to 27 per cent) and doctoral

Table 9.5. *Earned Degrees by Selected Fields: United States, 1971, 1979*

Field	Percentage awarded to women 1971				1979	
	BS	MS	PhD	BS	MS	PhD
Biological sciences	29.3	33.8	16.3	40.2	37.6	25.6
Computer and information sciences	13.6	10.3	2.3	28.0	18.8	12.7
Engineering	.8	1.1	.6	8.3	6.1	3.4
Mathematics	38.1	29.3	7.8	41.6	34.6	16.7
Physical sciences	14.0	13.4	5.6	22.5	18.1	11.3
Psychology	44.7	37.2	24.0	61.2	54.1	40.0
Social sciences	37.0	28.3	13.9	41.5	35.3	28.8

Source: The 1971 data are adapted from Brown (1979); and the 1979 data from National Center for Education Statistics.

degrees by 12 per cent (from 9 per cent to 23 per cent) (NSF, 1984).

During the same time period the propensity of men and women to finish graduate programs (attainment rate) also can be assessed. In 1972 and 1981 the attainment rate in both master's and doctoral programs was higher for men. However, during that decade, it fell for men and rose slightly for women. In 1982 the attainment rates for MS degrees were 14.7 per cent for women and 21.4 per cent for men; for PhD, degrees the attainment rates were 4.3 per cent for women and 6.4 per cent for men (NSF, 1984). In analyzing these apparent gender differences in attainment rates, the National Science Foundation applies two parity indexes, the results of which are shown in Table 9.6. The first parity index PI^1) assesses the extent to which the field distribution of women approximates that of men. A ratio of plus or minus 1.00 indicates the proportion of women respective to that of men. According to the data in Table 9.6, women earn proportionate to men more PhD degrees in both the life and social sciences. However, their attainment rate has dropped in the last decade. The second parity index (PI^2) measures the propen-

Table 9.6. Parity Indices for Women Earning Doctoral Degrees in Science and Engineering Fields: 1970 and 1982

Field	PI^1	PI^2
1970		
All science/engineering	—	.462
Physical science	.598	.387
Mathematical science	.685	.216
Engineering	.043	.800
Life science	1.402	.581
Social science	1.815	.539
1982		
All science/engineering	—	.744
Physical science	.583	.714
Mathematical science	.523	.336
Engineering	.200	1.270
Life science	1.132	.930
Social science	1.566	.893

Source: Committee on the Education and Employment of Women in Science and Engineering, National Research Council. Adapted from *Women and Minorities in Science and Engineering* (NSF 84–300) (1984) National Science Foundation, January, p. 174.

Notes: Parity indices are defined as follows:
  PI^1 = Percentage of women PhDs in field/
      Percentage of women PhDs in all fields.
  PI^2 = Percentage of women PhDs in field/
      Percentage of women PhDs in field (lagged t years).
  where:
    t = 6 yrs for physical sciences and engineering
    t = 7 yrs for life sciences and all science/engineering
    t = 8 yrs for mathematical and social sciences.

sity of women baccalaureates to complete a doctorate within a particular time period relative to a comparable sample of men. A ratio of more or less than 1.00 indicates whether women, in comparison to men, are more or less likely to complete a timely doctorate. Only in engineering are women more likely than men to complete a timely doctorate, according to the PI^2 ratios presented in Table 9.6. In 1982 the overall PI^2 index in science/engineering fields was 0.74, which indicated that women were 74 per cent as likely as men to complete quantitative doctorates within a specific time interval (NSF, 1984).

Matyas suggests in Chapter 4 that different types of graduate support may result in women taking longer to complete advanced degrees. Proportionately, more women, compared with men, hold teaching assistantships. It was suggested in Chapter 4 that teaching, in comparison with research, assistantships divert students' time and energies from their research and dissertations. However, a comparison of type of support by field with the parity indexes shows that that conclusion does not hold true today. In 1982, 57 per cent of male and 45 per cent of female graduate students received university support. Among the men, 35 per cent were teaching assistants while 55 per cent held research assistantships. The women were about equally divided between teaching and research assistantships. Women are more likely to be concentrated in fields such as the social sciences in which most of the support is awarded as teaching assistantships. Men, on the other hand, are concentrated in the physical sciences ($PI^1 = .583$) in which more research assistantships are found. In 1982 wide differences in type of support were not found between men and women in the same fields. For example, among doctoral students in the physical sciences 64 per cent of the men, compared to 59 per cent of the women, held research assistantships. Likewise, approximately half of both male and female graduate students in psychology and social sciences held teaching assistantships. The NSF report maintains that since women who received support were twice as likely as men (42 per cent vs 21 per cent) to be in psychology and social science, differences in type of support reflect field distributions (NSF, 1984).

Professional

As women enter scientific and technological careers, other factors affect their success. In Chapter 4 the author discussed the importance of a post-doctoral experience on a scientist's professional development. Again, recent data suggest improved opportunities for women. Between 1973 and 1981 the number of postdoctoral positions awarded to women increased by an annual rate of 16 per cent (from 900 to 2800). During the same time period, the number of men receiving postdoctoral positions rose at an annual rate of 6 per cent (from 4800 to 7800). However, the proportion of women postdoctorates in 1973 was 15 per cent, while in 1981 it rose to 26 per cent (NSF, 1984). As expected from the data in Table 9.6, most of the female gains were in the life and social sciences. When both male and female postdoctoral workers responded to questions assessing their reasons for taking such positions, they gave the following reasons:

1   in order to gain research experience;
2   in order to work with a particular scientist or research group;
3   in order to transfer to a new or related field;
4   inability to secure a permanent position (NSF, 1984).

Although few cited the last reason, changes have occurred; for in chemistry more men than women mentioned it.

Although it is positive that more women now secure postdoctoral positions, it is less positive that they stay in them longer. Twenty-three per cent of women, compared to 18 per cent of men, remain over three years in a postdoctoral position (NSF, 1984). Both men and women cite difficulties in finding employment as the reason for a long postdoctoral experience. However, other factors, identified and discussed in Chapter 4, which disproportionately affect the careers of women are found. For example, more married than single women stay in prolonged postdoctoral positions. Furthermore, although more than half of all women, compared to a fourth of all men, cite geographical constraints as part of their decision to accept a postdoctoral position, 70 per cent of married, compared with 30 per cent of single women, mention geographic constraints.

In addition to obstacles to equal education and postdoctoral positions in science, other professional barriers have been identified. For example, women scientists have less access to the rewards system. Lilli Hornig (1984) states that the explanation for the under-representation of women in the 1984 Sloan Foundation grants to young science faculty is inadequate. A representative of the Foundation has stated that the low proportion of women (6 out of 90 or 7 per cent) reflects the lack of women in most scientific disciplines. According to Hornig, 13 or 14 recipients should have been women, based on the number and quality of women PhDs in the relevant doctoral pool. She notes that the assumption that there are few women scientists is outdated and, furthermore, that young women scientists may be led to believe that they are ineligible for professional rewards. She suggests, on the other hand, that women's lack of representation may be traced to lack of employment opportunities (Hornig, 1984).

Employment

Many women in science today believe that although women have equal access to scientific training, sustained inequities remain in the work place, both academic and industrial. In 1982, 25 per cent of all scientists and 3.5 per cent of all engineers were women. These women were concentrated in the life (15 per cent), social (28 per cent), and psychological (42 per cent) sciences (NSF, 1984). Recently, women scientists have entered academia at increasing rates. For example, between 1975 and 1980 they constituted 25 per cent of newly hired faculty, while between 1967 and 1972, 17 per cent of newly hired faculty were women (Bruer, 1983). In Chapter 4 it was noted that more women, compared with men, scientists were hired by teaching colleges and universities. However, Bruer notes that at the fifty top universities, as ranked by research and development expenditures, women accounted for all net growth in science faculty at the assistant professor level. Furthermore, he states that similarly trained male and female scientists tend to be in equally prestigious academic institutions seven to thirteen years after receiving the PhD. However, he notes that their career development differs; that is, neither similarities in training nor in initial positions result in comparable scientific careers for men and women. Bruer reports that a 1981 survey of 1970–74 doctoral recipients showed the following percentages of men and women at the various academic ranks:

Professional rank	Men	Women
Full	17.2%	9.2%
Associate	50.8%	38.2%
Assistant	17.3%	31.7%

Source: Bruer (1983).

For this same group, 13.3 per cent of the men under 35 were tenured, compared with 9.4 per cent of the women. For those between 36 and 45 years of age, 80.8 per cent of the men, compared to 62.7 per cent of the women, were tenured or on tenure track (Bruer, 1983). Bruer concludes that women continue to face career development difficulties and that more attention must be given to elementary and secondary education as well as to the effects of societal differences before women can have equitable careers. As he states, 'The apparent discrepancy between the success rates of women and men in science is a tragedy for women and a loss of intellectual power for the nation' (Bruer, 1983, p. 1339).

Bruer's conclusions are supported by the most recent evaluation of women in science and engineering by NSF (1984). According to that report, twice as many men, compared to women, who hold quantitative PhDs were employed as scientists (22 per cent vs 11 per cent). However, in 1981, 60 per cent of female scientists, compared to 35 per cent of male scientists, reported less than ten years of professional experience. Although the National Science Foundation report attributes differences in the number of men and women who were managers in industry or who held tenure status in academia to lack of experience and youth, it states that sex differences endure even when men and women scientists are matched by type of institution, age, degree, etc. (NSF, 1984).

In addition to slower career advancement, women also face salary inequities. Average annual salaries, reported in Table 9.7, show inequities in favor of men in every field at both bachelor and master's degree levels, except for a B.S. in engineering. Considering salaries paid to all PhDs in science and engineering, women earn 75 per cent of what men earn. Furthermore, between 1975 and 1981 while the salaries of women PhDs increased 56 per cent, those of men increased 70 per cent (NSF, 1984). In academia, the average faculty woman made $5,374 less than the average man in 1983, and the pay gap has grown steadily since 1977–78 when the difference was about $3,500 (*On Campus with Women*, 1984). In industry, the average woman doctorate took home a paycheck that was $8,600 less than her male counterpart in 1981 (*On Campus with Women*, 1984). Overall, in 1982 women scientists earned 80 per cent of the salaries of their male counterparts.

Another way to compare equality in the work force is to assess participation rates of men and women scientists.[4] Although the gap between male and female participation has narrowed at all degree levels, differences exist. NSF reports the following participation rates for scientific personnel for 1981:

Degree	Women	Men
PhD	92%	96%
MS	95%	98%
BS	92%	97%

Source: NSF (1984).

Table 9.7. *Average Annual Salaries of Recent Science and Engineering Degree Recipients by Field of Degree and Degree Level*

Field of degree and degree level	Total employed	Men	Women
Total science/engineering			
Bachelor's	$20,700	$22,200	$17,300
Master's	27,400	28,500	23,800
Total science			
Bachelor's	18,000	19,200	16,300
Master's	25,500	26,700	22,900
Physical science			
Bachelor's	21,600	22,400	19,400
Master's	25,900	26,000	25,400
Mathematical science			
Bachelor's	22,100	22,800	20,800
Master's	28,700	29,800	26,400
Computer science			
Bachelor's	24,900	25,500	23,500
Master's	32,700	33,200	31,100
Environmental science			
Bachelor's	21,800	22,600	18,900
Master's	30,600	30,800	29,700
Life science			
Bachelor's	15,900	16,400	15,900
Master's	19,900	20,100	19,600
Psychology			
Bachelor's	14,800	16,700	13,700
Master's	22,100	23,500	20,300
Social science			
Bachelor's	17,000	17,700	15,900
Master's	23,400	24,900	20,000
Engineering			
Bachelor's	26,500	26,400	27,400
Master's	30,900	31,000	29,800

Source: National Science Foundation, unpublished data. Adapted from *Women and Minorities in Science and Engineering* (NSF 84–300) (1984) National Science Foundation, January, p. 151.

Note: Salaries computed only for full-time employed individuals. Data include combined 1980 and 1981 graduating cohorts exclusive of full-time graduate students. These are preliminary data, subject to revision.

Overall, 93 per cent of all women scientists and engineers are employed, compared to 76 per cent of all college educated women. However, when male and female scientists and engineers are queried about their reasons for not working, their responses differ. Most revealing, 71 per cent of men, compared with 11 per cent of women, scientists give retirement as a reason for unemployment. On the other hand, 36 per cent of women scientists, contrasted with 1 per cent of the men, give family responsibilities as a reason. Women continue to carry the burden of family and child responsibilities. A 1983 survey indicated that out of ten everyday tasks, men and women share equally only one, handling finances. Furthermore, Grey (1983) reports that a study of 232 married, professional women indicated that 77 per cent of them felt frequent strain in handling their personal and professional lives.

The effect of children on the participation rate of women scientists, however, is negligible in comparison to its effect on women in general. For example, the following data were collected for participation rates of women with children.

Ages of children	All Women (1981)	All S/E* Women (1982)	PhD S/E Women (1981)
Less than 6 years	48%	94%	90%
6–17 years	63%	82%	95%

*S/E indicates science and engineering

Women scientists and engineers, therefore, do not drop out of the work force after they have children. Yet, throughout this book we have seen that that bias has permeated the way others interpret and respond to the education and employment of women as scientists.

Although women scientists and engineers may not voluntarily leave the work force, they have fewer opportunities to enter it and more difficulties in remaining in it. Over the past decade, twice as many female as male scientists persistently have reported unemployment. Furthermore, as noted in Chapter 4, women have had more difficulties in finding scientific and technological jobs. They are both underemployed (working in non-scientific jobs or working part-time) and under-utilized (both unemployed and underemployed). According to the NSF (1984) report, in 1982, 6 per cent of all women scientists and 3 per cent of all PhD women scientists were under-employed, as compared to 3 per cent of all and 0.07 per cent of PhD male scientists. In the same year, 9 per cent of all female scientists were under-utilized, while 5 per cent versus 1 per cent of women and men doctoral scientists were under-utilized.

It is difficult to assess all the factors leading to lower employment and less career development for women, although throughout this book we have tried to identify them. However, when women scientists are asked why they leave science, certain factors stand out. According to Table 9.8, women doctoral scientists leave science and engineering jobs because of lack of opportunities (S/E not available) and geographical constraints (location preference). While the same reasons are given by all women scientists, they also state that they are 'promoted out' and that they leave for 'better pay.' Indeed, for full career opportunities and development, a woman scientist may have to leave science.

Table 9.8.   Reason for Non-Science and Engineering Employment of Women

Reason for non-science/engineering employment	Total non-science/engineering employed	Total	Men	Women
		Total scientists/engineers — 1982		
		(Percentages)		
Total	426,600	100	100	100
Prefer non-science/engineering	113,400	26.6	25.2	32.0
Promoted out	28,800	6.7	7.9	2.3
Better pay	42,100	9.9	9.7	10.3
Location preference	16,800	3.9	3.7	4.8
Science/engineering not available	41,200	9.7	7.7	17.2
Other/no report	184,400	43.2	45.7	33.4
		Doctoral scientists/engineers — 1981		
		(Percentages)		
Total	19,900	100	100	100
Prefer non-science/engineering	5,000	25.1	25.1	25.0
Promoted out	2,800	14.2	15.4	7.3
Better pay	900	4.6	4.9	2.9
Location preference	400	1.9	1.8	2.5
Science/engineering not available	1,400	7.1	6.1	12.6
Other/no report	9,400	47.2	46.7	49.7

Source: National Science Foundation, unpublished data. Adapted from *Women and Minorities in Science and Engineering* (NSF 84–300) (1984) National Science Foundation, January, p. 116.

Note: Detail may not add to totals because of rounding. Total science/engineering data are preliminary, subject to revision.

This observation is supported by recent data concerning minority women scientists. Although Chapter 5 presents the difficulties minority women face in obtaining a scientific or technological education, once it is achieved their opportunities are great. Black women scientists, for example, have higher labor force participation rates than either white or Asian women scientists.[5] According to NSF, the following participation rates were found in 1982 for women:

Race	All S/E	PhD.
Black	97%	95%
White	93%	91%
Asian	94%	95%

Source: NSF (1984).

In addition, black female scientists and engineers are more likely than their white or Asian counterparts to report management positions in industry (18 per cent, 15 per cent, and 11 per cent respectively). Although 69 per cent of black women quantitative PhDs, compared with 60 per cent white and 42 per cent Asian, were found in tenure track positions in academia, the same proportion of black and white women (less than two-fifths) report holding tenure. Last, Asian women scientists and engineers report higher salaries than all other women. The current status of women in science, regardless of race, may be seen in one statement in the Executive Summary of *Women and Minorities in Science and Engineering* (NSF, 1984):

> Labor market indicators . . . for women scientists and engineers vary in a fairly narrow range by race. For women [scientists and engineers], differences by race are less than the differences by sex within all racial groups. Hence, it appears that gender is a more significant factor than race in labor market behavior of minority women in [science and engineering] fields (p. viii).

Summary

In the past decade, dramatic gains have been made in equal education as well as in equal opportunities for women scientists and engineers. Few young women doctorates today would receive the well-meaning advice which a young Barbara McClintock gave to a new PhD recipient, Leonie Piternick in 1934.[6] During a visit to Stanford University, arranged by George Beadle, McClintock ate dinner with a group of graduate students. As Dr. Piternick recalls, at the end of a bottle of wine, she mentioned that she, too, wanted to do research. Dr. McClintock focused on her and remarked that since Piternick was a tall girl with long legs she would have opportunities to marry. McClintock urged her to do so because she would then have a husband who could support her while she did research. Piternick would not, continued McClintock, have to fight for grants to support her work. The professional and personal toll that McClintock's continual struggle for support to do research took is well documented in Keller's (1983) biography.

Today we would not advise a young woman scientist to marry in order to do research. However, we would have to mention the unequal status of women in scientific and technical fields in both academia and industry, and to caution her about limited child care facilities. Realistic advice also would include a comment about the disproportionate amount of time professional as well as non-professional women spend in child and home care tasks. The view of the status and role of women in science today is brighter than it has been in the past. Most educational barriers have been effectively removed. However, some obstacles have been resistant to change and these must be eradicated in the future.

A Vision of Tomorrow

> In my younger days, when I was pained by the half-educated, loose, and inaccurate ways which we [women] all had, I used to say, 'How much women need exact science,' but since I have known some workers in science who were not always true to the teachings of nature, who have loved self more than science, I have now said, 'How much science needs women.' (Maria Mitchell's presidential address to the Third Congress of Women in 1875, in Rossiter, 1982, p. 15).

Over a century ago, Maria Mitchell addressed the role of women in science. Her life and her work were attempts to remove one of the persistent barriers to women in science; that is, the sex role stereotyping of women and of science. Rossiter (1982) describes the situation in the following way.

> [T]he standard argument against women's participation in science stressed their supposedly delicate physical health, small and light brains, and greater 'Variability' in all measureable physical and mental traits. This 'evidence' purported to show either that women were not physically able to undertake the study of science, or, if they did, that their bodily and mental functions would be so seriously impaired as to endanger the future of the entire race (p. 13).

Sex role stereotyping affects women interested in pursuing educations or careers in science in two ways. First, as Rossiter discusses, the feminine stereotype of women as emotional, nurturing, artistic, and delicate suggests that women are not suited to science. Second, the masculine stereotype, analytical, pragmatic, logical, and rigorous, which is commonly used to describe science as masculine, may dissuade young women from entering science. Sex role stereotyping in either form is a persistent and subtle barrier to women in science.

Sex role stereotyping, however, is a pervasive societal factor affecting both the role and status of women in science and in other occupations. It is anticipated that as women's roles increase and their status improves, the stereotypes which have served to limit their potential contributions to science will gradually disappear. These changes provide us with a vision of tomorrow. Evidences of actual change or of concrete directions for change may be found in the three aspects of women in science we have selected to examine; that is, in educational opportunities, professional advancements, and employment concerns.

Education

The initial findings of a major English project, Girls into Science and Technology (GIST), propose specific changes in the science education of primary (elementary) students (Kelly, Smail, and Whyte, 1984). The researchers suggest that one way of encouraging girls' interests in physical science is to stress its relevance to human biology. They propose that elementary school science follow the lead of television science in order to find alternative ways of teaching popular topics. For example, although eleven-year-old girls, according to the GIST findings, are uninterested in finding out how machines work, they may be introduced to moments and forces by studying how muscles work (Kelly *et al.*, 1984).

In addition, Kelly and Smail (1984), find that girls are far more likely than boys to see science as sex neutral; that is, equally suitable for both sexes. Their findings suggest a positive change in the image of science among eleven-year-old girls. However, the same positive change is not noted for boys, who endorse items such as 'learning science is more important for boys than for girls' and 'girls who want to be scientists are a bit peculiar.' These results suggest new intervention strategies. As Kelly *et al.*, (1984) state:

> Boys' opinion that science is not really for girls may have profound effects on their female classmates; boys can be a powerful reference group for girls. If they think that girls are out of place in science lessons they may ridicule the girls and drive them away. So, attempts to change the masculine image of science — discussions, role models, and information about women in science — should be directed to boys at least as much as girls (p. 10).

Kelly *et al.* continue to present and discuss a range of sex differences found among science-related experiences reported by eleven-year-old boys and girls. For example, boys report far more 'tinkering experiences' with common tools (saws and screwdrivers), with everyday objects (bicycles and cars). and with manipulative toys (construction and electrical kits). They maintain that such experiences have a profound effect on later science studies, and they recommend that primary curriculum include 'tinkering experience' for all students in the future (Kelly *et al.*, 1984).

Another change suggested by the findings of Kelly *et al.* concerns the effect certain subjects and tasks have on the ability of girls to do science. They report that both boys and girls taking technical craft studies, compared with those taking non-technical subjects, increased their scores on spatial tests.[7] In addition, girls in the technical groups showed the greatest improvement in visualizing the top of a block model. As they state:

> The results ... indicate that there may be a whole range of skills, many of which are not specifically taught in the primary school, in which girls are, on average, relatively deficient. Many schools already recognize the importance of remedial reading provision and the building of language skills across the curriculum. Perhaps similar attention should be paid to the identification and development of the range skills involving eye-motor coordination and visuo-spatial ability (p. 14).

The GIST findings suggest changes in the organization and presentation of science in primary (elementary) schools. They recommend intervention strategies aimed at changing boys' image of science as inappropriate for girls and curriculum changes directed toward providing girls' experience with specific skills.

Certainly, the English vision of a primary education, which will expand the horizons and aptitudes of girls concerning science, is supported by the results of the study reported in Chapter 3. The American study of secondary school science, too, projects a vision of tomorrow's science classrooms. Based on the commonalities identified among teachers successful in encouraging girls to continue in science, four recommendations are made for the future.

1 Science textbooks must go beyond the token inclusion of women. For example, Barbara McClintock's work should be included in every chapter concerning genetics.
2 Special workshops, projects, and activities are still needed to eliminate sex-bias in and sex role stereotypes of science. These

activities also need to include boys, who demonstrate more stereotypic views than girls do.

3   The professionalism and education of the observed teachers suggests the need for continual, supported educational opportunities for secondary teachers. Whatever the format, the courses, workshops, or seminars must present solid science, include career information, and emphasize activities and topics which appeal to girls.

4   Teachers must be relieved of having to expend inordinate amounts of time and energy on securing supplies and equipment as well as space to store them. Then, they can direct their efforts to improving classroom instruction, to encouraging students in science, and to developing basic skills among their students.

The vision of tomorrow's elementary and secondary science education, then, includes specific recommendations for change. Recalling Berryman's (1983) admonition that the 'key for women is pre-high school interests' (p. 84), the suggested changes should increase the number of girls interested in science, the ability of girls to do science, and the acceptibility of science as a woman's career.

Professional

In 1983, Oberlin College (Ohio), American's first coeducational institution, celebrated its 150th year. *The New York Times* chronicled the festivities, noting in particular the advances academic women have made in that period. However, the same article reported that Alice Rossi, professor of sociology at the University of Massachusetts, identified one continuing problem; that is, the dearth of female faculty members, particularly in the senior ranks. While Oberlin College, according to Professor Rossi, had 23 per cent women on its faculty, only 4 per cent of its full professors were women. On the other hand, at Smith College, a women's college, 23 per cent of the full professors were women and six departments were headed by women. Research reported in this book suggests that the lack of women full professors at Oberlin is reflected at most coeducational institutions. As the article concluded, 'And so, the revolution begun 150 years ago at Oberlin over the questions whether young women should be educated in college now turns to the role of women in educating them and their male classmates' (Hechinger, 1983, p. 20)

In the future, the number of women entering science careers should affect their opportunities for professional advancement. For example, both a substantial pool for potential full professors, managers, and administrators will be formed, and a broader group for collaborating, supporting, and mentoring other young women scientists will be available. Table 9.9 shows the dramatic increases in numbers of women entering science and engineering professions between 1972 and 1980.[8] In addition, in one year (from 1983 to 1984) the percentage of women who were full time pharmacy students rose 2 per cent to a total of 34 per cent. Furthermore, the rapid influx of women into engineering schools in the United States resulted in women receiving 13.2 per cent of all bachelor's degrees in engineering in 1983. Of particular importance is the fact that women engineers entered graduate study at approximately the same rate as U.S. white males did (*Manpower Comments*, 1984).

Table 9.9. *Percent Female of Science and Engineering Occupations in 1972 and 1980*

Occupation	Percent Female	
	1972	1980
Computer Specialists	16.8	25.7
Engineers	0.8	4.0
Life and physical scientists	10.0	20.3
Chemists	10.1	20.3
Social Scientists	21.8	36.0

Source: Table 675 US Bureau of the Census, *Statistical Abstract of the United States: 1981* (102nd edition), Washington, DC, 1981, p. 402.

(Adapted from Berryman, S.E. (1983). *Who Will Do Science?* New York, The Rockefeller Foundation, p. 87.)

Although we have seen that the salaries and promotions of women in science are consistently lower and slower than those of men, it is hoped that increases in the pool of women scientists will affect both conditions. One way in which change may come is that there will be more women who function as principal investigators on funded projects, who head university search and screen committees, who adjudicate tenure decisions, and who serve as section managers or as department heads. Due to low numbers, the impact of women in such positions cannot be assessed. However, the lack of women in higher positions may have contributed to the finding that letters of recommendation for women applying for assistant professorships, in comparison with those for men, are seldom found to be 'very positive' but are often categorized as 'ineffective' (AAC, 1983).

One measure of the professional advancement of women in academia in the United States has been the number of women appointed as chief executive officers (CEO) or presidents of colleges and universities. The American Association of Colleges reports that between 1975 and 1982 that number rose from 148 (5 per cent of the total) to 247 (9 per cent of the total). Although a slow increase, real gains can be found. For example, in 1975 two-thirds of the women CEO's were in religious orders, while religious orders accounted for only one-third of the women in 1982 (AAC, 1983). When these figures were released in 1982, the Office of Women in Higher Education pointed out that the rate of increase was approximately one new women chief executive per month. Continuing at that rate and assuming that the number of institutions remained constant, the Office estimated that women would hold 16 per cent of all college presidencies by the year 2000.

Although the projected gains were modest, indications are that they will not be met. For example, only seven women joined the ranks of chief executive officers between 1983 and 1984. The lack of women appointed to those positions was not due to lack of openings. A recent survey of college and university presidents and chancellors by the College and University Personnel Association found that 54 per cent of the 1300 chief executives responding had held their current position less than five years (*Manpower Comments*, 1984). In both academia and industry, women continue to be underrepresented in administrative and/or managerial positions. Their absence is illustrated by the data concerning chief executive officers. The demographics suggest that factors other than job turnover affect the promotion of women to positions of power and prestige and that their numbers in such positions will not increase adequately in the foreseeable future.

There are evidences, however, that women themselves are attempting to improve their professional situations. One way is by mentoring. Women scientists as well as other women professionals are beginning to understand both the impact and importance of being a mentee and of serving as a mentor. Gornick (1983) eloquently explains the situation in the following way.

> It is the rare women scientist who feels she can simply ignore or deny the question of women in science, no matter how intellectually or psychologically distant from it she may feel; there is embarrassment rather than self-assurance if one is not a partisan. The issue of women in science is alive in the profession. Those who address the issue directly are numerous and their positions are endless (p. 147).

The term, mentor, is taken from Homer's *Odyssey*. King Ulyssees' trusted friend, Mentor, cared for and educated Ulysses' son in his absence. In addition, Mentor introduced the son to other leaders in order to insure him of his rightful place. Therefore, a mentoring relationship goes beyond skill development to include personal, professional and civic development. In academia, the model for mentoring has been the extended relationship that often develops between graduate student and professor. As Matyas points out in Chapter 4, graduate women have had less access to mentors. According to a special publication of the Project on the Status and Education of Women (1983), the problem of women both finding and serving as mentors is threefold.

1 Male faculty tend to select and affirm male students more frequently than they do female students.
2 The overvisibility of women students in some fields (due to their scarcity) may cause senior persons to avoid choosing a female protegee, whose career may be easily followed and whose success or failure will reflect on them.
3 The lack of senior women may lead to an overload of mentees as they are sought out by increasing numbers of junior women. This overload can affect the success of the mentoring relationship.

These three obstacles leading to a lack of mentoring relationships for young women caused one to lament,

> [T]his [lack of senior women faculty] to serve as professors or advisors had been the single most important deficit of the PhD 'experience.' I have no sense that my advisor and/or department supports my professional efforts, believes in my ability or cares whether or not I succeed. I would say this feeling is more pervasive with female students. (Project on the Status and Education of Women, 1983, p. 4).[9]

In order to improve the situation for tomorrow's female scholars, the Project on the Status and Education of Women (1983) recommends the following model programs.

> *Massachusetts Institute of Technology: An informal, institution-wide program which encouraged mentoring for all students, staff, and faculty. Some of its special features are:
> Fostering networks of women.
> Establishing close liasons between women's networks and top administrators.
> Training and guiding junior women to find their own sponsors.

*City University of New York: A project which matched women and minority faculty with little research experience with senior scholars with national reputations. Special features include:
> Presenting seminars by mentors about research.
> Matching mentors and mentees on basis of research interests.
> Providing support services for mentees (proposal writing, statistical methods, etc.)
> Giving visibility to the mentee on his/her own campus.

*HERS — New England (Higher Education Resource Services): A career cooperative model which provided a mutual support group as well as a personal network. Among its unique features are:
> Providing skills to obtain first academic position.
> Evaluating competencies necessary to advance professionally.

*State University of New York College at Cortland: A career development program for women students which included a three part model of coursework, advising, and role models. Its special aspects involve:
> Presenting a strategy course for credit.
> Providing intensive consultation between first-year women students and women faculty and administrators.

*Alverno College (Wisconsin): A peer advising program which was developed for women students. Its features include:
> Selecting and training second semester students to be peer advisors.
> Providing peer advisors with guidelines and sources of assistance.
> Offering peer advisors and their mentees back-up assistance from counselors and faculty.

If intervention programs during early grades continue to be successful, the number of women students choosing scientific majors will increase in the next few decades. These young women, however, may face personal obstacles in their advanced training and in the early stages of their careers. Since it is doubtful that adequate numbers of senior women faculty will be available as mentors, the alternate approaches, described above, provide a positive view for the future.

Although a mentor relationship may ease the professional adjustment and improve the professional options of a women scientist, it does not alleviate other constraints. For example, pragmatic concerns such as child care facilities affect the professional performance and, therefore, advancement of many working mothers. As Ellen Galinsky, a director of a project on work and family life at the Bank Street College of Education, has stated, 'Managers are generally aware of the issues in only extreme cases. They don't realize the toll the everyday issues, such as picking up kids from school, take on employees' (Johnson, 1984). In 1983, only 40 per cent of all two-year and four-year US campuses had some kind of child care facility, and only about 100 US corporations provided one (AAC, 1983; Johnson, 1984). In contrast, in 1983 over 60 per cent of American mothers with children under six worked outside the home. In addition to the lack of competent daily care, the stress of juggling a career with family responsibilities is amplified by emergencies such as a child's illness.

A vision of tomorrow, however, is provided by the current situation in Sweden where steps have been taken to foster family life. Since 1968, Sweden had had a governmental policy which attempts to foster economic independence for both men and women and to maintain family life. For example, Swedish parents receive a nine months leave and the right to return to one's position after the birth of a baby. The leave may be divided between the parents. However, since it became an option in 1983, less than 25 per cent of the eligible fathers have taken advantage of it. Swedish policies, also, provide up to 60 days' leave each year for child illness, and an extra two weeks leave when a child enters school or a day-care facility. In this case, fathers have shared the responsibility more equitably with mothers, since approximately equal numbers have taken child sick-leave.

Although such policies will alleviate many identified sources of stress for working mothers, they also may result in their increased productivity. A working mother of young children faces each day not knowing whether an emergency will interrupt her experiment, her data analysis, or her journal report. Plans to attend professional meetings may be aborted or simply not made due to problems with child care. Personal experiences attest to the toll both the uncertainty and the lack of concentration may cause on one's productivity. A colleague, noting the professional growth of a woman in the one year after both of her children left for college, asked about it.[10] She replied that her concentration was not interrupted by school plays or track meets, by emergency trips to hospitals, by serving refreshments at ball games, or by baking cookies for school dances. When those types of responsibilities are multiplied by the more fundamental needs of a young child (trips to doctors and to dentists, daycare, etc.), the productivity of a young professional women may be adversely affected.

Without adequate governmental or institutional support, the emerging pattern in the United States is for professional, dual career couples to postpone childbearing until the woman is well established in her career and the couple can personally afford quality child care. For example, when asked during a graduate seminar, a young women professor stated that she delayed her pregnancy until after her tenure decision.[11] She explained that she could not have completed the necessary research concommitant with child care responsibilities. Our vision of tomorrow, then, may include one of several outlooks: improved, accessible child care or lowered birthrates among professional women. Although other alternatives may emerge, precedents for these two possibilities exist.

The future professional life of a woman in science involves many diverse factors. In conjuring up a vision of it, we anticipate continued improvement in the early and secondary science education of girls with a concommitant increase in the numbers of young women with the prerequisite skills and aptitudes to pursue science majors at college. As these newly trained young women move into the professional world, more of them should be assisted by supportive mentor relationships. However, based on available data, our vision cannot include rapid professional advancement for these emerging young women scientists. Until the number of professional women in senior positions defuses the commonly held sex-stereotypes and until institutions accept responsibility for different scheduling patterns and for child care facilities, the professional development and advancement of young women in science will be partially constrained by societal barriers.

Employment

The obstructions faced by women scientists in the job market have been less subtle than the professional ones they have encountered. In the past, many women scientists simply could not obtain a scientific or technical position. Even today we find women scientists, compared with their male counterparts, underemployed and underutilized. According to recent data, progress is slow, particularly in some disciplines (*Manpower Comments*, 1983). For example, although women earned over 10 per cent of the doctorates awarded in chemistry between 1970–1 and 1982–3, the faculties of chemistry departments offering doctorates included only 4.1 per cent women in 1982–3.[12] Perhaps more disheartening is the fact that almost half of the 177 institutions offering doctoral studies in chemistry have no women on their faculties.

While women earn 25 per cent of the PhDs awarded in biochemistry, they make up only 8.5 per cent of the full-time faculty in biochemistry departments. Since their numbers have decreased during the past several years, employment opportunities seem dim in the future. Although employment opportunities for US women chemists in industry have improved, women who made up 8.1 per cent of the doctoral chemists in 1981, hold only 4.4 per cent of the chemical positions in industry (*Manpower Comments*, 1983). Employment opportunities in some areas of science continue to exclude women, and nothing indicates that major changes will be made in the future.

However, one fundamental change is occuring in the United States which eventually will affect the employment status of all women including that of female scientists. This change is the concept of pay based on comparable worth. Briefly, comparable worth theory goes beyond equal pay for equal work to include equal pay for different jobs of comparable value.

Before discussing comparable worth theory and its potential effect on the work force, let us consider its relationships to women scientists. Throughout this book we have noted consistent and widespread differences in the pay of male and female academics at all ranks and in the pay of men and women scientists in industry. However, we have not suggested that the women were doing different jobs, simply that their work was valued or rewarded less. The substantiated difference in male and female salaries in equal positions is affected by the permeating societal attitudes which undervalue 'women's work.' In this section, then, our vision of tomorrow will be a broad perspective on the changes which can accrue with wide acceptance of both the theory and the underlying assumption of comparable worth.

In the US in 1982, full-time working women earned an average of 62 cents for every dollar paid to men. This overall discrepancy is partly due to the fact that 80 per cent of the women in the work force are found in only 20 of the 427 job categories, identified by the US Labor Department (Lewin, 1984). This crowding of women into certain positions has created the 'pink collar' ghetto of women who support themselves, and often their families, by waitressing, clerking, nursing, etc.[13] In science a similar 'lab coat' ghetto consists of women, regardless of training, who settle for technician, instructor, and long-term postdoctoral positions. In spite of recent gains, Table 9.10 shows that women continue to be underrepresented in well paying science-related professions. As stated earlier, female scientists earn approximately 80 per cent of what male scientists earn.

One positive view of the future can be based upon what has

Table 9.10.   *Women and Minorities in the Sciences: Women's Proportion of Occupations*

	Percent Female	
Occupation	1970	1980
Engineers	1.7	4.6
Physicians	9.7	13.4
Veterinarians	5.3	13.3
Math/Computer Scientists	16.7	26.1
Natural Scientists	13.6	19.9
College Teachers	29.1	36.6

Source: Adapted from *Manpower Comments,* 21 (4), p. 16, 1984.

happened recently in Europe. Although little change has been made in the wage gap between American men and women in the last decade, Swedish women have increased their earning power by 17 per cent. Swedish women now earn 90 per cent of that of their male counterparts.[14] Perhaps Sweden's supportive family policies have helped more women reach their potential.

Another vision of the future includes the extension of comparable worth theory both across and within job categories. Supporters of the comparable worth theory say that the only way to eliminate the remaining pay bias is to revalue all jobs on the basis of the skills and responsibilities they require. Comparable worth involves formal job evaluations under a point factor system; this is, certain factors present in a job are represented by points. According to the document, *Comparable Worth: A Summary* (1983), factors include items such as skill, effort, responsibility, and working conditions, Jobs receiving equal points are considered to be of equal value and, therefore, receive equal pay. Examples of comparable worth positions by points and by existing salaries are shown in Table 9.11. According to the data in Table 9.11, all of the positions commonly held by women are undervalued and, therefore, underpaid. Overall, the 1974 comparable worth study of Washington state employees found that women's salaries were approximately 20 per cent lower than those of men in positions of comparable worth.

The 1974 comparable worth study in the State of Washington eventually led to the legal decision by the US Supreme Court that sex-biased wage discrimination claims need not be limited to equal pay for equal work. Consequently, Title VII of the Civil Rights Act of 1964 became the vehicle for achieving comparable worth action. Subsequently, major industries, the federal government, and several states have investigated their pay scales. However, the price for equality is high. It

Table 9.11. *Representative Jobs in Comparable Worth Evaluations by Points and Monthly Salary*

Job Title	number of points	monthly salary
MINNESOTA		
Registered Nurse	275	$1,723
Vocational Ed. Teacher	275	2,260
Typing Pool Supervisor	199	1,373
Painter	185	1,707
SAN JOSE, CAL.		
Senior Legal Secretary	226	665
Senior Carpenter	226	1,040
Senior Librarian	493	898
Senior Chemist	493	1,119
WASHINGTON STATE		
Licensed Practical Nurse	173	1,030
Correctional Officer	173	1,436
Secretary	197	1,122
Maintenance Carpenter	197	1,707

Source: National Committee on Pay Equity
(Adapted from *Manpower Comments*, 21 (4) p. 17, 1984)

is estimated that it will cost employers as much as $150 billion a year to raise women workers to the same levels as men in jobs with comparable skills, responsibilities, and efforts (Lewin, 1984). Therefore, labor lawyers, representing employers, warn them of the danger of a comparable worth study. As one labor lawyer explains, 'I tell clients that they shouldn't start a job evaluation if they're not going to have the money to carry through on remedying any undervaluation they find. Once you have the study, it can be used against you to make a much stronger legal case of sex discrimination' (Lewin, 1984, p. F15). In spite of legal advice to the contrary, comparable worth is an idea whose time has come. Although it may not be directly applicable to the situation of many female scientists, it will directly affect the salaries of some. In addition, its focus on worth, based on skill, responsibility, and effort rather than on gender, is bound to improve, when appropriate, the salaries of women working in science.

Summary

Our vision of tomorrow for women in science includes both bright and gloomy prospects. Today's experimental and action research provide suggestions for interesting more girls in science. Therefore, we anticipate that more girls may develop the prerequisite skills to do science by tinkering with mechanical and electrical toys and by enrolling in mechanical drawing, shop, and industrial arts classes. Within science classes, teachers, assisted by intervention programs, may begin to project a positive view of science, accessible to all capable students. As Cecily Cannan Selby (1982) has said, 'Science must be presented as not only basic but beautiful, as those of us whose lives and professions have been touched by this beauty are so proud and privileged to know'. That description portrays science as neither masculine nor feminine, and new approaches in teaching science must present its egalitarian image as well as provide equal educational opportunities.

As more girls acquire the skills to do science, it is anticipated that more will select elective science courses which can lead to science majors and to science careers. The development of a critical mass of women scientists seems crucial before the next step. That is, before tomorrow's vision of women in science can include professional women employed, promoted, and paid at rates comparable with those of their male counterparts. In the future, we anticipate that more women will be assisted in the complicated adjustment from student to colleague by other women. However, eradication of the resistant barriers of equal pay and promotion has been slow and unsuccessful. New approaches, involving both legislation and judicial decisions, indicate that eventually these persistent obstacles to women, including women scientists, may be overcome.

Improving the status and increasing the role of women in science will change both the image of science and the image of women as scientists. Both views are constrained by sex-role stereotyping which, both research studies and changing policies, indicate are antiquated. Tomorrow's vision, then, rests firmly on today's research, which has identified changes needed in the education, the professional advancement, and the employment of women scientists. Perhaps, a vision of science for tomorrow is best expressed by a fifteen-year-old American girl, who responded in the following way to a question about women's role in science:

> There are some women scientists; but men have been in it longer. Women can do the same job as men. They may have a different way of thinking and might improve science (Kahle, 1983b).

Notes

1 BERRYMAN (1983) ran a variety of analyses to identify a key to equalizing disciplinary choices among racial and ethnic subgroups in the United States.

Her conclusions were that the different non-Asian-American minorities behaved similarly with regard to a college major and that they did not behave like other minority groups nor like whites.

2 In the United States, approximately 96 per cent of all elementary teachers were women, whereas only 24 per cent of all secondary science teachers were women in 1977.

3 DUNTEMAN *et al.*, (1979) identified 'hard' sciences in their study as physical sciences, engineering, mathematics, and life sciences (Berryman, 1983, p. 81).

4 Labor force participation rates measure the fraction of the S/E population in the labor force; that is, all those either working or seeking employment (NSF, 1984, p. 17).

5 Minority women represent a small share of employed women scientists and engineers. In the US, there were approximately 437,000 employed women scientists and engineers in 1982. Of these, about 85 per cent were white, 7 per cent were black, 6 per cent were Asian, and less than 1 per cent were native Americans. The remainder were in another category or did not report their racial group (NSF, 1984, p. 8).

6 PITERNICK, L. (1984). Personal communication, Seattle, WA.

7 Technical crafts include woodwork, metal work, and technical crafts (Kelly *et al.*, 1984).

8 In the US, women began outnumbering men on campuses in 1979, and by 1981, there were 108 women in college for every 100 men. In 1972, there were 72 women for every 100 men enrolled in college (Bureau of the Census, 1984).

9 Quotation taken from 'The Quality of Women's Education at Harvard University: A Survey of Sex Discrimination in the Graduate and Professional Schools', June 1980.

10 DOUGLASS, C., and KAHLE, J.B. (1979). Personal communication, West Lafayette, Indiana.

11 PUTNAM, L. (1984). Personal communication, West Lafayette, Indiana.

12 In 1970–71, the faculty of chemistry departments awarding doctoral degrees included only 1.5 per cent women.

13 According to the 1980 Census, 18.9 per cent of all children in the US are from single parent families and over 50 per cent of black children reside in single parent homes.

14 Between 1972 and 1982, American women increased their average wage from 59 per cent to 62 per cent of American men's average wage. In that same period, the average Swedish woman's paycheck rose from 73 per cent to 90 per cent of an average male's paycheck.

References

ASSOCIATION OF AMERICAN COLLEGES (AAC). (1983) *Project Newsletter*, 13, 5, Summer.

BENBOW, C.P. and STANLEY, J.C. (1980) 'Sex differences in mathematical ability: Factor or artifact?' *Science*, 210, pp. 1262–64.

BENBOW, C.P. and STANLEY, J.C. (1983) 'Sex differences in mathematical reasoning ability: More facts', *Science*, 222, pp. 1029–31.

BERRYMAN, S.E. (1983, November) *Who Will Do Science?* Washington, DC, The Rockefeller Foundation.

BRUER, J.T. (1983) 'Women in science: Lack of full participation', *Science*, 221, p. 1339.

Comparable worth: A summary (1983, December 29) Unpublished paper, Seattle, WA, Washington State Joint Select Committee on Comparable Worth Implementation, House Office Building, Rm 203-A.

Contributions to the second GASAT conference (1983) Oslo, Norway, Institute of Physics, University of Oslo.

DAVIS, B.G. and HUMPHRYES, S. (1983) *Evaluation Counts: A Guide to Evaluating Math and Science Programs for Women*, Oakland, CA, Mills College.

DUNTEMAN, G.H. *et al*. (1979) *Race and Sex Differences in College Science Program Participation*, Triangle Park, NC, Research Triangle Institute.

FOX, L.H. (1980) *The Problem of Women and Mathematics*, New York, Ford Foundation.

GORNICK, V. (1983) *Women in Science*. New York, Simon & Schuster.

GREY, J.D. (1983) 'The married professional woman: An examination of her role conflicts and coping strategies,' *Psychology of Women Quarterly*, 7, 3, pp. 235–43.

HARDING, J. (1983) *Switched Off: The Science Education of Girls*, School Council Programme 3, York, England, Longman Resources Unit.

HEAD, J. (1979) 'Personality and the pursuit of science,' *Studies in Science Education*, 6, pp. 23–44.

HECHINGER, F. (1983) 'Oberlin College pointed the way 150 years ago', *New York Times*, p. 20, 26 April.

HORNIG, L.S. (1984) 'A bias that hurts women scientists', *New York Times*, p. 20, 20 March.

HUEFTLE, S.J. RAKOW, S.J. and WELCH, W.W. (1983) *Images of Science: A Summary of Results from the 1981–82 National Assessment in Science*. Minneapolis, MI, Minnesota Research & Evaluation Center.

JOHNSON, S. (1984) 'Working families in Sweden and US' *New York Times*, p. 30, 31 May.

KAHLE, J.B. (1983a) *The Disadvantaged Majority: Science Education for Women*, AETS Outstanding Paper for 1983, Burlington, NC, Carolina Biological Supply.

KAHLE, J.B. (1983b) *Girls in School: Women in Science*, Washington, DC,

National Science Board, Commission on Precollege Education in Mathematics, Science and Technology.

KELLER, E.F. (1983) *A Feeling for the Organism,* San Francisco, W.H. Freeman and Company.

KELLY, A. with ALEXANDER, J. AZAM, U. BRETHERTON, C. BURGESS, G. DORNEY, A. GOLD, J. LEAHY, C. SHARPLEY, A. and SPONDLEY, L. (1982) 'Gender roles at home and school', *British Journal of Sociology of Education,* 3, pp. 281–95.

KELLY, A. and SMAIL, B. (1984) *Sex Stereotypes and Attitudes to Science Among Eleven Year Old School Children,* Unpublished paper, Manchester, England; Girls into Science and Technology, 9A Didsbury Park.

KELLY, A. SMAIL, B. and WHYTE, J. (1984) *Initial GIST Survey: Results and Implications,* Published report, Manchester, England, Girls into Science and Technology, 9A Didsbury Park.

LEWIN, T. (1984) 'A new push to raise women's pay', *New York Times,* Section 3, pp. 1 and 15, 1 January.

LINN, M.C. and PETERSEN, A.C. (1984) 'Emergence & characterization of gender differences in spatial ability: A meta-analysis', Unpublished paper. Berkeley, University of California.

LINN, M.C. (1984) 'Fostering equitable consequences from computer learning environments', *Sex Roles,* (in press).

Manpower Comments (1982) Washington, DC, American Association for the Advancement of Science, September, p. 20.

Manpower Comments (1983) Washington, DC, American Association for the Advancement of Science, October, p. 19–20.

Manpower Comments (1984) Washington, DC, American Association for the Advancement of Science, May, p. 17–30.

National Assessment of Education Progress (NAEP) (December, 1978b) *Science Achievement in the Schools* (Science Report No. 08-S-01), Denver, CO. Educational Commission of the States.

National Assessment of Education Progress (NAEP) (May, 1978a) *The Third Assessment of Science, 1976–77,* (Released Exercise Set), Denver, CO, Educational Commission of the States.

National Science Foundation (NSF) (1984) *Women and Minorities in Science and Engineering,* (NSF 84–300), Washington, DC, National Science Foundation, January.

On Campus with Women, (1984) Project on the Status and Education of Women. Washington, DC: Association of American Colleges, Winter.

PALLAS, A.M. and ALEXANDER, K.L. (1983) 'Sex differences in quantitative SAT performance: New evidence on the differential course-work hypothesis', *American Educational Research Journal,* 20, 165–182.

PROJECT on the STATUS and EDUCATION of WOMEN (1983) *Academic Mentoring for Women Students and Faculty: A New Look at an Old Way to Get Ahead,* Washington, DC, Association for American Colleges.

Report on Education Research (1983) 'Growing gender gap observed in computer research', Arlington, VA, 14 September, pp. 6–7.

Report on Education Research. (1984) 'US students improve in science, new study shows', Arlington, VA, 6 June, pp. 1–2.

ROSSITER, M.W. (1982) *Women Scientists in America: Struggles and Strategies to 1940*, Baltimore, Johns Hopkins Press.

SELBY, C.C. (1982) 'Turning people on to science,' *Physics Today* p. 26, July.

SKOLNICK, J. LANGBORT, C. and DAY, L. (1982) *How to Encourage Girls in Math and Science*, Englewood Cliffs, NJ, Prentice Hall.

SMAIL, B. and KELLY, A. (1984) *Sex Differences in Science and Technology Among Eleven Year Old Schoolchildren: II Attitudes*. Unpublished paper. Manchester, England, Girls into Science and Technology, 9A Didsbury Park.

STAGE, E.K. (1982) *Women and Mathematics: Strategies for Future Program Development Based on Research and Successful Program Models*, Paper presented at the meeting of the American Educational Research Association, New York, 20 March.

STEINKAMP, M.W. and MAEHR, M.L. (1984) 'Gender differences in motivational orientations toward achievement in school science: A quantitative synthesis', *American Educational Research Journal*, 21, pp. 39–59.

TREAGUST, D.F. (1980) 'Gender-related differences of adolescents in spatial representational thought', *Journal of Research in Science Teaching*, 17, pp. 91–7.

WILCE, H. (1983) 'Girls less keen on science after puberty.' London, *The Times Educational Supplement*, 11 November, p. 5.

WILLSON, V.L. (1983) 'A meta-analysis of the relationship between science achievement and science attitude: Kindergarten through college.' *Journal of Research in Science Teaching*, 20, pp. 839–850.

Notes on Contributors

Jane Butler Kahle   In recognition of Jane Butler Kahle's work concerning women in science, she was named a Fellow in the American Association for the Advancement of Science (AAAS) in 1981 and was awarded the Distinguished Service to Science Education award of the National Association of Science Teachers in 1984. In that same year, she received the Helen B. Schleman Gold Medallian Award, Purdue University, for promoting the concerns of women. In 1983 Dr. Kahle won the Implications of Research for Educational Practice award of the Association for the Education of Teachers in Science for her paper. *The Disadvantaged Majority: Science Education of Women*. She is currently serving as a member of the Steering Committee for the third International Conference for Girls and Science and Technology (GASAT). Dr. Kahle has served as president of the National Association of Biology Teachers and of the Hoosier Association of Science Teachers, Inc. She is chairman of the Board of Directors of the Biological Sciences Curriculum Study, a Member-at-Large of the Science Education Section of AAAS, and a member of the Governing Council of the American Institute of Biological Sciences. Her leadership of the Role and Status of Women in Biology Committee produced the studies and surveys reported in this book.

Marjorie Perrin Behringer is Professor Emeritus of Biology at the University of North Dakota. Dr. Behringer has extensive biology teaching experience at both the secondary and collegiate levels. In addition to numerous biological research articles, she published *Techniques and Materials in Biology* (1973, McGraw-Hill; 1982, Krieger Publishing). Her commitment to improving secondary science education led to her extensive work with the Biological Sciences Curriculum Study and directorship of several National Science Foundation Summer Science Institutes for high school science teachers. She is particularly interested in increasing young women's interests in science courses and careers.

230

Mildred A. Collins is an Assistant Professor of Biology at Stillman College in Tuscaloosa, Alabama. She has completed advanced studies at Tuskegee Institute (Tuskegee, Alabama), the University of Alabama (Birmingham, Alabama), and Purdue University (West Lafayette, Indiana). Ms. Collins has had thirty years experience in teaching biology to secondary and undergraduate students. She has been the academic advisor for more than one hundred students who have completed medical school or PhD programs; half of these students were minority women. Currently, she serves as a consultant on teaching effectiveness and classroom management for the School of Education, Alabama A and M University, Huntsville, Alabama.

Claudia B. Douglass is Professor of Biology at Central Michigan University, Mount Pleasant, Michigan. She is currently completing research on the relationship of hemispheric dominance and academic test performance. Her previous research has included the development of alternative instructional materials for urban middle and secondary school students. In addition to serving on the Role and Status of Women in Biology Committee of the National Association of Biology Teachers, Dr. Douglass serves as a member of the Board of Directors of the School Science and Mathematics Association.

Marsha Lakes Matyas recently received the doctorate degree in biology education from Purdue University, West Lafayette, Indiana. Her research interests include factors affecting the attrition of undergraduate women from biology majors and methods for encouraging secondary school students to continue in science courses and careers. She has presented her research findings on women in science at national and local meetings. Currently, she serves as a member of the Role and Status of Women in Biology Committee of the National Association of Biology Teachers and of the special interest group, Research on Women in Education, of the American Educational Research Association.

Ann Haley-Oliphant is a doctoral student in science education at the University of Cincinnati, Cincinnati, Ohio. She holds a Bachelor of Science degree in biology and biology education from Purdue University, West Lafayette, Indiana. In 1984 she chaired the Role and Status of Women in Biology Committee of the National Association of Biology Teachers. Ms. Haley-Oliphant has developed activities for use in classrooms and museums which are designed to increase science interest among girls; these activities have been published in newspapers, presented at national educational meetings, and used in various education facilities.

Frances S. Vandervoort teaches biology and physical science to gifted students in a magnet program at Kenwood Academy, a Chicago, Ilinois public school. She obtained her bachelor's and master's degrees in zoology from the University of Chicago and has studied curriculum and educational administration at the same institution. In addition to the problem of motivating girls in science, she is interested in scientific literacy and issues of science and society.

Author Index

Subject Index

academic barriers
  to women in science, 81–4
Academy of Science [USSR], 179
Adams, J., 8
Adult Nowicki-Strickland Scale, 63
affirmative action
  federal policies for, 22
  and minority women, 119
  and women biology teachers,
    160–1
Africa
  importance of women in agriculture
    in, 181
agriculture
  women's role in developing
    countries in, 181–2
Al-Ahram science clubs [Egypt], 184
Albion [college], 12
Alverno College (Wisc.), 219
American Anthropological
  Association, 138–9
American Association for the
  Advancement of Science
  Science Manpower Commission of
    the, 77
American Association of Engineering
  Societies
  Engineering Manpower
    Commission of the, 139, 140, 141
American Association of
  Immunologists, 130, 18

American Association of Physics
  Teachers
  Committee on Women in Physics of
    the, 137–8
American Astronomical Society (AAS)
  Committee on the Status of Women
    of the, 130–1
American Chemical Society (ACS)
  Women Chemists' Committee of
    the, 133

American College Test, 141
American Geological Institute
  Women Geoscientists Committee
    of the, 135
American Meteorological Society,
  136, 137
American Pharmaceutical Association
  (APhA), 2, 129
American Physical Society, 137–8
  Committee on the Status of Women
    in Physics of the, 137
American Society of Biological
  Chemists, 130
American Society for Cell Biology,
  130
American Society for Microbiology,
  127
Anderson, A.G., 17
anthropology, 6, 138–9
Antioch [college], 12

239

Vassar College, 9, 11
Veterans Administration, 129

Washington [State]
    comparable worth study in, 223–4
Wellesley [college], 9

Western Europe
    programs to encourage girls in
        science in, 174–8
    women in science in, 186
    women university students in, 184
white male doctoral scientists
    distribution by field of, 114, 118
William and Mary [college], 9
Williams College, 11
Wisconsin, University of, 12
*Woman in Science . . . Women's Long
    Struggle for Things of the Mind*, 4,
    10
women
    see also girls; women scientists
    ability of, 7
    and achievement in science, 27–48
    and admission to medical schools,
        16–17
    and anthropology, 138–9
    and astronomy, 130–2
    attitudes to in East and West
        Germany, 186
    and biological sciences, 126–30
    and biology education, 1
    as biology teachers, 129–30,
        148–68
    and chemistry, 132–3
    and choice of science careers,
        144–5, 169–92
    college education for, 9–10
    constraints on in science, 77–101
    degrees in chemistry of, 133
    degrees in science of, 202–3
    and dual roles, 84–6, 187–8
    education of, 5–18
    elementary education for, *see*
        elementary schools

    and engineering, 139–43, 216
    and family responsibilities, 84–6
    in 'feminine' professions, 187
    first degrees awarded to, 9
    and geoscience, 133–5
    graduate education for, 13–14,
        77–86
    graduate support for, 83–4, 204
    in history of science, 18–19
    and immunology, 138
    interest in science of, 27–48
    and job mobility, 94, 209
    in labor-short occupations, 185–6
    and life sciences, 126–7
    and meteorology, 135–7
    and microbiology, 127–8
    and 'micro-inequities', 82–3, 84, 86
    numbers in various professions of,
        20–1
    and pharmacy, 128–9
    and physical sciences, 130–8
    and physics, 137–8
    and professional attainment, 93
    in professional scientific
        organizations, 124–47
    professional training for, 15–18
    retention in science of, 49–76,
        81–4
    and science careers, *passim*
    secondary education for, 8–9,
        11–12
    self-image of, 86
    and tenure, 24
    'triple penalty' against, 125
    as 'undedicated' students, 81–4, 86
    wages of in Sweden, 226n14
    wages of in United States, 226n14
women astronomers
    job satisfaction of, 131
    and marriage, 131
    publications by, 131–2
    salaries of, 131
    status of, 131
women biology teachers
    and administrative positions,